ATHLETIC JOURNAL'S
ENCYCLOPEDIA OF BASKETBALL

ATHLETIC JOURNAL'S
ENCYCLOPEDIA OF BASKETBALL

edited by
Tom Ecker
and
Don King

Parker Publishing Company, Inc. West Nyack, New York

Parker Publishing Company, Inc.
West Nyack, New York

Library of Congress Cataloging in Publication Data
Main entry under title:

Athletic journal's encyclopedia of basketball.

1. Basketball coaching–Addresses, essays, lectures.
I. Ecker, Tom. II. King, Don . III. Athletic journal. IV. Title: Encyclopedia of basketball.
GV885.3.A87 1983 796.32'3'077 82-14373
ISBN 0-13-049882-3

Printed in the United States of America

WHAT THIS ENCYCLOPEDIA OFFERS YOU

When the *Athletic Journal* was first published back in 1921, an important new vehicle was established for the dissemination of sports knowledge among America's coaches. Immediately, the magazine gained wide acceptance and has since grown from its original issue of only twelve pages to its present status as one of the most respected publications in the coaching field.

The *Athletic Journal's* original concept—to exchange ideas without categorically stating that there is only one right way or correct idea—has been maintained throughout the years. It is with that concept in mind that this Encyclopedia of Basketball has been compiled. Within these pages you will find many "right ways" and "correct ideas"—all designed to improve your basketball coaching knowledge and skills.

By culling through some 2,500 basketball articles, consisting of nearly four million words, we were able to put together the *best* of basketball from the *Athletic Journal.* Contained in this one volume is invaluable information for you—the basketball coach—provided by 42 of the country's top basketball authorities.

Many of the game's top names are included, such as Jerry Tarkanian, Lynn Nance, Paul Lambert, Neil McCarthy, Gene Keady, Virgil Sweet, Jim Dutcher, Red Severson, John Benington, Dick Vitale and George King. But there are also many contributors whose names may not be immediately known to all, but who have made notable contributions to the game of basketball. All in all, this Encyclopedia provides the best available information on basketball coaching from a broad cross section of basketball authorities.

As a student of the game of basketball, you will find this timeless resource guide yet another valuable contribution from the *Athletic Journal.*

Tom Ecker
Don King

CONTENTS

PART FOUR—Fast Break

PART FIVE—Special Situations

ATHLETIC JOURNAL'S

ENCYCLOPEDIA OF BASKETBALL

part ONE

Conditioning and Fundamentals

Chapter 1

PRE-SEASON CONDITIONING

by Ed Hager

Our program consists of two parts. One part is conducted outside, using the track and stadium facilities; the other part is conducted inside, using the basketball court. If for no other reason than the uncertainty of the weather, we think two programs are necessary.

In preparing to conduct this type of pre-season program, the following factors should be considered: 1. There is a need for two coaches. 2. Physical examinations and insurance must be taken care of early. 3. Cold weather, and its effects on unconditioned muscles and respiratory systems, must be considered. 4. Proper clothing to meet cold weather conditions must be secured for the players. 5. The use of outdoor facilities must be arranged.

We conduct the pre-season program four days a week, for three weeks. At the end of the difficult first week, the players are advised to run on their own over the weekend in order to continue the conditioning process.

The outside program consists of the following: A. Run a mile (groups of 5, single file). B. Sprints—twelve 10-yard sprints; eight 20-yard sprints; and six 30-yard sprints. C. Run a mile.

A possible change in the outdoor program could be: A. Run a mile. B. Two to four 440's, with walking in between. C. Run the stadium steps four times. C. Run a mile.

By using this program, the coach learns which players are willing to work. Thus, a degree of purpose is established. The players are doing extensive running on a soft surface as opposed to the hardwoods.

At the end of the three-week period, have all the players run a mile for time. By comparing the time with the time posted when they came out the first time, the coach and the player can see the rate of improvement.

On the days we are not outside, an active program is conducted inside. The program consists of eight stations, with an aspect of conditioning at each station. The floor layout in Diagram 1-1 shows how the stations are arranged.

Station 1: Agility Drill—(working with 4 or 5 in a group). a. Face the board. b. Shuffle to the corner. c. Sprint to the key. d. Back-pedal to the end line. Repeat individually until each player has executed the drill four times.

Station 2: Rebound Release Drill. a. Throw the ball against the board, rebound, and release to the outlet man. b. Sprint to the free throw line taking a pass back from the release man. c. Turn, hit the release man again, and drive back for the board. d. Take a return pass for the lay-up.

Station 3: Running the Steps. There are about 35 steps, which are run a minimum of five times.

Station 4: The Bench or Rope Jump. a. Use either a bench or a rope tied between two chairs. b. Stand parallel to the rope, jump over, and back quickly, and use as many repetitions as possible.

Station 5: Jump Rope. Have the same number of ropes as there are players in the group and then jump rope.

Station 6: Shuffle Drill. Checking on defensive position, move the players according to the follow-the-leader principle, or hand direction. Have them shuffle back and forth, to the side and back, using constant movement. The number of times the drill is run is up to you, but there should be a minimum of three repetitions.

Station 7: Tipping Drill. a. Split the groups in order to use both sides of the basket. b. Tip the ball against the board using both hands as many times as possible.

Station 8: Whistle Drill. a. All five players run at the same time. b. They should sprint until they hear the whistle, and on the whistle reverse themselves as quickly as possible, being careful to remain in a line. Do this several times ending at the starting point. c. Repeat the drill three times.

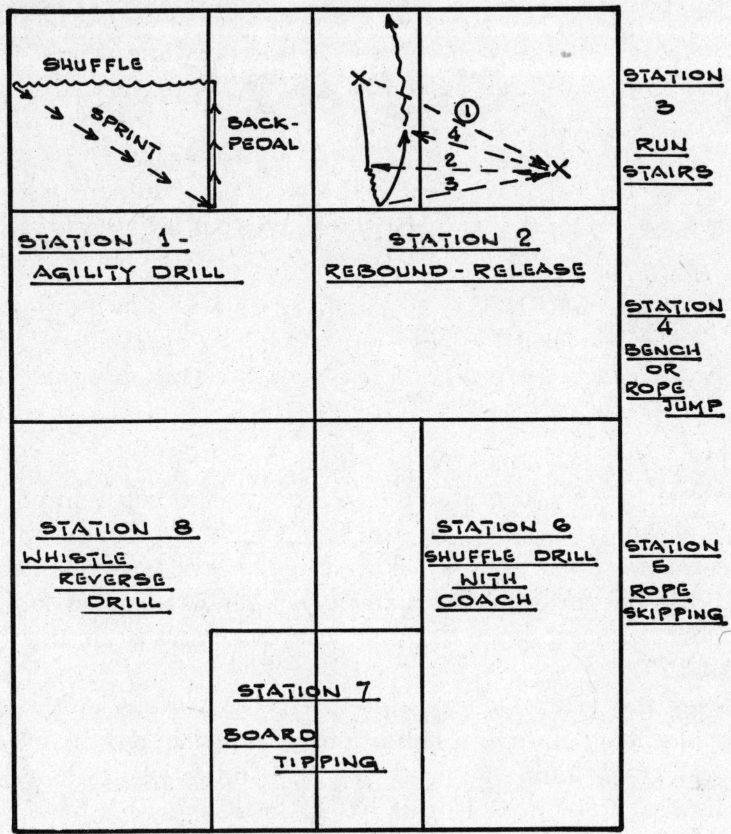

Diagram 1-1

This is the schedule that is followed for three weeks prior to the start of organized practice. The closer the actual starting time approaches, the more time is devoted to indoor work. During the third week the players run two miles outside, and come back into the gymnasium for the indoor work.

A relatively short length of time is required for any part of this program. Both programs can be run off in 35-45 minutes.

Chapter 2

BASKETBALL CONDITIONING DRILLS

by Leonard MacPhee

Because basketball is an intense and demanding sport, coaches agree that conditioning is one of the most important aspects of winning games. In order to achieve top condition, the players must execute complex skills at high speeds and often these skills must be performed after a player has run long distances. Thus, the winning team is often the one that is in the best condition.

Over the years we experimented with various methods of getting our team into top condition. Since it is our belief that basketball conditioning has both physical and mental dimensions, the following sequence of drills has given us what we have been seeking.

This sequence of drills is used for three to four weeks at the beginning of the practice season each fall. One hundred percent effort is demanded from every player throughout the entire sequence. Although very few players enjoy this part of practice, they do seem to take pride in the fact that they go through it. The results of this program are both physical and mental. Each player must develop the mental self-discipline to push beyond what is comfortable physically. This becomes extremely important in the late stages of a close game when players who lack self-discipline are likely to let up as they become tired. This type of effort also develops tremendous physical condition.

Another advantage which our conditioning sequence gives us is team morale. When a group goes through something difficult, the participants begin to depend on each other. They encourage each other and team morale develops.

In addition, this drill sequence sets the tone for team discipline. It enables the coaching staff to establish the idea that each player has the responsibility of giving 100 percent of his potential effort. These drills are not unique to our system; in fact, most of them are used in various ways by many coaches. However, what is unique is that the sequence we developed yields the highest possible physical and mental condition for basketball. It should be mentioned that the drills are used for 15 minutes after a full one and one-half hours of practice.

Speed dribbling in which the team is divided into two groups is the first drill. Each player in the first group has a ball and lines up on the baseline. The players are instructed to dribble the length of the floor and back at top speed, using only the weak hand. After one group finishes, the other starts. Keeping the head and eyes up and pushing the ball out in front on the dribble are emphasized. Each group usually goes two or three times. When going full speed with the ball, the player is not only developing dribbling skill, but is also developing leg muscles and lung conditioning. The primary function of speed dribbling in the drill sequence is that it sets the stage for the following drills.

The second drill, called the sea gull, includes defensive sliding and sprint running. The players start (leaving about 6 feet between players) at one end of the court and sprint up the sideline to half-court (Diagram 2-1). Then they slide in a defensive position, facing the same end of the court to the center circle, touch the palms of both hands simultaneously to the floor, turn so that they

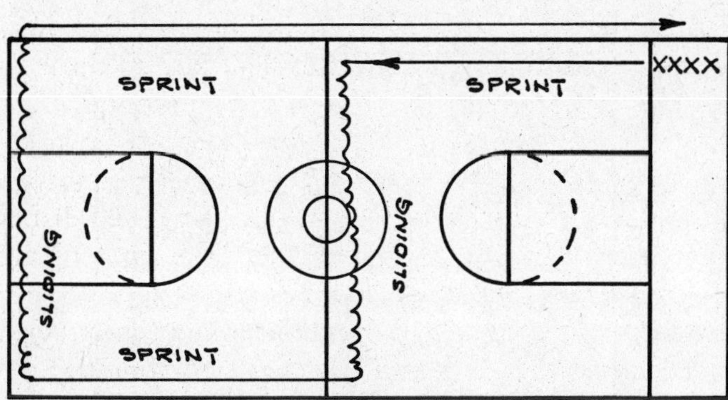

Diagram 2-1

are facing the opposite end of the court, and slide to the far sideline at half-court. From that point they sprint to the far corner of the court, take a defensive stance, and slide to a point under the far basket. At this time the palms hit the floor, the turn is made, and they slide the rest of the way across the baseline to the sideline. Then the players sprint the entire length of the sideline back to the point where they started. Two or three sea gulls are usually done each day during the conditioning sequence.

In this drill good defensive positioning of the body is emphasized, because the players have a tendency to cross their feet when sliding and are also likely to straighten up as they become tired. The idea of 100 percent effort on the sliding and sprints is also emphasized.

The third drill is the six-man passing drill. It involves passing and shooting lay-ups, as well as conditioning. Six players are stationed on the court as passers (Diagram 2-2). Two players are

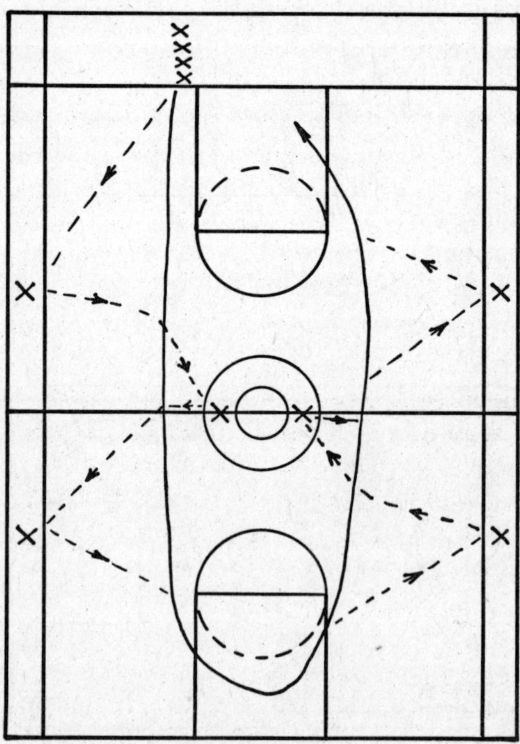

Diagram 2-2

placed on each sideline about halfway between each end line and half-court. The other two are placed in the center circle back to back. All of the other players have basketballs and the drill starts under one basket. The first man starts by passing the ball to the first sideline man and breaking toward half-court. He receives a return pass at about quarter-court, passes to the man in the center circle facing him, receives a return pass at half-court, passes to the sideline man at three-quarter court, receives a return pass, and goes in to score the lay-up. The player gets his own rebound, passes to the man on the opposite side of the court, and starts back down the other side. When the first man makes his second pass, the second man starts. After each man completes the loop, he gets back into line. With a squad of 12 players, usually there is no waiting time. All players make three rounds and then the challenge can be made to the group with the mandate that each lay-up must be made and all passes must be good on a round before the drill is stopped. Once this is accomplished, places are swapped and the passers become the players making the rounds. This drill can be run in both directions so that the players shoot both left- and right-handed lay-ups. Also, it should be pointed out that this drill requires concentration or bad passes develop as the rounds continue.

At this point the players go to sprints for the fourth drill in the conditioning sequence. From one to three of these are used and we really bear down on the team because they are tired and tend to let up. One hundred percent effort on each drill must be attained or the players are not accomplishing what we want accomplished relative to mental conditioning and discipline. Therefore, the players are watched closely, because we want to push them as far as possible, yet still attain 100 percent effort from them. Sprints start at the baseline at one end of the court. The players sprint one-fourth of the court, stop, and run backwards to the baseline. Without stopping, the next sprint is to half-court and the return is backwards to the baseline. As soon as they hit the baseline, the players sprint to the three-quarter court mark and return running backwards. This is followed by the full-court sprint and a backward run to the starting position at the baseline. The players are challenged by being told that they should do a sprint in 30 seconds. Again 100 percent effort is demanded. When the team finishes, the squad walks to the center circle for the final drill in the conditioning sequence.

This drill is called foot fire and it builds team spirit as well as physical and mental conditioning. The team forms a tight circle around the captain. When the whistle blows, each player holds his arms up (elbows shoulder high) and with his knees bent makes his feet go up and down as rapidly as possible. The players knees do not come up very far and their feet never get more than two or three inches off the floor. Also, while the foot fire is taking place everyone yells, the idea being to encourage each other and build team spirit. This drill is done for 15 seconds, the players stop for 10, and go again. The number of times the drill is practiced is built up from 5 to 10 as the team gets into better shape. It is our feeling that this drill, with the individuals helping and encouraging each other, builds pride in the team and program.

We believe in a two-dimensional conditioning program for basketball—physical and mental. Our drill sequence is intense and demanding to the extent that the players take pride in being able to complete it, encourage each other, team morale develops, and the stage is set for team discipline.

Chapter 3

TEACHING THE BASIC FUNDAMENTALS

by Charles R. Luce

Something must be added to fundamental basketball drills in order to make them as much like game play as possible. When repeating something over and over without a challenge, it is only natural merely to go through the motions. Improvement comes much faster when the stimulus of competition is present.

When they are on offense, players must be able to execute the fundamentals of passing, catching, stopping and pivoting, shooting, and dribbling. A few little wrinkles have been incorporated into our fundamental drills to make them more interesting and realistic for our players.

After the first few days of practice, the accompanying drills are used to increase the team's efficiency.

1. *Pressure Shooting:* Practically every coach has had a player who could make most of his shots when no one was on him defensively. As soon as a little defensive pressure is applied, his touch is gone. For this reason we have our boys shoot while undergoing some degree of defensive pressure. The defense is instructed not to try to block the shot, but to play close enough so that the shooter must use good shooting habits, protect the ball in order to get the shot off, and hit the target. This is not a game of one-on-one. Our players are told what shot they are to work and from what offensive spot. It may be a jump shot in place, a jump shot off a drive to the left, etc.

2. *Pressure Lay-Up:* Most high school and college basketball players can take the ball on an uncontested lay-up and score easily. The trouble is that this situation does not arise often in a game.

Almost every time a player drives to the basket in a game, there is some defensive pressure which will create a less desirable angle. Diagram 3-1 shows the drill which is used to teach this situation. A man is placed at the basket and instructed to disconcert the player with the ball as he drives in for the lay-up. He is not to block the shot but may heckle, jump, and fake at or bluff the shooter any way he desires. We want our players to learn that they must take the ball to the basket and protect it. This drill has assisted us in getting the point across.

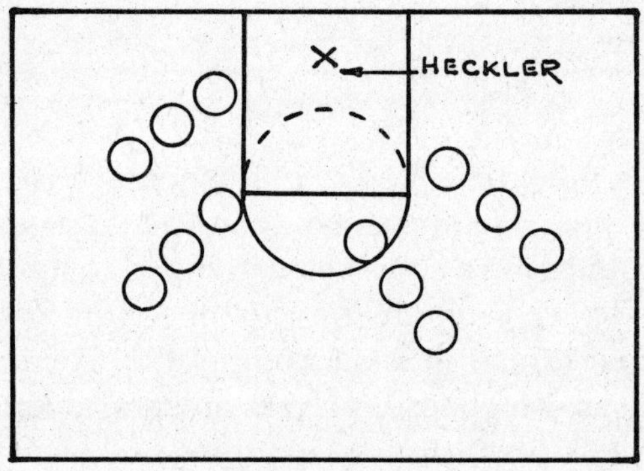

Diagram 3-1

3. *Pressure Foul Shooting:* Achieving game-like pressure in free throw shooting practice is the aim of all basketball coaches. We have not found the complete answer to this situation, but do think our boys are able to cope with the noise of the crowd. It is our custom to stop practice several times and conduct free throw shooting. No player is ever permitted to take more than one shot at a time, and the boys who are not shooting are told to make all the noise they can. They try in every way possible to break the concentration of the free throw shooter. Thus, everybody is kept active, free throw shooting is interesting, and comes as close as possible to emulating the noise that is present on game night.

4. *Dribble in Congested Area:* Boys who play on the basketball squads in most schools have the ability to dribble in an open area at a reasonable rate of speed. Most mistakes occur when a player is dribbling into the congested area on a drive or to force the defense to tighten down so the team can get the good percentage shot. These mistakes are made because the dribbler does not protect the ball from a defensive man who is in good position or

from the extra hand of another defensive man who is helping out. The drill used to simulate this situation is shown in Diagram 3-2. We start our players from a four-spot setup and send men on drives to the basket. The other men are scattered around the key. These players do not try to steal the ball, but slap, fake, and harass the dribbler.

5. *Footwork:* Over the years, our teams have been hampered by loss of the ball as a result of poor footwork. Most of this trouble is because the man with the ball is shuffling his feet before the initial push off. Most players shuffle in order to get a different foot back to drive off. As a corrective measure, we have an offensive player catch the ball and drive by a defensive man. The defensive man assumes a stance and allows the offensive man to get by after the initial step. In this drill, the defensive man watches the offensive man's feet and checks for the foot violation. As shown in Diagram 3-3, he is making the offensive man conscious of his feet by acting as a defensive man and as an official.

6. *Catching:* The fumble at the critical time in a basketball game always hurts. When working in play patterns, the freeze, fast break, and in passing drills, different size balls are used. All coaches are guilty of assuming their players can catch a ball. The different size balls, especially those that are smaller than normal basketballs, accentuate the importance of watching the ball as it goes into the hands and keeping the fingers spread.

Improvement in fundamentals comes from concentration and precision. We have found that these variations have helped make our players better performers.

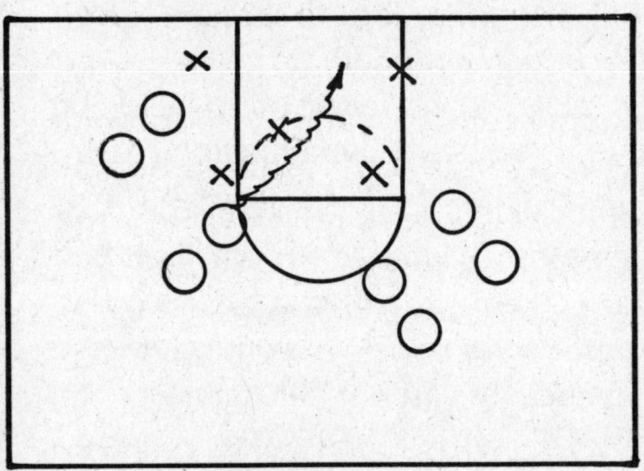

Diagram 3-2

Diagram 3-3

Chapter 4

THE ASSOCIATED AND PROGRESSIVE DRILL THEORY

by M.G. Severson

Successful basketball coaches operate from a common core of fundamental skills, but this skill knowledge as such is not sufficient in itself to win basketball games. The coach must do something sound, fundamentally speaking, with the basic skills. What might this fundamental soundness be? Apply the drills in the teaching-learning situation with proved psychological learning factors. One technique that should be emphasized is the associated and progressive drill practice. Learning is accelerated when the drill takes the learner from a point of development to greater achievement, and the time allowed for repetitive and remedial learning is increased when drills are associated with a common symbol. One symbol might be an adopted name for a drill.

Through the technique of associating each of the drills with a name, you assist the players in their readiness for each drill. Each player recalls the organization of the drill from past association. You can attempt to assist in the communication to the players through the associated drill practice. A core of five lay-up drills may be used. Each lay-up drill has a name. The core consists of the two-line lay-up drill, the two-line dribble in lay-up drill, the one-ball pivot lay-up drill, the two-ball pivot lay-up drill, and the two-ball baseball pass lay-up drill. Each practice in which you choose to use or repeat any of these drills, you merely call out the name of the drill. This tends to reduce the verbiage employed to get the drill under way; consequently, time is saved.

Diagram 4-1 shows the two-line lay-up drill.

The two-line dribble in lay-up drill is shown in Diagram 4-2.

The one-ball pivot lay-up drill is shown in Diagram 4-3. The player at the free throw line follows the shot and rebounds the ball. He passes it out to the first man in line B. A player from line B always moves up to the free throw line waiting for a pass from line B.

Diagram 4-4 shows the two-ball pivot lay-up drill. The second player in line B has a ball and passes it to the player on the free throw line as soon as he can.

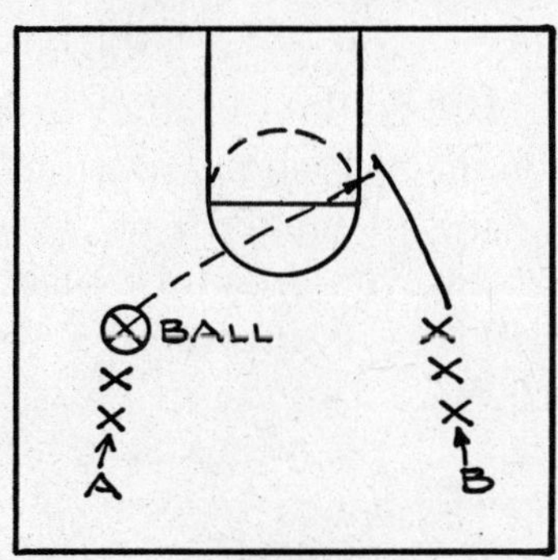

Diagram 4-1

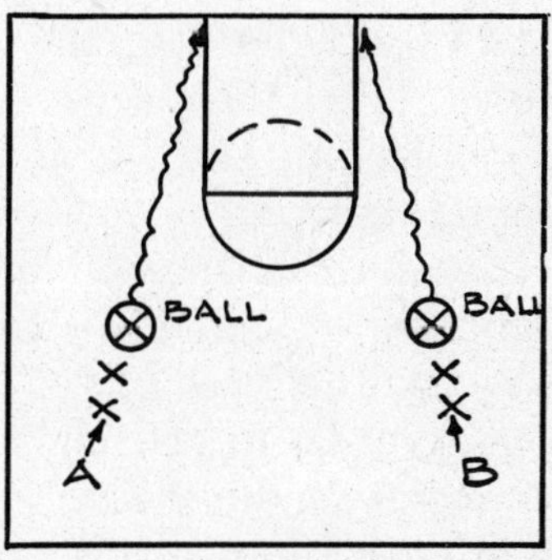

Diagram 4-2

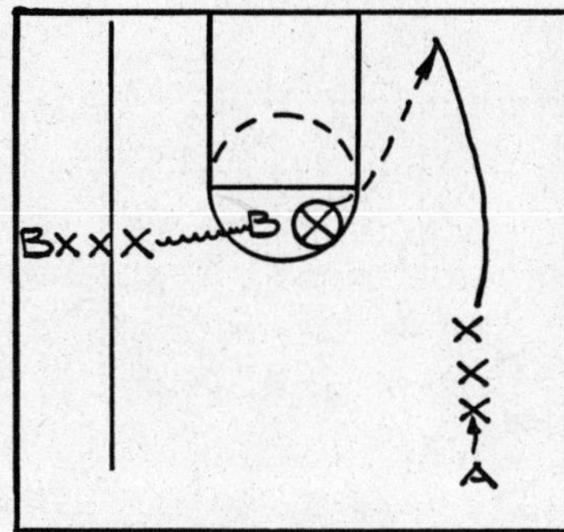

Diagram 4-3

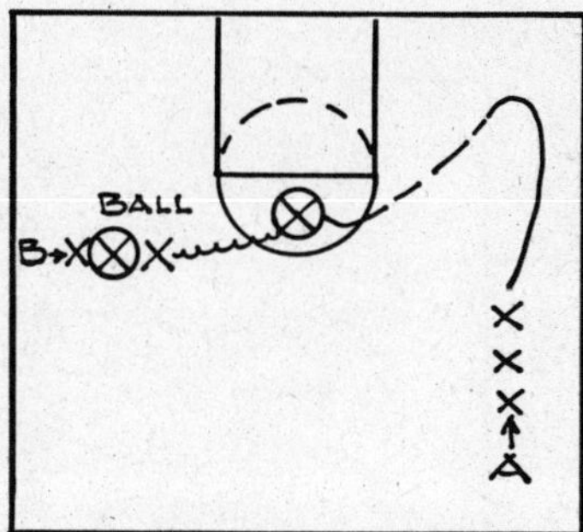

Diagram 4-4

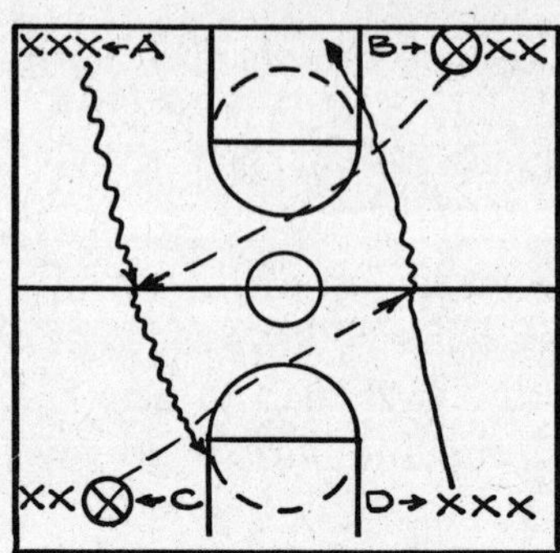

Diagram 4-5

The two-ball baseball pass lay-up drill is shown in Diagram 4-5. Lines A and D break up the court while lines B and C baseball pass to them. When the receivers catch the ball on the run, they dribble in for a lay-up. Lines C and B rebound. The shooters go to the rebound line.

In the fundamental drill practices, you may also use the progressive technique within each drill for the purpose of improving the skills of each player. It is not necessary to search for many different drills to accomplish this goal. However, you must be resourceful in advancing the skill performance of your players within the basic structure of the core of drills. Diagrams 4-6, 4-7, and 4-8 show the progressive theory.

Diagram 4-6 shows the two-line lay-up drill.

Progression of the drill is shown in Diagram 4-7. This drill

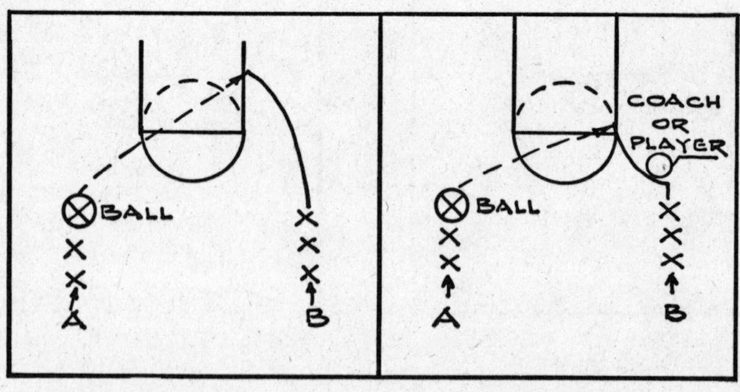

Diagram 4-6 Diagram 4-7

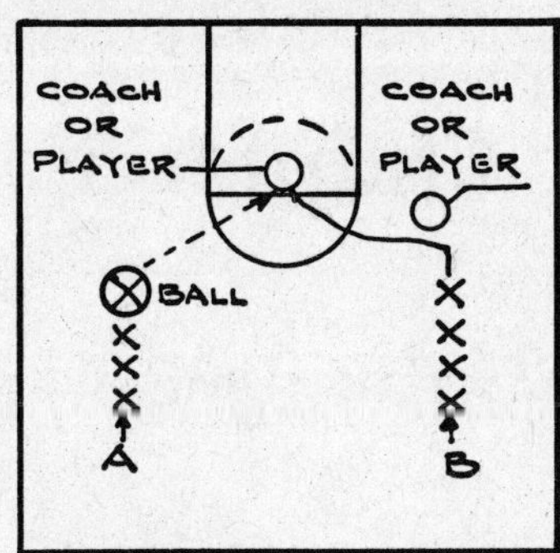

Diagram 4-8

teaches a player to head-shoulder and step-fake free of his man in order to receive the pass.

Diagram 4-8 shows further progression of the drill. After a head-shoulder step fake, a player in line B receives a pass. He must complete a pivot to the right or left of the man in front of the basket before he dribbles for a lay-up.

This progression has no limit in increasing the degree of complexity of the learning of fundamental skills. Its greatest contribution stems from your evaluation as to the progress, or lack of progress, in certain skill areas, and then you find the method for advancing the needed skill within the drill. These drill practices provide more time for teaching important techniques. The value of drills is to teach what is necessary for a specific group of boys in the easiest and most economical manner.

Chapter 5

FREEING THE JUMP SHOOTER

by George King

There are five basic moves or fakes which utilize a player's ability to elude a defender. We call these individual basic offensive maneuvers. A player must develop the ability to go either to the left or right equally well using any of these maneuvers.

Basic Fake Series

1. Fake right, go left. Fake left, go right. 2. Fake right, (hesitate) go right. Fake left, (hesitate) go left. 3. Fake right-left, go right. Fake left-right, go left. 4. Rocker step right, go right. Rocker step left, go left. 5. Fake a shot, go right. Fake a shot, go left.

Each day during the pre-practice season, and periodically during the season, a specific drill is set up for the players to use in working on this fake series. By positioning a coach facing the players (Diagram 5-1), every player is watched carefully as he executes each of the maneuvers. Each player must learn to keep the pivot foot planted firmly on the floor to eliminate the possibility of traveling or walking.

1. Fake Left, Go Right:

The first in this series of individual basic offensive maneuvers is a simple fake left, go right. The player uses the head and shoulder fake and a short jab step with the left foot. After he comes back to the right with a cross-over step, the player explodes off his

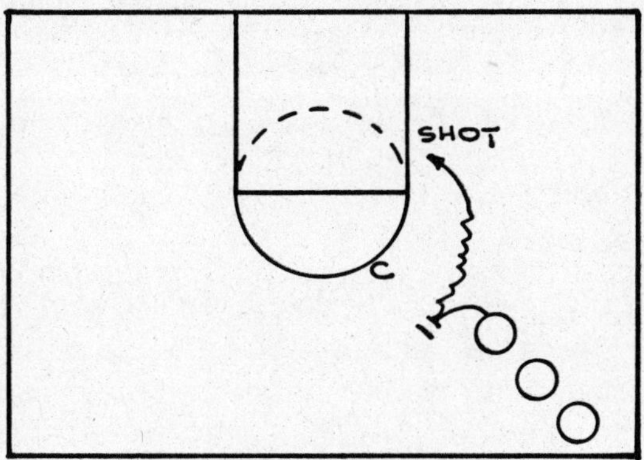

Diagram 5-1

right foot and reaches out with the first bounce on the dribble. He must penetrate on the dribble to a spot within his shooting range. The initial step is taken by planting the left foot and bringing the right foot to a planted position beside the left foot, insuring body balance. Then the explosion straight up should take place and the player should release the shot at the peak of the jump. We insist that the player come down on the identical spot from which he left the floor, thus curtailing any drift or floating motion of his body during release of the shot while he is still in the air.

Notice in this particular move that the first step and dribble after the fake should be quick and as long as possible. The ball should be projected out as far as possible, away from the defender with an explosive move past the defender. We emphasize that the player make his penetrating move appear the same with the exception that the fake would be to the right and the movement to the left.

2. Fake Left, Go Left:

The second in the series of basic maneuvers is the fake left, (hesitate) go left. Its counter is, of course, the opposite, fake right, (hesitate) go right. Proper execution of this maneuver is the use of a short jab step with the left foot, a slight hesitation, and then continued movement to the left. As in all of the individual basic offensive maneuvers, it is important for the player to use the technique of ball protection, making it appear as though he is going all the way to the basket. Penetration should be to a point in the shooter's range on the dribble, then a quick stop to gain balance with an explosive move up for the jump shot.

3. Double Fake:

Third in this series is the double fake. Facing the defensive man, the offensive player should fake left, fake right, and then go left. In the initial move, we like him to use the head and shoulder fake along with the short jab step with his left foot. The head, shoulders, and body should be brought back to the right in the second part of the maneuver and then the explosion should take place to the left using a straight-out step with the left foot. Continuation of the factors carrying through the shot itself are the same as those used in the previously mentioned fakes and maneuvers. The counter to the double fake left would be the fake right, fake left, then go right.

4. Rocker Step:

The rocker step is the fourth of the individual maneuvers. In the rocker step left maneuver, proper technique involves using a fairly long step with the left foot, rotating the body away from the defender on the ball of the right foot, and bringing the left foot completely behind the body. During the maneuver, the player must be careful to protect the ball from the defensive player. As the move lures the defensive man in, the offensive player should explode out with his left foot past the defender. From this point on, the continuation factors involving protection of the ball on the initial dribble and dribble penetration to the shooting area are all the same as in the other maneuvers. Of course, the counter to the rocker step left maneuver would be the rocker step right, again trying to develop the player's ability to go to the right equally.

5. Faked Shot:

The last maneuver in this series is the use of the faked shot. Facing the defender, the player utilizes the ball in a synchronized movement (fake) with his head and eyes toward the basket in order to draw the defender up off-balance to protect against the shot.

Then the offensive player should explode past the defender to the left executing properly all continuation factors on his penetration drive for the jump shot. The counter to this move is the fake shot and go right.

Additional Maneuvers

In addition to the five basic individual offensive maneuvers discussed, we work daily on other ways to penetrate for the open jump shot. One maneuver is set up in a drill which utilizes the cross-over dribble. This is an effective move which requires emphasis on the proper execution of the low bounce of the ball when moving the dribble from the left to the right hand in front of the defender. From thc point of technique, we continue to emphasize the importance of the quick explosive move by the defender on the dribble penetration into the shooter's range, while making the move appear as though the player is going in for the lay-up. The offensive player must maintain ball control when he comes to a stop and regain body balance as he explodes directly up to the peak of his jump for a shot release. We emphasize the necessity of controlling body movement in any direction other than the straight-up, straight-down movement.

A reverse point move is also used, and it is executed off the dribble, both to the left and to the right. All the specific points of emphasis following the dribble reverse itself are the same to the point of penetration desired for the jump shot.

Equally important, a player must be able to free himself from the defense when he does not have the ball. Within this concept, he must develop similar fakes to elude the defender and move quickly to an area where he may receive a pass and immediately shoot the jump shot. In the drills, setting up the defensive man is emphasized through the use of the fake left before movement to the right and receiving the pass.

The two-man game is also used to develop our jump shooters. In this situation, the intended shooter shoots over the screen set by a teammate (Diagram 5-2). Player A1 will bring the ball to our jump shooter with a dribble concentrating on good penetration in player A2's shooting range. A front screen is used by player A1, and then he should toss a short flip pass over his shoulder to the jump

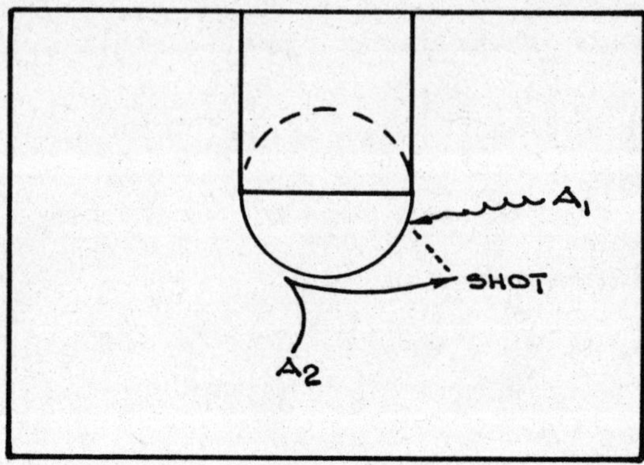

Diagram 5-2

shooter who is moving in behind the screen. It is important that A2 set up his man away from the ball as diagrammed, and come in behind the screen with good body balance, ready for the reception of the ball and explosion up for the jump shot.

In addition to this particular maneuver where A2 shoots over A1's screen, considerable time is spent working with the jump shooter to duck and hide behind the screen. Then he should explode out off the screen away from a jump switch by the defense, for one or two dribbles, a quick stop, and explosion straight up for the jump shot (Diagram 5-3).

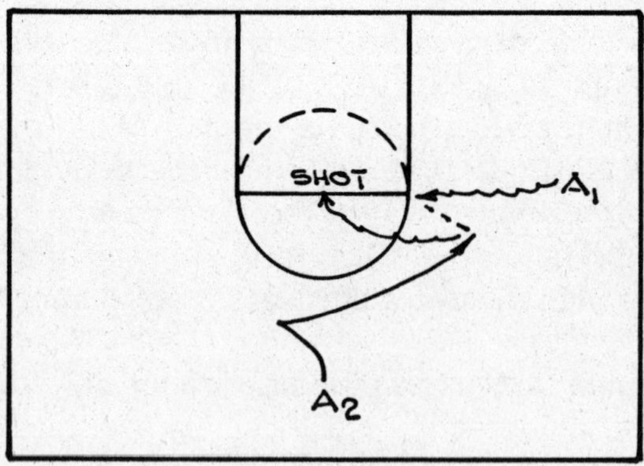

Diagram 5-3

Chapter 6

FREE THROW SHOOTING

by Virgil Sweet

It is a common practice to have the players shoot free throws after they have run laps, scrimmaged or taken part in a vigorous drill. We do not. Free throw shooting is done when the players are fresh; they do not shoot free throws when they are tired.

Everyone knows that free throw shooting accuracy in a game depends to a great extent upon the confidence of the shooter. If he is to have the correct frame of mind in competition, then he must have achieved a high degree of accuracy in practice. For this reason it is made as easy as possible for the players to shoot free throws in their daily workouts; therefore, they shoot free throws at the beginning of practice.

Developing a muscular pattern is important in the execution of any fundamental, expecially free throw shooting. The only way to train the muscles to function the same way each time is through high repetition of an activity. Our players shoot at least 25 free throws before moving from the line. When they miss a shot, they are not permitted to chase the ball.

A record is kept of the number of consecutive free throws made by each player and recognition is given for certain plateaus that are reached. The ultimate goal of each player is to hit 100 consecutive free throws without moving so he can become a member of the 100 club.

Free throw shooting is time-consuming. Seven or eight players are permitted to shoot at one time, standing side by side. It means that the player may be using a different distance each time and therefore develops better control of his muscles. Greater impetus is required when standing toward the end of the free throw line then in the middle. Thus, the players learn just how hard to shoot the ball.

Players are required to stand in the center of the line in games, because it is easier to make the shot in a symmetrical environment.

There is no such word as *relax* in the vocabularies of our players. Great athletes perform with controlled tension, and this is especially true in free throw shooting.

To develop hand control in shooting, it is necessary to grip the ball tightly. This means the ball will not be resting entirely on the fingers but must touch the pads of the hands at the base of the fingers and thumbs.

During the execution of the shot, the ball must not be rolled to the finger tips and released from there. Impetus is actually applied by the entire fingers enabling the shooter to adjust his shot at the point of release if he has the feeling it has gone awry. This method is also helpful in field goal shooting where contact may occur on the shot.

The symmetrical arch which so many coaches and players strive for may be thrilling to the spectators. On the long field goal attempts the ball will travel nearly to the rafters and will barely move the net on successful free throw tries. However, we prefer that the ball travel in a non-symmetrical trajectory and reach the highest point of its arch two-thirds of the way to the basket.

To enable players to visualize the highest point of the free throw shot, parallel bars can be placed across the free throw lane 5 feet from the basket.

This type of trajectory means that the ball is traveling the shortest possible distance while still entering the basket at a feasible angle. It also means that the players are shooting the ball outward toward the basket and thereby are better able to judge the distance it will travel. Players who have a symmetrical arch are throwing the ball upward hoping it comes down somewhere around the basket.

Chapter 7

THE ANATOMY OF THE ONE-ON-ONE

by Phil Worrell

In modern-day basketball, the 1-on-1 has become an integral part of almost any successful basketball offense.

The precision accuracy of the jump shot and the increasingly frequent use of the power lay-up, along with the knowledge of how and when to use an assortment of age-old offensive fundamentals, provide offensive players a distinct advantage in 1-on-1 situations.

When to Use the 1-on-1

Almost any man-for-man offense, from the free-lance to the shuffle, wheel, or other continuity patterns, can and will yield many opportunities to use the 1-on-1. Zone offenses usually have fewer chances to use the 1-on-1; however, a wise coach will not completely discount the possibilities.

If a team is in a zone offense, and the man with the ball is open, or is 1-on-0, then he is in a near perfect position and the shot should be taken. If he is being guarded by two men, a teammate will be open and movement of the ball in a prearranged manner will usually find that player. The remainder of the time some of the 1-on-1 maneuvers can be used either to get a shot or to force two opponents to take the ball-handler, leaving a teammate open.

In a match-up, a combination, or a multiple defense situation, the defense will automatically present many 1-on-1 conditions.

Procedure of the 1-on-1

In many situations, the offensive player will be moving laterally, or away from the basket when he receives the ball in a 1-on-1 situation. Unless he is within a 10-foot radius of the basket when he receives the ball, his first move should be to pivot into the starting position. Ideally, his inside foot should be slightly forward with his weight on the ball of the foot and the toes. His body position should be a semi-crouch with the hips lowered, shoulder forward, knees bent, and head normal. The ball should be cradled against his outside hip, and his hands should be holding it in a shooting position.

The offensive player's next move is to notice the defensive man's immediate distance and his footwork. If the situation indicates a jump shot, the offensive player's move should be smooth, quick, and continuous. The ball should be pulled in a straight motion in front of the center of his chest and face, then into the jump shot position, and released with proper follow-through. His knees and hips should be straightened into a short jump which accompanies the shot. The jump need not be high due to the quickness of the shot.

The key to the move of the offensive player is the movement of the defensive man. The previously mentioned move should be made if the defensive man is far enough away and is not moving toward the offensive player, or if he is on his heels. If, however, the defensive man makes a move toward the offensive player with either of his feet or his hands in a forward motion, then the offensive player should make his move. The success of the drive depends mainly on the timing of the move. Also, the length of the first dribble and step is important. Both should be longer than normal, placing the body position of the offensive player even with or beyond that of the defensive man. Once the offensive player is even with the defensive man, he should be in control. Now, the offensive player may take the moving jump shot, the straight driving lay-up, the wrong foot lay-up, or the power lay-up. At this point, even if the defensive man does recover, the change-of-pace dribble and the quick jumper should be successful.

When he is at the beginning position, if the offensive player encounters an exceptional defensive man who is in position to stop the jumper, but also has the equipment to curb the drive, he can use several effective equalizers. Well-drilled players can use an assortment of the rocker step, head fake, cross-over step, stutter step, change-of-pace, and other good beginning moves to get the defensive man to commit himself and therefore be off-balance. Also effective at this point is an occasional pick by a teammate. These will give the defensive man an additional possibility to think about and look for, and will make the 1-on-1 more effective.

The Power Lay-Up

Use of the power lay-up is becoming increasingly popular. This is one of the best inside moves in basketball. After he has become proficient in its use, the offensive man can employ it from any angle. However, it is used best when the position of the defensive man is behind and slightly to one side of the man with the ball. In preparing to take this shot, the offensive player will usually turn his body away from the basket. The move should be started with a head fake and dribble to get the defense moving. The defense must be moving so that if there is contact when the actual lunge is made, an offensive foul will not result. Of course, if the defense does not move, then a simple drop step and pivot will place the offensive man in an excellent shooting position.

The offensive player's move to the basket must be quick, and his body position from which it starts has to vary. He should remember that the surprise element is very important. With both feet set, he should start his lunge. His body should be in a position revealing the basket to the shooter, slightly in front of the defensive man. The defensive man still has only a shoulder to guard. With his arms extended outward at a 45° angle away from the defensive man, the offensive player should release the ball using a wrist motion only, against the board.

Each of the previously mentioned fundamentals can be learned and perfected by any basketball player who has average ability, a desire to learn, and enough self-discipline to spend many off-season hours on the basketball court.

Chapter 8

BIG MAN POWER DRILLS

by Ted Zigler

1. *Tip Drills*. a) the player does ten tips with each hand, then tries to score on the last tip; b) figure-8 tip drill (Diagram 8-1); c) four-player tip drill (Diagram 8-1A)

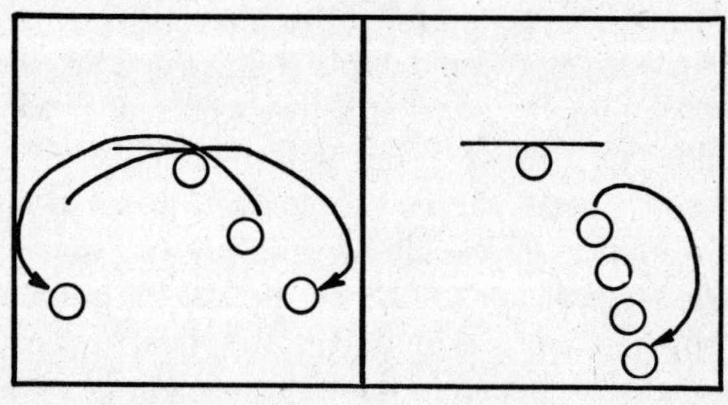

Diagram 8-1 **Diagram 8-1A**

2. *Mikan Drill*. The player executes a short hook shot, rebounds and shoots another hook shot from the other side. He continues in this fashion for a certain time or number of shots. The ball should never hit the ground.

3. *Superman Drill*. This drill consists of rebounding, side to side, across the lane (Diagram 8-2). The player must go back and forth, catch the ball, turn, put it up and go catch it again. The player is not trying to make a basket.

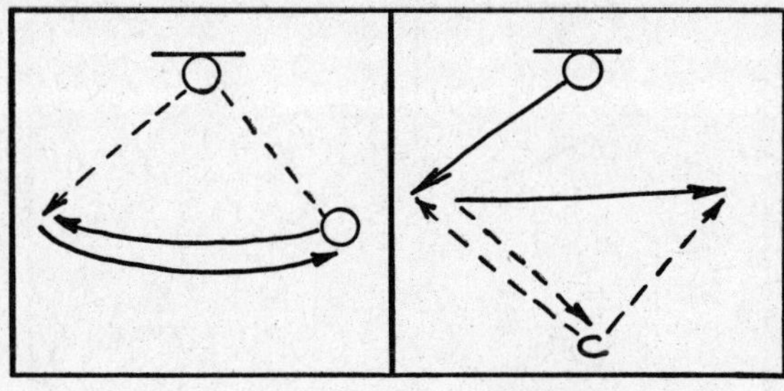

Diagram 8-2 **Diagram 8-3**

4. *Pick-Ups*. The coach rolls two balls in different directions as rapidly as possible. The player must gather up one ball, pass it back and then go get the other ball (Diagram 8-3).

5. *Etzler Drill* (Diagram 8-4). In this drill there is a ball on each block. The player must get the ball, power it in, go get the other ball and power it in, then back again. Two other players rebound the balls. This drill should be performed for a certain length of time. In a variation of this drill the player must shoot over the upstretched hands of the rebounders. The rebounders can also give a shove or push, making contact as if in a game situation.

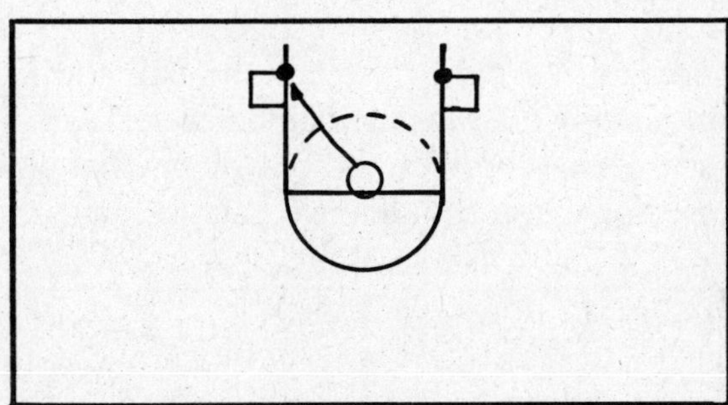

Diagram 8-4

6. *Three Basic Low Post Moves* (Diagram 8-5). These moves should be practiced often. a) power move—drop-step with dribble; b) turn-around jump shot; c) quick move to the middle of the lane

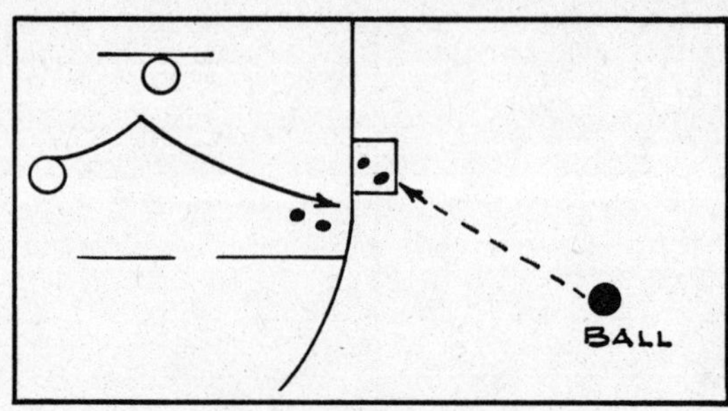

Diagram 8-5

for jumper/hook/stab. On all of these moves the offensive player should be taught to attempt to get to a position where his baseline foot is on or very close to the block. This is the spot he should aim for when he flashes to the low post.

7. *DeVoe Drill* (Diagram 8-6). This drill enables the player to work on the three basic low post moves alone. The player tosses the ball out with a reverse spin, jumps out and lands on two feet in a proper jump stop. He grabs the ball and executes one of the three moves.

8. *Get Open Drill* (Diagram 8-7). The offensive player must move strong to get the ball, working on pinning the defensive player on his side or behind him and giving a hand target to the passer. On one side the player catches the ball and passes it back out, then immediately goes for the ball on the other side, catches it and tries to score on the defensive player on that side. The drill ends on a score, or when the defense gets the ball.

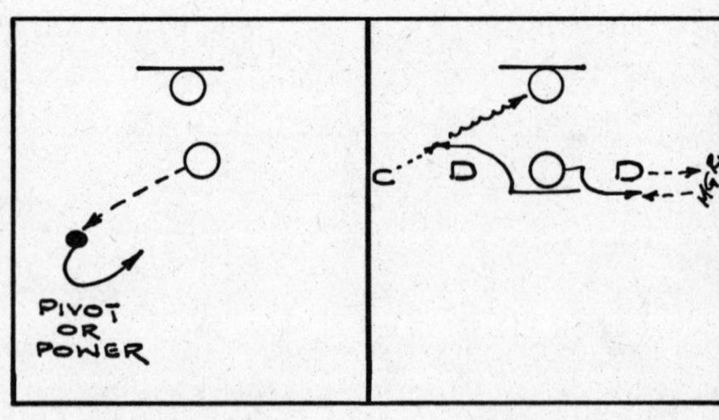

Diagram 8-6 Diagram 8-7

9. *Get Big Drill* (Diagram 8-8). The offensive player comes to the ball, working on pinning the defensive player behind him or on one side, and on giving the hand target. The player must spread out, making himself as big as possible, taking up as much room as possible. Once the offensive player gets the ball, it is one-on-one to a score or defensive rebound.

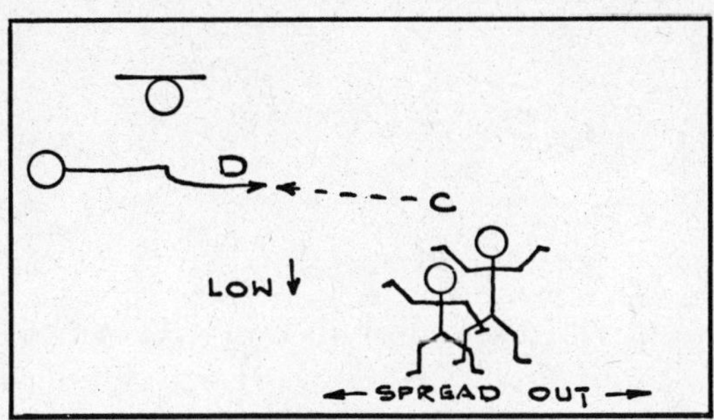

Diagram 8-8

10. *Getting to the Power Blocks* (Diagram 8-9). In this drill, teach the player to get to what we call the *power blocks* for his shot. He catches the ball in the power block, goes off both feet for a strong power shot; or, he may catch the ball and take one dribble to get into the power block for his muscle shot. This drill should also be done with the offensive player giving a head fake and then going up for a shot.

It should be emphasized in practice that the players always square up, facing the basket when at the high post or on the wing.

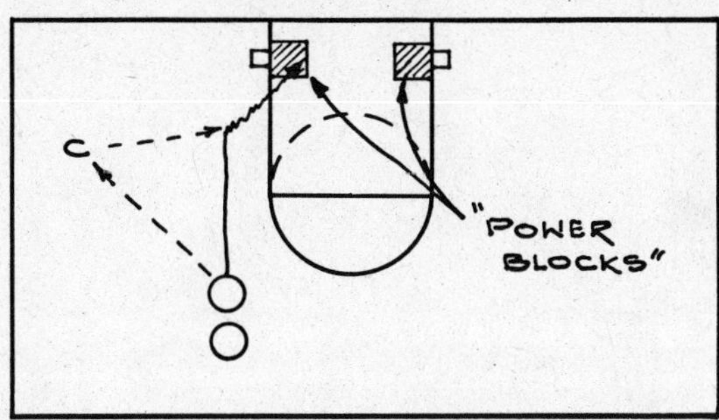

Diagram 8-9

Chapter 9

REBOUNDING DRILLS

by Dr. Walter J. Nitardy

The box-out whistle drill is shown in Diagram 9-1.

Using the three circles on the court, pair off players of similar size and assign three or four pairs to each circle, with a manager or assistant coach at the center of each circle with a whistle.

When the manager blows his whistle, the offensive rebounders outside the circle attempt to get around their partners and touch the manager. Their partners act as defensive opponents and try to box and ride the offensive players out of the circle for approximately three seconds. The managers blow the whistle a second time after a 5-second count to stop the drill.

Rotate offensive and defensive assignments. Competition can be added to the drill by not rotating if the offensive rebounder gets into the circle and touches the manager.

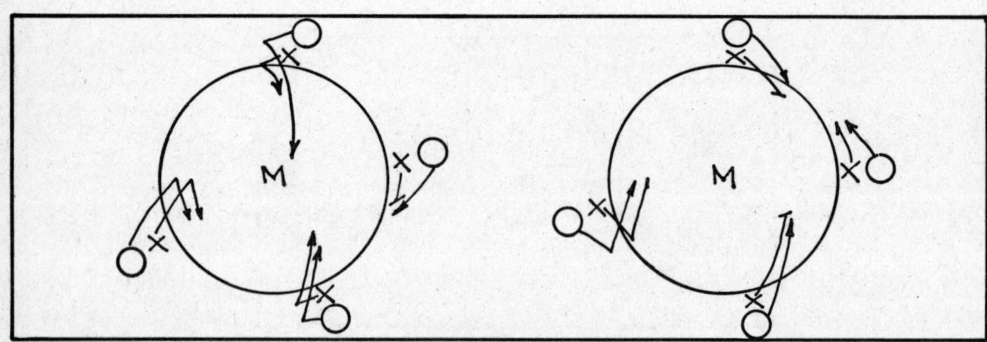

Diagram 9-1

Have the manager or assistant coach keep the whistle at his mouth to avoid anticipation by the rebounders.

Offensive rebounders must attempt to maneuver legally around the defensive players, not over their backs.

The defensive rebounder must sight his opponent and pivot in front of him. A back, or reverse pivot, on the foot closest to the offensive rebounder will prove most satisfactory. The defensive man's arms should be held out to the side of his body and bent at the elbow. In this manner, they may be used to feel for the movements of the opponent but not to hold him.

The defensive rebounder must make contact with the offensive rebounder by placing his butt into him and ride his offensive movements without backing into him. The elbows are out to help feel for the opponent but must not be swung at him.

Diagram 9-2 shows the dummy rebound drill.

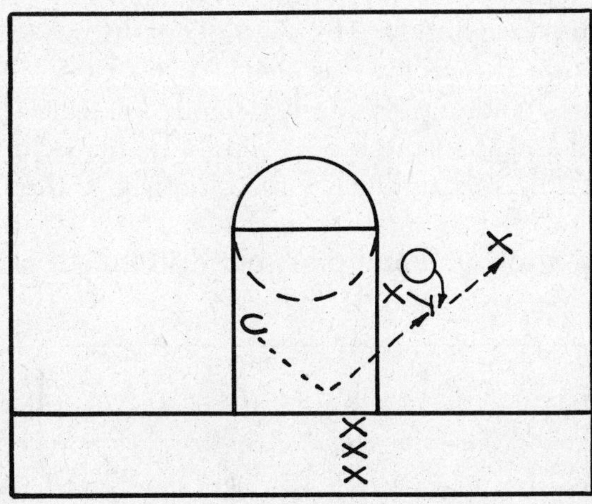

Diagram 9-2

Position yourself on one side of the basket and place a defensive rebounder and an offensive rebounder on the other side, approximately 8 feet from the basket. The offensive rebounder should offer only simulated movements to the basket so that the defensive rebounder must box him but can concentrate on controlling the ball and making a good pitch-out to a third player along the nearest sideline. Try to carom the rebound off the backboard.

Other forwards should wait out of bounds to rotate into the drill from defensive rebounding to offensive rebounding to receiving the pitch-out. Use several balls to keep the drill moving.

The defensive rebounder must box-out the offensive rebounder at least 6 to 8 feet from the basket and deeper, if possible, so that the rebound does not go over his head.

The defensive rebounder must go up to meet the ball at an angle toward the basket. If the defensive rebounder takes the rebound directly over his head, the offensive rebounder may be able to steal or slap the ball out of his hands.

As the defensive rebounder comes down with the ball, he should pivot away from the basket, keeping the ball at eye level with his elbows out. He should not bring the ball down below his chest. A defensive rebounder who brings the ball down below his chest may have it stolen, or he may be tied up and a jump ball will be the result.

In order to start a fast break, the rebounder must get rid of the ball quickly but accurately. He should not throw the pitch-out away, but be sure the receiver is clear for the pass. The pitch-out should be a one-handed pass or a two-handed sidearm pass thrown from the shoulder. Most pitch-outs should be made to the nearest sideline unless the rebounder is forced to pivot to the inside as he rebounds.

The 3-on-3 rebound and pitch-out drill is shown in Diagram 9-3.

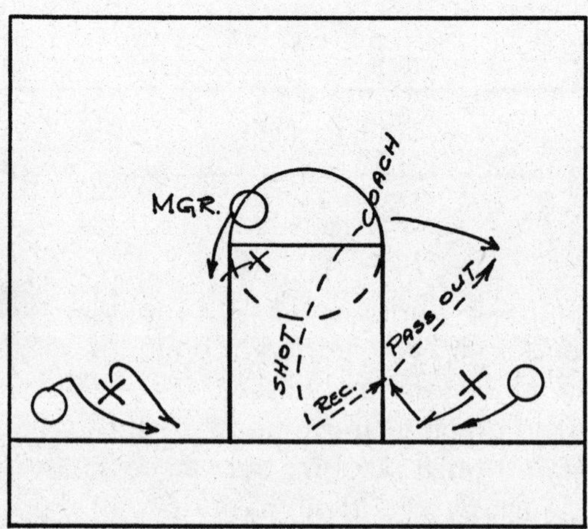

Diagram 9-3

Divide the team or just the forwards into groups of three of approximately equal size and weight. Three players act as offensive rebounders maneuvering aggressively to get the rebound, with three opponents attempting to box and ride them off the boards and control the ball.

Start the offensive rebounders approximately 15 feet from the basket. At times allow one offensive rebounder to assume a medium or low pivot position.

One or two players are used outside without defense to act as shooters and to receive the pitch-out. They may be coaches, managers or guards.

When a defensive rebounder gets the ball, he pitches it out to one of the outside men. If an offensive rebounder controls the ball, he may shoot or pass the ball back out.

In order to rotate off defensive rebounding, the defensive rebounders must control two successive rebounds, at which time the teams change assignments.

The outside shooters attempt to hit the rim of the basket, not score. They may occasionally feed offensive rebounders so they can take the shot in order to keep them honest.

If all defensive rebounders check, box, and ride their opponents off the boards as soon as the shot is taken, it is possible for the ball to fall on the floor untouched. However, the objective is for each defensive rebounder to keep his man away from the boards until the direction and distance of the rebound are established, and the closest defensive rebounder can jump to meet the ball.

Timing is most important. The defensive rebounder must not charge in for the rebound or leave his feet too soon.

Do not look immediately at the basket when the shot is taken. It takes a second or more for the shot to reach the basket and rebound. A defensive player should use that time to check the movement of the offensive rebounder and establish body contact between him and the basket. A reverse pivot on the foot closest to the offensive player is best used to establish legal contact immediately and ride the opponents off the boards.

The defensive rebounder must go to meet the ball and keep it up at eye level after grasping the rebound. Two hands should be used to grab the rebound. Body control must be established before a quick and accurate pitch-out can be made. Although anticipation of a shot and the direction of a rebound are important characteristics of successful offensive rebounding, the offensive rebounders should not be allowed to cheat too much on this drill. Occasionally, the ball should be thrown to them for the shot. By the same token, the defensive rebounders must start from the correct defensive position before boxing out, depending upon where the shot is taken.

Diagram 9-4 shows the free throw line rebound-and-break drill.

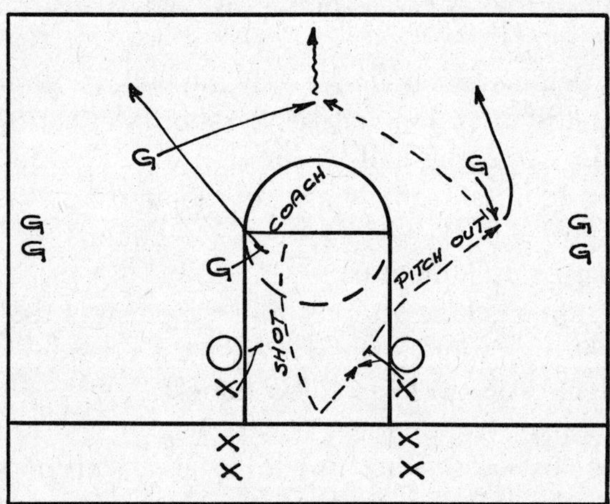

Diagram 9-4

The forwards rotate under the basket as defensive and then offensive rebounders. Guards rotate outside and on the free throw line box-out to receive a pitch-out and break down the court on a three-man break. The coach or manager acts as a free throw shooter. A fast break from out-of-bounds after a successful free throw may also be practiced.

One or two defensive guards can be added to this drill to hamper the fast break.

As a rule, the offensive guard nearest the rebounder with the ball receives the pitch-out and the opposite guard takes the center lane. The guard who is boxing out the free throw shooter takes the opposite side lane. However, any offensive pattern may be used, and several alternatives should be practiced.

After a rebound has been pitched out and three men have executed the fast break down the court, new guards take their places on the court and the forwards rotate as the coach receives the ball to put up another free throw shot.

A quick step-in and strong box-out by the defense after a free throw attempt hits the rim is essential and must be practiced regularly throughout the season. The assignment for boxing-out the free throw shooter must be clarified, and usually is the job of a forward or the tallest guard. Therefore, the forwards should work along with the guards on the free throw line box-out position.

The pitch-out must be quick and accurate but the rebounder must be sure that his teammate is clear and no opponent is in a position to steal the pass. As a rule, the guard receiving the pitch-out is responsible for meeting the ball, unless a long lead pass is possible.

This drill can be run by having five offensive and five defensive players on the court, with one team practicing the free throw line fast break in one direction, and then the other team practicing a return break. Players can take turns shooting the free throw shot. A fast break pattern should be established from out-of-bounds after a successful free throw.

part TWO

Offense

Chapter 10

THE SINGLE POST OFFENSE

by Kenneth A. Hunter

Over the years we have developed a highly successful single post man-for-man attack. Any well-executed offense will meet with some degree of success; however, we believe our single post attack includes practically every possible option, and is so versatile that only a defense with superior personnel is able to defense it effectively.

The basic alignment is shown in Diagram 10-1. The center, 01, is positioned on the free throw line as a high post. 02 and 03, both forwards, are at a point which is approximately 10 feet from the baseline and 15 feet from the sideline. The guards, 04 and 05, are both 15 feet from, and directly in front of, the forwards. When using the single post, our attack is always started from the floor position shown in Diagram 10-1.

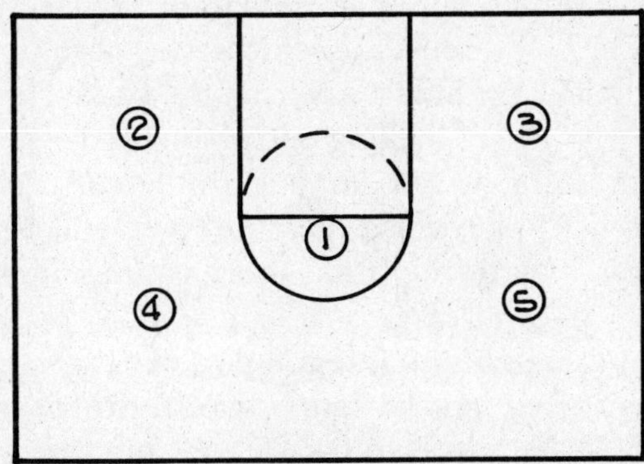

Diagram 10-1

The first offensive maneuver is the high split. 04 passes the ball to 01, cuts sharply off the stationary post, and immediately returns to the center court for defensive purposes. The second cutter, 05, gets an angle and crosses over the high post in the hope of rubbing his man on 01. By getting an angle, we mean the offensive maneuver of a player who takes his defensive opponent behind a stationary screen before cutting over the top, and prevents the defense from stepping up and sliding through. If 05 is successful in rubbing his defensive man on 01, then he will drive for a lay-up; however, if the defensive man, X5, slides behind 01, then 05 will pull up and take a 15-foot jump shot over the screen. The on-side forward (the forward who is on the same side as the ball) clears to the opposite side, taking his defensive opponent with him, thereby allowing the guard to score on a uncontested lay-up.

The only defensive player who can prevent the lay-up resulting from the high split is X1. If X1 switches and prevents the lay-up, then 05 drops the ball off to 01, who has rolled toward the basket for the score. The high split can be run to both sides.

If X1 applies defensive pressure and prevents the pass into the high post man, then 01 rolls out to the on-side. This offensive maneuver is called the weak-side guard play. As the center, 01 clears to the on-side, the guard, 05, passes to the forward, 02, who comes up to the high post. In order to prevent an interception or deflection, this pass must not be thrown directly at the forward, but to his outside. Then 04 cuts directly for the basket, receives a bounce pass from 02, and scores on a lay-up. The weak-side guard can also be run to both sides.

Forward action is automatically initiated any time a guard passes to a forward. Whenever forward action is started, the center clears to the off-side (the side away from the ball). Then the on-side guard has the privilege of making one of four choices. After passing to the forward, he may set an outside screen, go behind the forward, which is the key for a double screen clear, so that a one-on-one situation may develop for the forward, or remain in the same position.

The double screen is an integral part of our forward action. 05 passes to 03 and goes behind him while 01 nd 02 are setting the double screen. As 03 passes to 04, 05 rubs his man on the double screen, receives a pass from 04, and takes a 10-foot jump shot.

Whenever a guard passes to a forward and goes through, in effect, a give-and-go play results. In these situations the forwards should always be alert to take advantage of a possible defensive mistake by making a quick return pass to the guard, as he cuts toward the basket, for an easy two points.

When a guard passes the ball to a forward and clears to the off side, an automatic one-on-one situation develops. As shown in Diagram 10-2, 05 passes to 03 and clears, thereby providing 03, after maneuvering X3 out of position, with an opportunity to score. In early season practice sessions, several one-on-one offensive drills, which enable the forwards to be effective in this phase of our attack, are stressed.

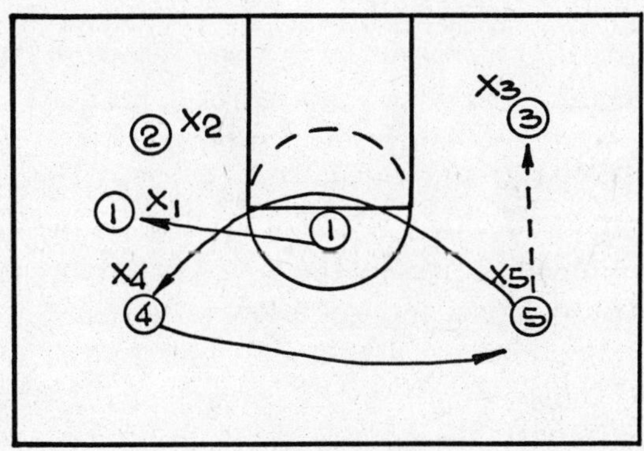

Diagram 10-2

If 05 remains in the same spot after passing to 03 and receives a return pass, then an inside screen takes place. As shown in Diagram 10-3, 03 sets a screen for 05. If X5 slides behind 03, then 05 takes an 18-foot jump shot. However, if X5 attempts to fight over the top and is rubbed, then 05 drives in for a lay-up. If X3 switches and prevents 05 from driving in, then 03 immediately rolls to the basket, receives a return pass, and scores.

In our forward action repertoire, there is also a basic maneuver, which we call the reverse. If the defensive player, X3, attempts to prevent the pass from 05 to 03, then our players automatically look for the reverse. The guard fakes a pass to the forward, who leans toward the ball, but does not move his feet. Then the

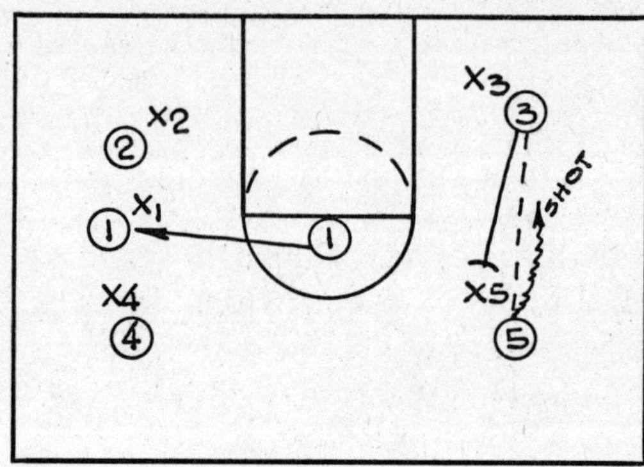

Diagram 10-3

defensive forward invariably steps out to block or intercept the pass. O5 reverses immediately, cuts directly for the basket, receives a bounce pass from the guard and scores. This play, as all others in our single post attack, can be run to both sides.

Our last basic maneuver (Diagram 10-4), resulting from forward action, is the low post split. When an inside screen does not develop following a pass by the guard to the forward, our center attempts to come across and get a low post position. We prefer to have the forward make the initial pass into the center for two reasons: first, it is difficult for the defense to steal or deflect the pass from that angle; second, we prefer to have the guard take the shot, because he is moving toward the basket, and not away, as is the case with the forward. The low post split has been very

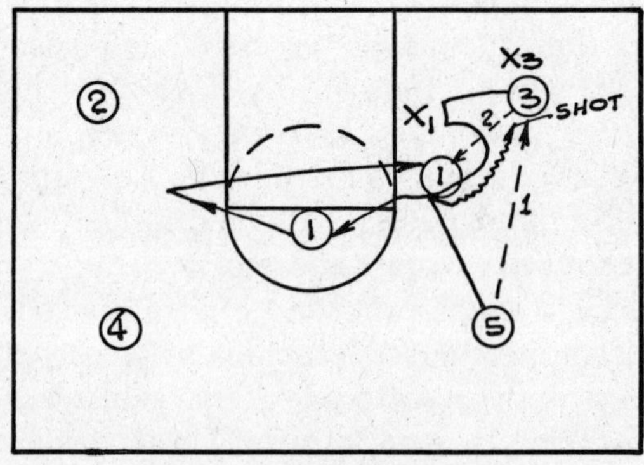

Diagram 10-4

effective, especially against sloughing or collapsing man-for-man defenses.

The fact that the success of any offense is dependent upon its execution cannot be overemphasized. During early season practice the various options are isolated, and sufficient time is devoted to perfecting them. For example,when teaching the high post split, our centers are stationed approximately 15 feet apart and the guards and forwards (cutters) form two lines in front of each center. During this drill we concentrate on footwork, getting a proper angle, and timing. A basketball is not used. Once the basic skills have been perfected, then a ball is inserted and defensive players are used. All other options of the single post attack are broken down in a similar manner.

Obviously, more time is allocated during early season practice for such drills; however, we do not hesitate, when a certain phase of our attack begins to sputter during the season, to isolate immediately for making corrections.

Chapter 11

THE DOUBLE POST OFFENSE

by Larry Forsythe

The strengths of the double post offense are excellent rebounding position, simple continuity, good floor balance, with all players afforded an opportunity to score. If there is a weakness, it is that some adjustments are necessary in order to contain an excellent fast break.

The basic floor arrangement is shown in Diagram 11-1. 01 is the head of the circle, and 02 is on the right wing. Usually, 02 plays fairly high, about straight out from where the circle joins the free throw line. 03 plays just about opposite 02 on the left side of the court. The two tallest players are left to fill the double post positions and become 04 and 05.

In regard to the placement of personnel, 01 should be tall, a good rebounder and shooter, and an excellent ball-handler.

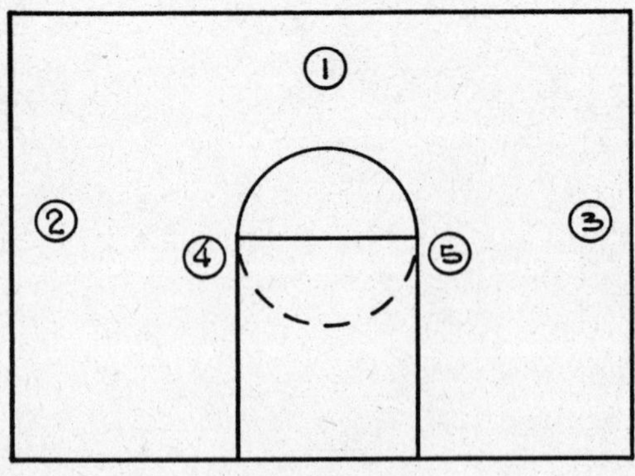

Diagram 11-1

02 should be the best outside shooter and a good rebounder.

Usually, 03 is the best defensive guard and a good ball-handler. If you have a weak outside shooter who has other outstanding qualities, this is where you should play him.

As a rule, 04 is the best big player and we like him to be an excellent shooter and strong rebounder.

05 has to be a strong rebounder, and if he is a good shooter, so much the better.

In the play shown in Diagram 11-2, 01 starts the offense by dribbling and then passing to 02. Then 01 cuts to the corner, passing close to 04 as he remains alert for a return pass from 02. On arriving in the corner, 01 receives a pass from 02 if he did not receive the ball during his cut. When 02 passes to 01 in the corner, 04 breaks down the side of the lane to the low post, looking for a lob pass from 01. If 04 does not receive the pass from 01, he crosses to the low post on the side with 05.

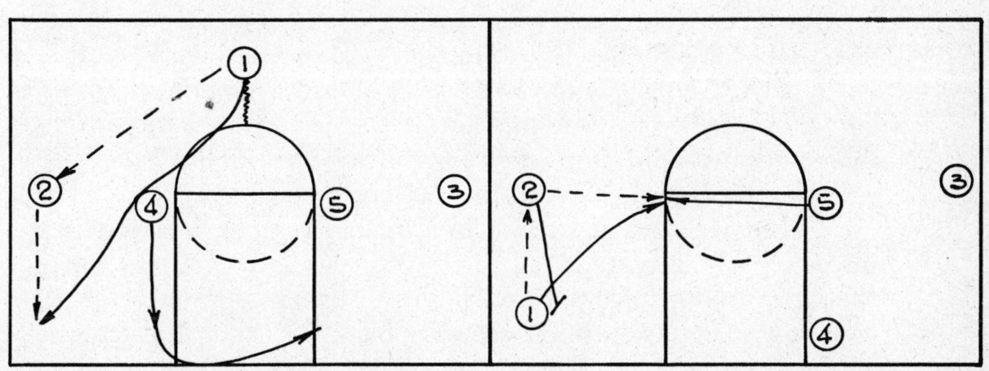

Diagram 11-2 **Diagram 11-3**

As shown in Diagram 11-3, 01 is unable to hit 04, so he returns the pass to 02. When 02 receives the ball, 05 breaks across the lane to a spot near 04's original position, looking for a pass from 02. If 02 is able to hit 05 breaking across the lane, he moves quickly to set a screen for 01 in the corner. 01 comes off the screen and 02 either turns and shoots or gives to 01 off the screen for the good jump shot.

In the continuing action shown in Diagram 11-4, 02 is unable to hit 03 breaking across the lane. When 03 realizes this, he breaks to 01's original position and 02 passes to him as he breaks. When 04 sees 03 in position at or near the top of the circle and in possession

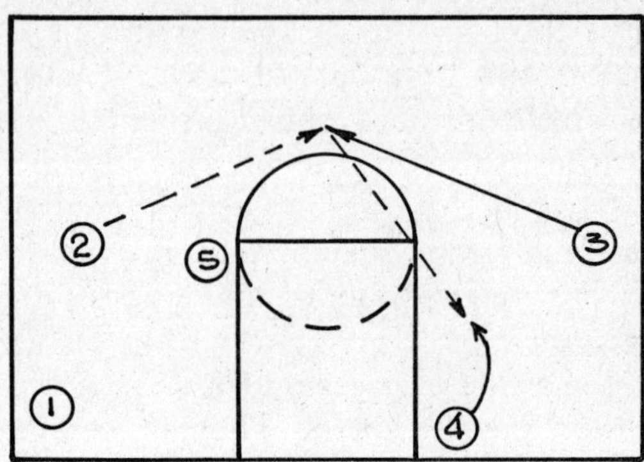

Diagram 11-4

of the ball, he breaks out from the low post and receives a pass from 03. The option is effective against zone defenses when the ball is brought rapidly around from the far corner.

04 is unable to shoot when he receives the ball. At this point, 01 breaks along the baseline to the low post on 04's side. If he does not receive the pass at the low post position, he continues to the corner where 04 passes to him and breaks to the low post position 01 has just vacated, and looks for the lob pass from 01 and the resulting short jump shot or hook, (Diagram 11-5).

As shown in Diagram 11-6, 01 is unable to hit 04 breaking back into the post position. At this point 03 breaks down from the top of the circle to the angle position and receives a pass from 01,who in turn moves on 03's outside, receives a hand-off, and dribbles to the

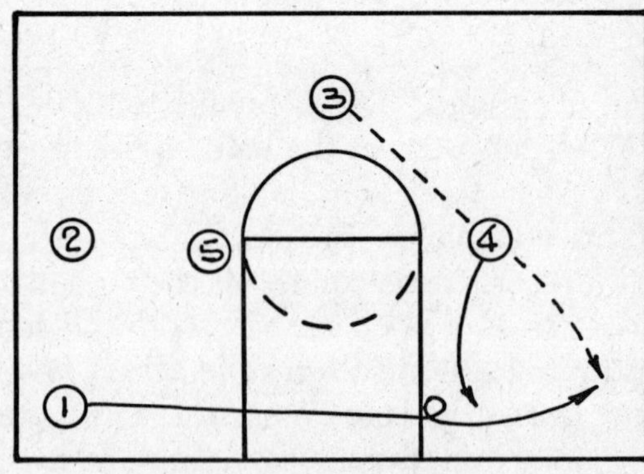

Diagram 11-5

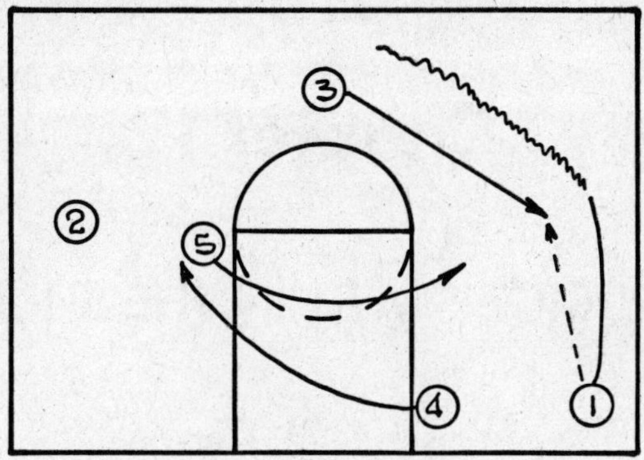

Diagram 11-6

top of the circle. As this takes place, 04 and 05 exchange positions and the team is back in the original floor arrangement.

Any time a shot is taken, the players are instructed to go to the boards, with the exception of the deepest man, who is normally the man at the head of the circle or the weak-side angle player.

Chapter 12

VARIATIONS WITHIN THE SHUFFLE

by Glenn M. Carson

The secret of any successful offense is intelligent use of the available personnel in order to take advantage of an opponent's weaknesses. This is one of the responsibilities coaches must accept if they expect to win games against strong opposition.

One or two well-learned patterns which have simple variations will work more successfully than many patterns and alignments. At the present time more teams are using the same alignment and patterns against both the man-for-man and the zone defense. We use the shuffle alignment and pattern against both of these defenses. (Diagram 12-1).

In the basic pattern (Diagram 12-2), 02 passes to 01 and starts

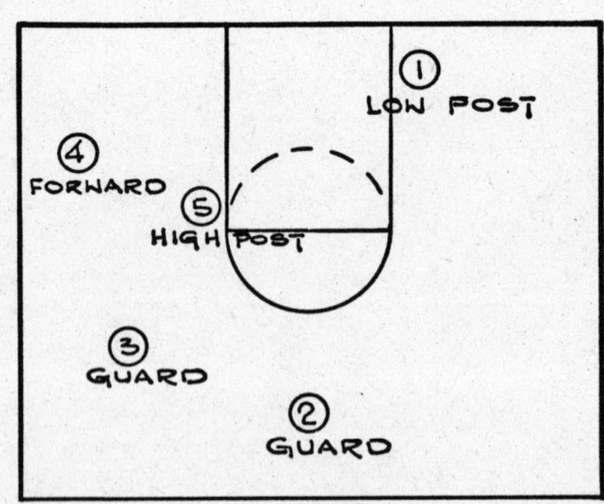

Diagram 12-1

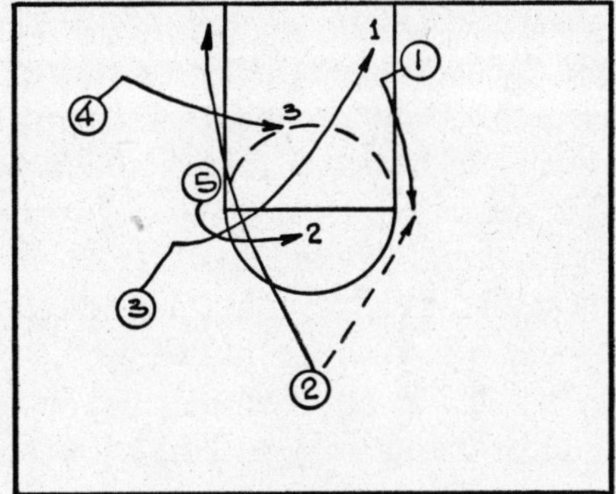

Diagram 12-2

his screening moves for 05 and 04. If 02 is tall, he will be able to rebound on missed shots, 03 cuts off 05 either way on a lay-up for the first scoring opportunity. 05 cuts over 02's screen for a 15-foot jump shot on the second scoring opportunity. Then 04 cuts off 02's screen for a short jump shot in the lane for the third scoring opportunity. If no shot is taken, the turnovers are shown in Diagram 12-3. 01 and 05 become the guards, 03 becomes the forward, 04 becomes the high post, and 02 becomes the low post. This pattern can be continued from left to right until a good shot is secured.

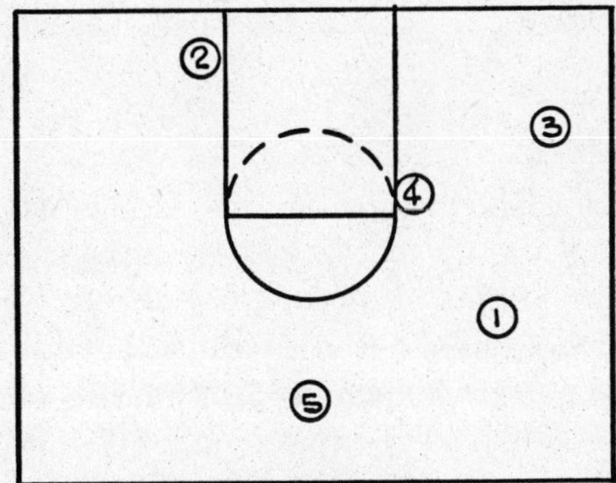

Diagram 12-3

Our first variation is a four-man rotation, which is used for two reasons. The first one is to play a small guard and not have to send him to the board to rebound, and the second is to take a tall defensive man from the board to give the offense an advantage in rebounding. This variation is shown in Diagram 12-4. In the turnover of this variation, 02 remains constant. If a team has a small guard who is an excellent ball-handler, a good outside shooter, or a good defensive man, this variation of the shuffle pattern will work advantageously. It will not be necessary to send him to rebound against larger opponents on offense. This pattern can also be used to draw a tall defensive man away from the board by stationing the offensive man who is being guarded by the tall defensive man at the 02 spot. The turnover of this variation is shown in Diagram 12-5. 02 remains as a guard, 01 becomes the other guard, 03 becomes the forward, 04 becomes the high post, and 05 becomes the low post.

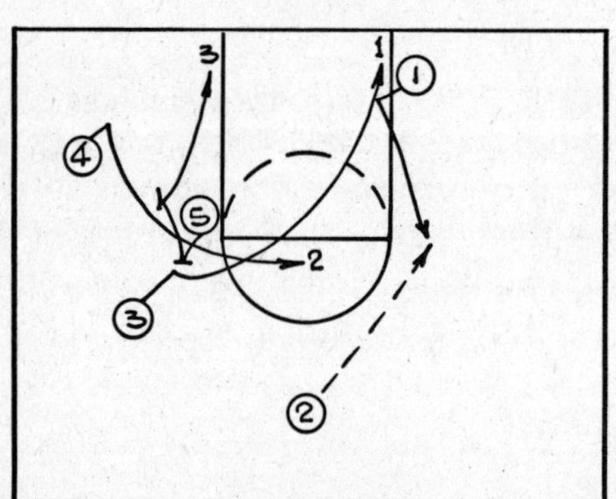

Diagram 12-4

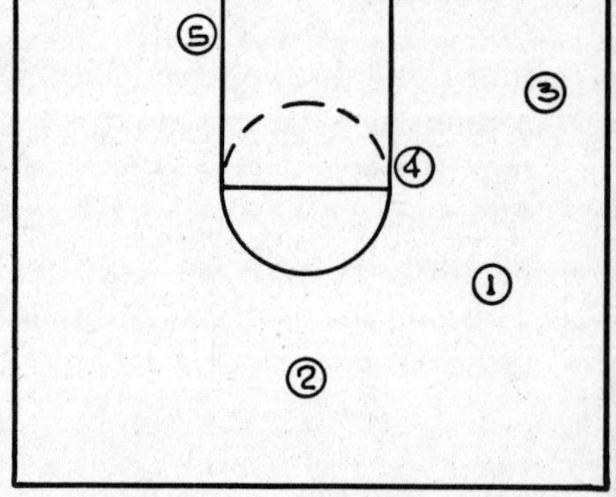

Diagram 12-5

The variation shown in Diagram 12-6 is used to keep a tall offensive player at the 05 spot to take advantage of his rebounding, tipping or short-shooting ability. It may also be used to keep a tall player inside who does not play outside effectively. The only change from the pattern shown in Diagram 12-4 is that 04 cuts back toward the weak-side baseline to screen for 05 if 04 does not receive the ball at the free throw line for a jump shot. The turnover for this variation is shown in Diagram 12-7. 02 remains as a guard, 01

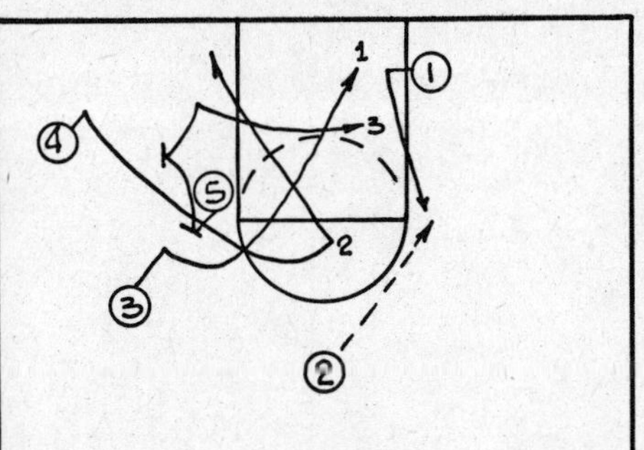

Diagram 12-6

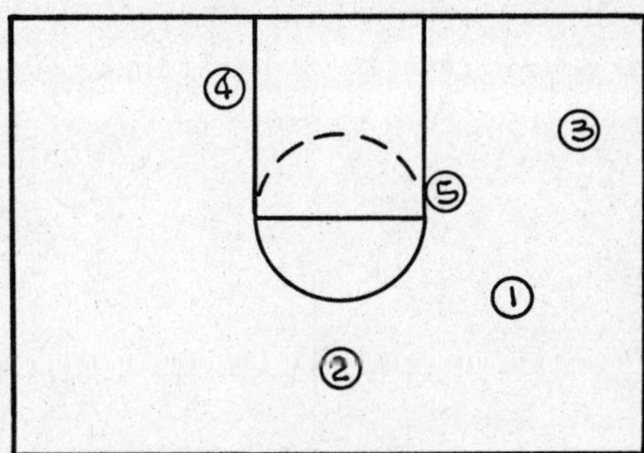

Diagram 12-7

becomes the other guard, 03 becomes the forward, 05 stays at the high post, and 04 becomes the low post.

Diagram 12-8 shows a variation which allows a tall guard who has height advantage over his defensive man to go inside and attempt a high-percentage shot. The only change in this variation from the pattern shown in Diagram 12-2 is the cutback and screen by 04 for 02. 04 is responsible for starting the variations shown in Diagrams 12-6 and 12-8. The turnover for this variation is shown in Diagram 12-9. 05 and 01 become the guards. 03 becomes the forward, 02 becomes the high post, and 04 becomes the low post.

Diagram 12-10 shows a variation which can be used in three ways. First, a good player at the No. 1 position is given more scoring opportunities by screening for him. The second is to keep the tall 01 and 05 players inside, and the third is to keep the smaller 02, 03, and 04 men playing outside. The pattern starts (Diagram

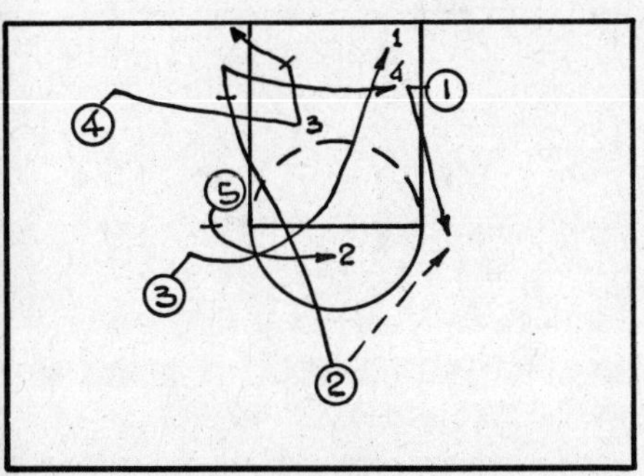

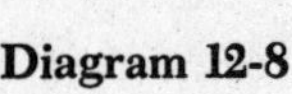

Diagram 12-8

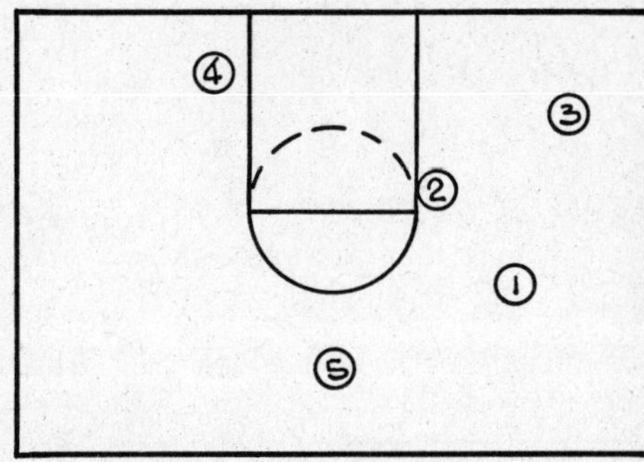

Diagram 12-9

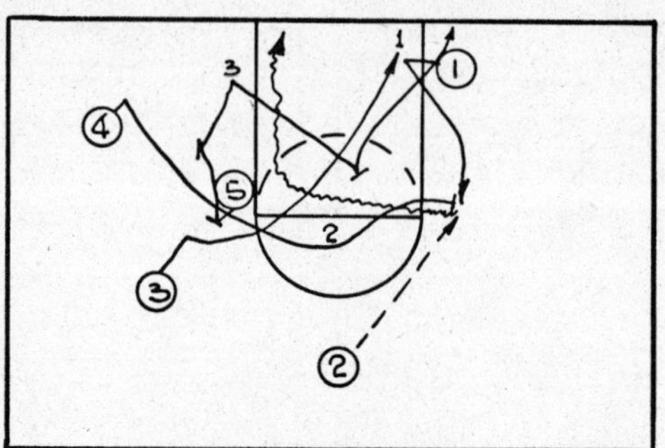

Diagram 12-10

12-4) as 01 looks for 03, 04, and 05 in that order. If these options are not open, 04 continues across the lane to screen for 01. If 01 cannot get a shot, 05 comes across the lane to set a moving screen and rolls. Again, 01 shoots, drives, passes to 05 for a shot, or out to 02 if none of these scoring opportunities is open. The rotation is shown in Diagram 12-11. 02 remains as a guard. 04 becomes a guard, 03 goes to forward, 05 stays at the high post, and 01 stays at the low post. This variation keeps 01 at the low post and 05 at the high post position at all times.

Many defensive teams will overplay 01 to keep him from receiving the ball. The offensive team must have a maneuver to counter this defensive move. Diagram 12-12 shows how 01 is overplayed, and cannot receive the ball from 02. Then 01 moves across the lane to screen for 05 who receives the pass from 02. 01 becomes the high post player who screens for 03 as he cuts through. Then

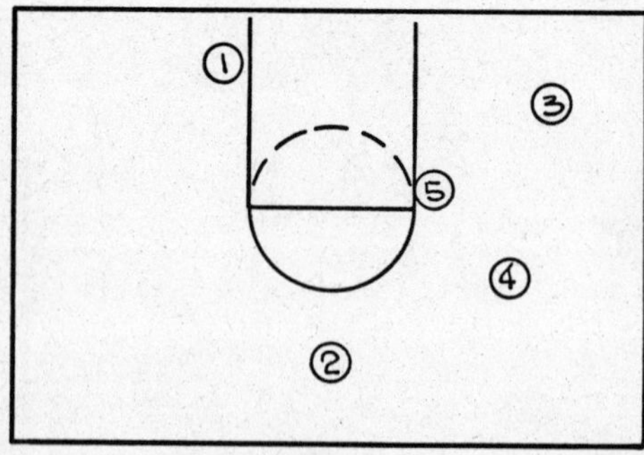

Diagram 12-11

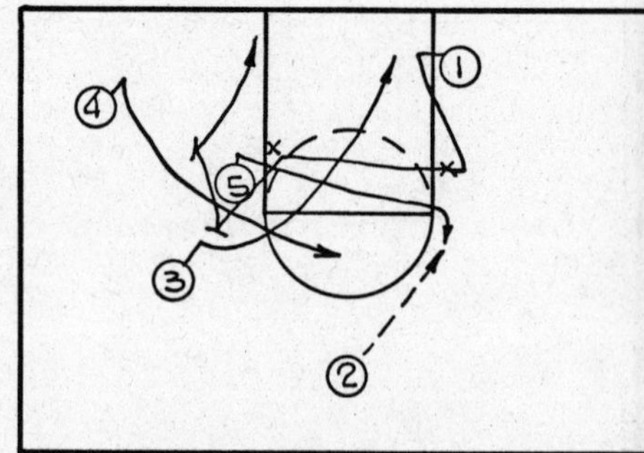

Diagram 12-12

the pattern can continue with any of the patterns or variations previously described.

We have presented simple shuffle variations which can be used to take advantage of defensive personnel or weakness in a man-for-man defense. These variations also give the offense an advantage in being able to use players at positions where they can perform best.

Every coach is looking for an all-purpose offense which can be used against the man-for-man and zone defenses with equal effectiveness. This is especially true as many teams change defenses often during a single game. Having one offense can make players more effective because they have only one offense to learn. More time can be devoted to fundamentals, shooting, and defense since less time will be required to work on team offense. When practice time is limited, this is a great timesaver.

Our zone attack will work against all zones and thus saves valuable time. Diagrams 12-13 and 12-14 show a simple but effective move against a 1-2-2 or 1-3-1 zone. Either 02 or 03 feeds 05 who turns, shoots or passes to 01 or 04 who has cut under the goal for a shot.

Many teams used to move only the ball against zones but today with improved zone defenses, both the ball and the players should be moved. The shuffle accomplishes this maneuver very well. It also uses the overload principle of attacking zones with its starting alignment and moves into a 1-3-1 alignment when 03 cuts to the baseline.

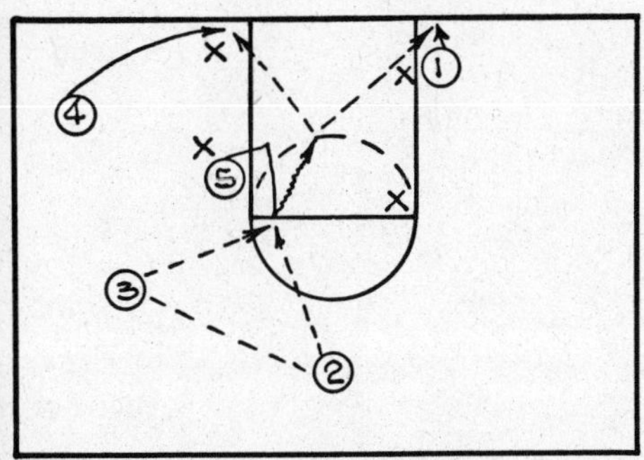

Diagram 12-13

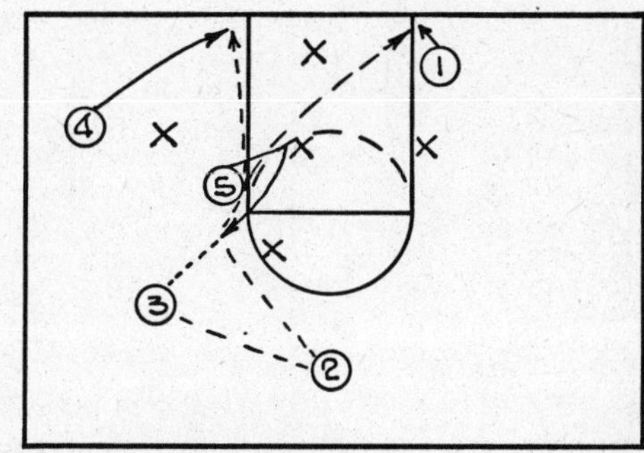

Diagram 12-14

Diagrams 12-15, 12-16, 12-17, 12-18, and 12-19 show the progression and shooting opportunities against a 2-1-2 or 2-3 zone when the ball is fed to 01. 01 breaks wider against the zone than he would against the man-for-man-defense. 03 also breaks faster to the

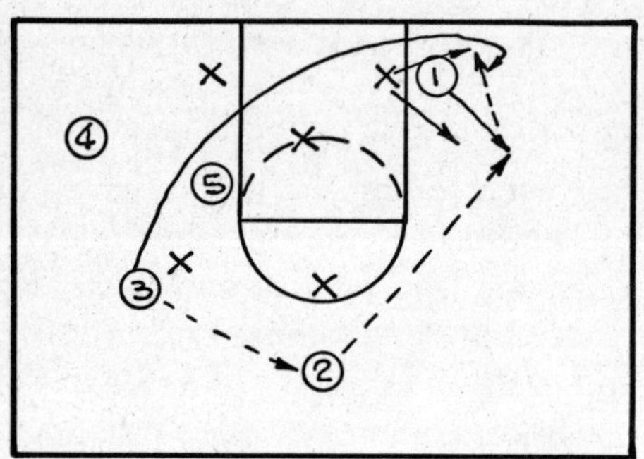

Diagram 12-15

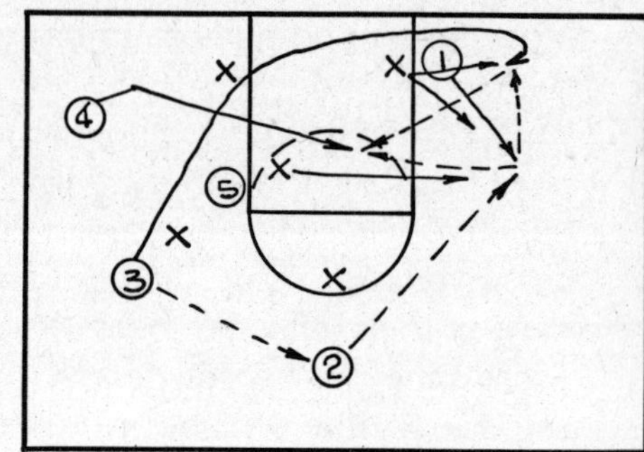

Diagram 12-16

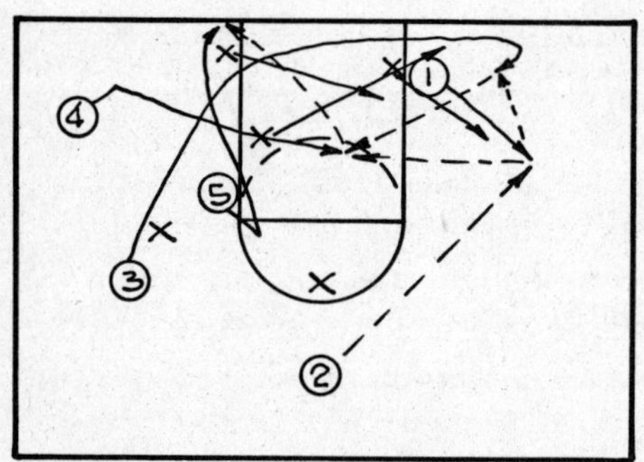

Diagram 12-17

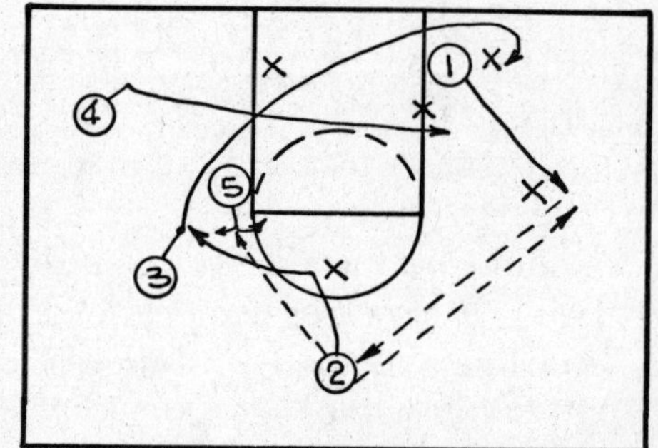

Diagram 12-18

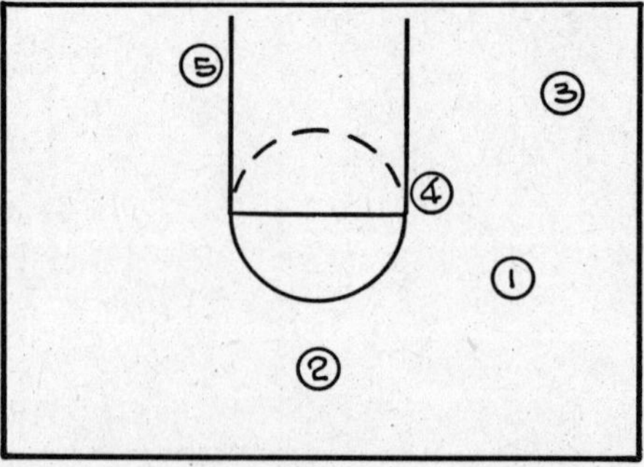

Diagram 12-19

baseline so 01 will not have to pass to him. 03 does not use 05's screen against zones. The baseline defensive man must cover 01 and 03, since both players are in his zone. Diagram 12-15 shows that 01 should shoot if left unguarded, or pass quickly to 03 if he is guarded. In turn 03 shoots. If the middle defensive man covers 01 or 03, then 04 is breaking quickly into the area that the middle defensive man has just left (Diagram 12-16). Then 04 is open for a pass from either 01 or 03. 04 will be given the opportunity to make a good short jump shot from just in front of the basket. If the weak-side baseline defensive man moves to cover 04 in the lane, then 05 should roll back to receive a pass from 04 for a lay-up (Diagram 12-17). If the 2-1-2 or 2-3 zone covers 01 with an outside man (Diagram 12-18), a quick pass back to 02 and a reverse of the ball to 05 who shoots or passes to 02 who shoots over 05 will get results.

Diagram 12-19 shows the rotation if no shot is taken. It is the same rotation as the man-for-man pattern shown in Diagram 5. This pattern will also work effectively against a 1-2-2 or 1-3-1 zone.

It is important for 01 to receive the ball so low that an outside man in the zone defense will have difficulty covering him. This also holds true in the case of 04. 04 tries to align himself in the vacant space extended between the baseline and the front defensive man. This move causes some indecision as to which player is supposed to cover him.

Diagram 12-20 shows a simple but effective man-for-man pattern we have used to the strong side. An adaptation of this pattern is also used against zones. The first part of this strong-side zone pattern is shown in Diagram 12-21. 03 passes to 04 and cuts off

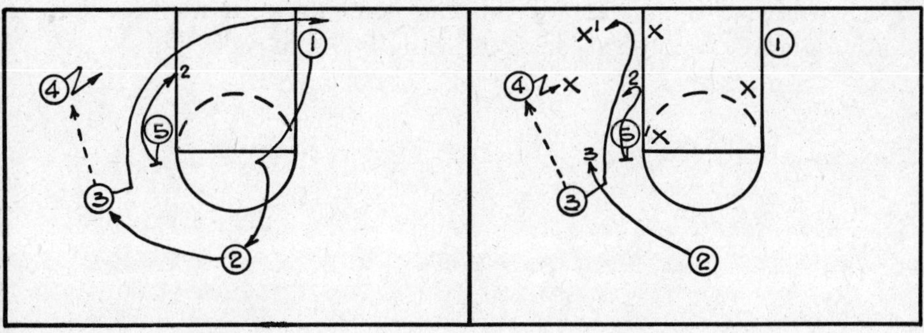

Diagram 12-20 **Diagram 12-21**

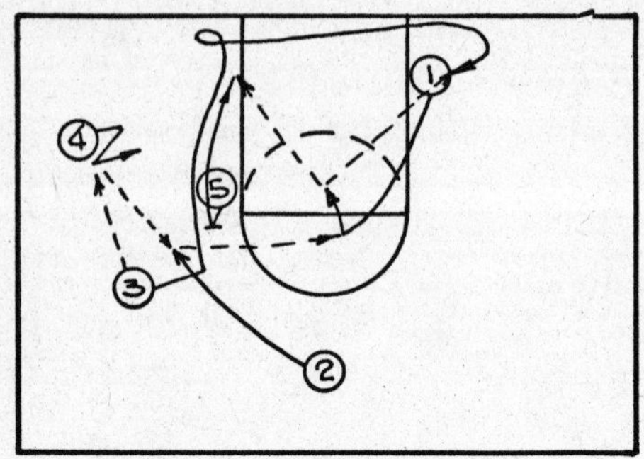

Diagram 12-22

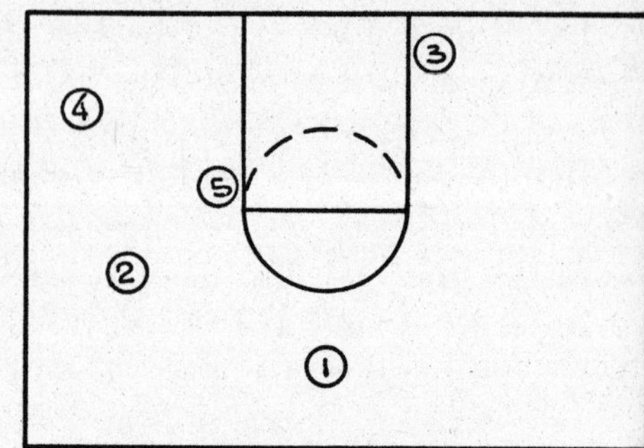

Diagram 12-23

05 to the baseline. If a baseline man covers 04, 03 may be open on the cut. If he is not open, then he fishhooks at the baseline for a possible pass. 05 rolls back down the lane a step or two for a possible pass and 02 cuts in front of 03's position. 04 looks for 03, 05, and 02 in that order, for a shot. On this overload, 05 will be open frequently.

If 04 cannot pass to 03 or 05, then he passes to 02 for a possible shot. If 02 cannot shoot, he looks for 01 who is breaking to the free throw line. In turn, 01 shoots or passes to 03 or 05 (Diagram 12-22). If no shot is taken, the rotation is as shown in Diagram 12-23.

These patterns may look complicated, but they are ready to master if the drills are worked out to use these movements. We have even used them successfully on the junior high school level.

Other advantages of these patterns are that they provide good team movements, a good percentage shot, rebounding strength, and defensive balance to stop the fast break. Simplicity is the key to successful basketball, and if you can combine your man-for-man and zone attack patterns, learning time is cut in half.

Chapter 13

THE PICK-AND-ROLL CONTINUITY OFFENSE

by Joseph D. McKay

Basketball coaches are faced with the problem of developing an offense which not only maintains floor balance, but also possesses continual offensive thrusts. Therefore, the pick-and-roll continuity offense should be considered by both the beginning coach as a basic offense, and the veteran coach as an effective replacement or supplement to his present offense.

Although this offense was developed for the standard single post (2-1-2) offense, it can easily be adapted to the other basic offenses. Various basic options are available, as shown in the accompanying diagrams, and the alert coach can devise additional options to match his personnel as his players master the basic pick-and-roll continuity options.

The offense offers an effective, floor-balanced, rotating offense which can succeed against the straight or the switching man-for-man defenses. It incorporates both the horizontal and vertical modes of attack, thereby rendering it useful against either defense. In addition, it can be operated to either side.

The offensive attack always begins with a guard hitting the forward who has faked into the basket and returned to the side for the pass. Diagram 13-1 shows the right side attack. For option one, the guard passes to the forward and step fakes for the basket, going all the way for the fundamental fake give-and-go if the defense does not take the fake.

If the defense does take the fake, option two begins as the guard sets a pick for the guard who cuts off him and off the pivot man who is at the free throw line (Diagram 13-2).

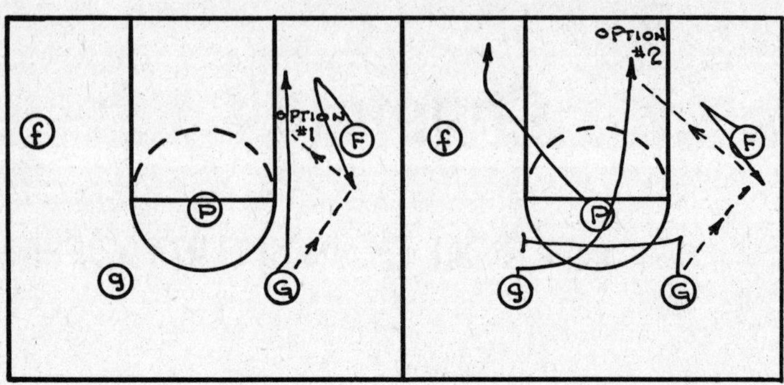

Diagram 13-1

Diagram 13-2

Then option 3 develops, because as soon as the cut by the post man is made, the pivot man picks to the negative side (away from the ball) for the forward who cuts off the pick into the lower or upper part of the key (Diagram 13-3). The positions of the five players are indicated by the letters in Diagram 13-4 as option 3 concludes and option 4 begins.

To begin option 4, the guard comes back to his original position, and the pivot man moves to the top right of the key area. It is essential that the guard move to the right of the basket so that he has the proper driving angle for the next thrust. The pivot man may position himself on the free throw line or on the corner of the side of the free throw area rectangle, facing the guard. Then the

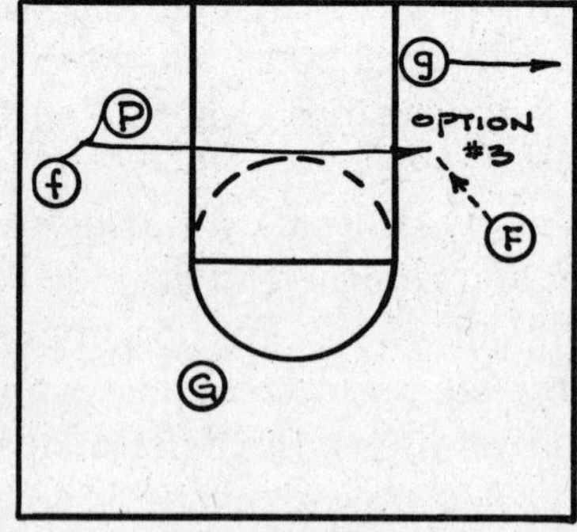

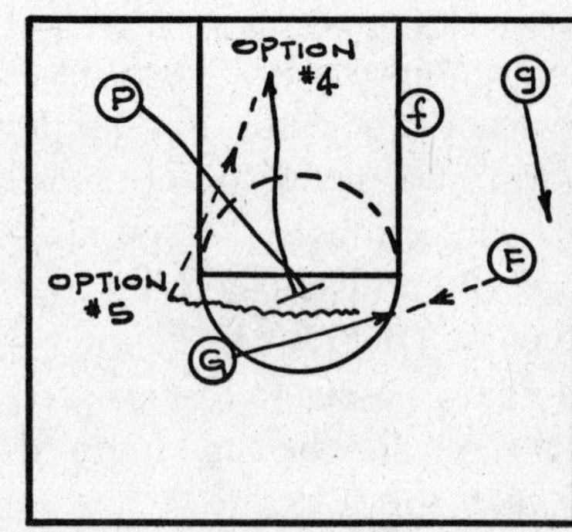

Diagram 13-3

Diagram 13-4

forward passes to the guard who fakes a drive right and drives left at an angle to drive his defensive man into the pivot. Here the pivot man keys on the guard's defensive man. If the defense switches, the pivot man reverse pivots, keeping the guard's defensive man on his hip, and rolls to the basket for the pass (option 4) from the guard. If no switch occurs, the pivot man merely contains the guard's defensive man with his pick and pivot as the guard drives for the lay-up (option 5).

Next, if options 4 and 5 do not develop, the forward cuts off the other forward for the pass in option 6 as shown in Diagram 13-5. At this time the guard has returned to the outside for primary defensive responsibility.

If option 6 fails to develop, the forward comes to the side, and the mirror effect of the offense and the floor balance are evident as the guard can pass to the forward and begin the left side pick-and-roll continuity, or the guard can pass to the other guard, who can initiate the right attack again. Diagram 13-6 shows the resumption of floor balance and the preparation for the new attack.

When executed properly, these movements develop a pick-and-roll continuity offense which contains the enviable and fundamentally essential qualities of floor balance, continual attack both horizontal and vertical, and the defensive alignment safety valve feature. Six effective options are available to either side.

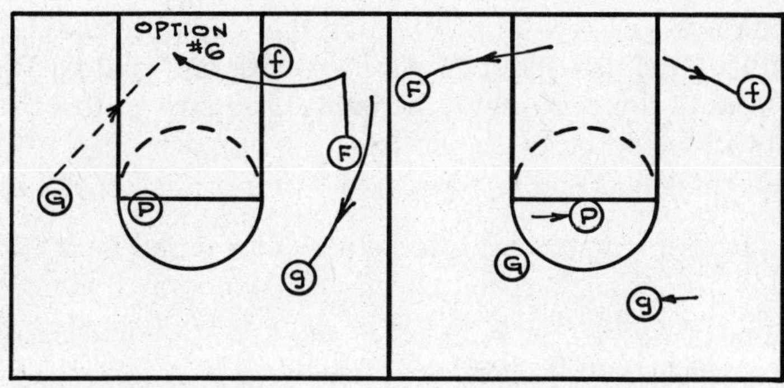

Diagram 13-5 **Diagram 13-6**

Chapter 14

THE FREEDOM WEAVE

by John Benington

Every coach spends considerable time trying to think of new things that will make his offense more effective. Whether it is a new option, a special play, or some other coach's idea does not matter, as long as the variation answers a need. Most coaches have a basic style of offense and would rather add variations than start some new offense.

At a time when the players are a little stagnant or play becomes stereotyped, and you need something that will give you more four-and five-man movement, especially lateral movement, try the freedom weave.

Start by using a four-man weave with the guards and forwards and let your center move with the ball along the baseline. Later on, the center can be moved to a high or long post position at the free throw line and used as a screener. In this way, the basket can be cleared for possible cutaways by the forwards and guards. Then, in order to work the center into the weave, you may go to a five-man weave, which will be explained later.

Advantages of the freedom weave are:

1. The team is given something else to fall back on when things are not going well with the normal offense.
2. A good team move where each individual gets a chance to handle the ball is provided.
3. The problem of lack of motion is lessened to a certain degree.

4. Opponents have something else for which they must prepare a defense.
5. Through practice, ball-handling is improved.
6. The players get good defensive practice while playing against the weave.
7. The center is given relief when he is being two-timed or is having trouble getting the ball.
8. A good moving center can be given additional scoring opportunities by moving him into the five-man weave.
9. The weave helps players understand the importance of floor balance.

There are always disadvantages along with advantages in any offensive move. Lack of good rebounding position and the chance of error through many ball-handling exchanges are two disadvantages found in this weave. Even with these weaknesses, our players have been able to play an entire game, using nothing but the four-and five-man freedom weaves.

Any move in basketball must be applicable to the personnel at hand. The better the personnel, the more freedom is allowed, and more ball-handling is encouraged. If the center is not capable of doing a good job, he does not handle the ball in the five-man weave.

In early practices, the freedom weave is introduced by a four-man drill, using two guards and two forwards (Diagram 14-1). It is simple to run after a team has been using it for several weeks. Timing and floor position are important. The first few times the players usually end up at mid-court for the shot instead of under the basket. The move is started by having one guard dribble to the other, who in turn dribbles to the forward. As shown in Diagram 14-1, 01 dribbles to 02, 02 to 03, 03 to 04, and 04 to 02 who is now coming back from the side of the court. At first, the players are kept dribbling laterally and going to the side of the court after they hand the ball off. Once they get the idea of handing off the ball and keeping spread, we ask them to penetrate toward the basket when they get a hand-off and have the next man come close for the hand-off. A few days are necessary for the players to learn to execute the drill properly.

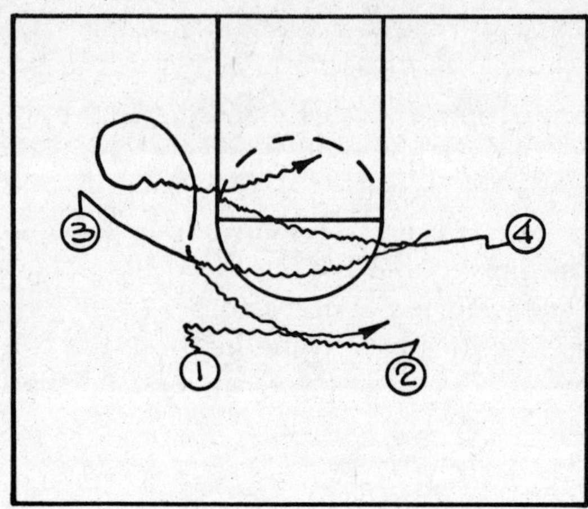

Diagram 14-1

Players are given the following rules on the drill: 1. Each player should fake before he comes to get the ball. 2. The dribbler goes on the inside. 3. After handing off, go to the side of the court. 4. Hand off the ball, do not throw it. 5. A player should penetrate when he has the ball. 6. Dribble with the outside hand for protection and also for an easier hand-off. 7. Stay low. 8. Hand off the ball at the side of the circle to enable the player who gets it to have a drive for the basket.

When the defense is added, the players are instructed to play man-for-man and slide through. We have always found this to be one of our best defensive drills. It also helps develop confidence in the weave as an offensive move, because early in the season the defense is always behind the offense.

Once the move is fairly well learned, the defense is allowed to switch. Instead of trying to give the players separate moves against a switching defense, we try to give them more freedom in initiating the weave and in a sense eliminating the effective switch. The drill may start as shown in Diagram 14-2, but 02 is allowed to cut to the basket as 01 starts toward him. Then 01 dribbles on to 04, realizing that we still may have the switch, although it might not be quite as effective as the first switch. 04 will dribble to 03 who can also cut to the basket, with 02 coming back from the side to receive the second hand-off.

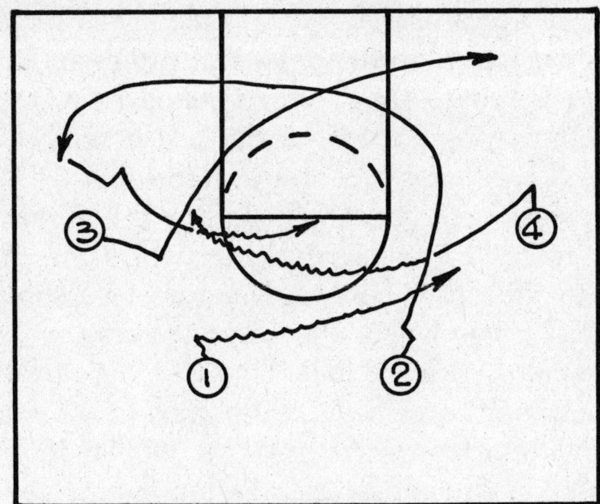

Diagram 14-2

You may also allow 01 to initiate the weave by starting to the forward, 03, (Diagram 14-3), and have 03 dribble to 02, who can also cut, leaving 04 to get the second hand-off. By keeping the defense guessing which way the move starts and by adding the threat of cuts to the basket, you help to eliminate the switching problem. Naturally, our players expect to be stopped at times with a quick switch, and are prepared to go into a pass-and-cut sequence to confuse the defense further.

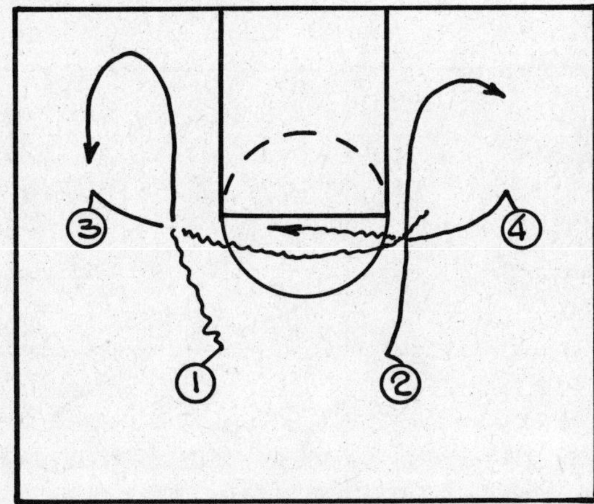

Diagram 14-3

Once the players are far enough along with the weave, the center is inserted to add to the defensive problem. When employing the four-man move, the center is used as a screener. He is instructed to move to the side of the circle ready to cut to the basket in case the defensive center switches off.

It is very easy for the team to go into a five-man weave with the center open. Have one guard go through to one corner and the center move to the other corner. Diagram 14-4 shows the initial position. Usually, two players are run to the corners as the team is coming up the court with the ball. Thus 01 is able to start the move in either direction off a dribble. If he goes to 02, 02 cuts for the basket, setting a temporary screen for 04. 04 may look for the shot, or drive as he takes the hand-off, or he may continue the weave by going on toward 03. 03 usually cuts for the basket, setting a temporary screen for 05, who is coming out of the other corner. This pattern is shown in Diagram 14-5. The best guard usually handles the ball in the middle, which gives him the freedom of driving directly to the basket if he thinks he can out-maneuver his man. The two forwards do not have to cut away every time, but may fake the cut and take the first hand-off from the guard, who is starting the five-man weave. In other words, 02 may fake a cut to the basket and take the first hand-off from 01.

By mixing the four- and five-man weaves properly, a variation is achieved which helps make the offense more flexible and more effective. It does provide a good change-of-pace.

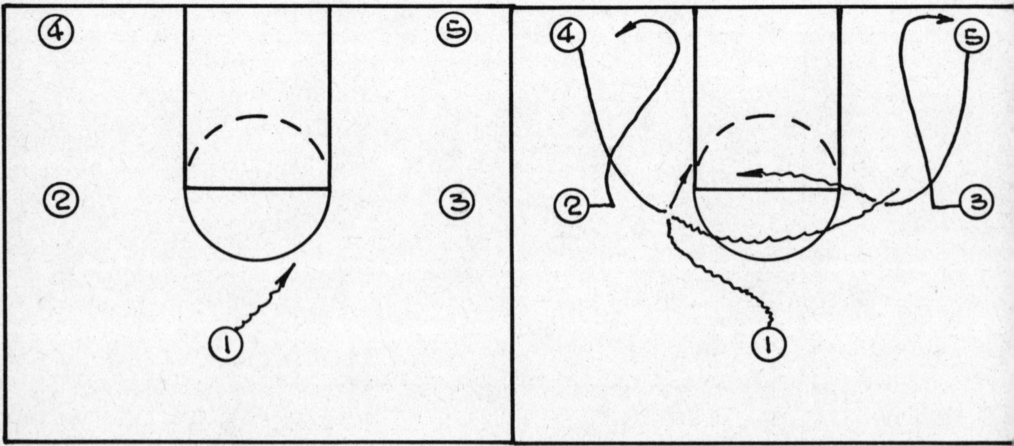

Diagram 14-4 Diagram 14-5

Chapter 15

THE MIXER OFFENSE

by Neil McCarthy

The mixer is a multi-purpose zone offense that can be used effectively against all standard and match-up zone defenses. It is a pattern offense incorporating player specialization and featuring the continuous movement of players in a predetermined plan.

After a study of the structure and movement of standard and match-up zones, it is evident that certain weak spots are present in all these alignments. The problem, of course, is to design a single offense that is capable of exploiting these inherent weaknesses. That is why the mixer evolved.

The mixer is based on the following principles:

Overloading. More offensive players are placed in an area than there are defensive players to guard them. The offensive pattern develops a continuous overload situation which rotates from one side of the court to the other.

Player Movement. The purpose of continuous player movement is to develop well-defined passing lanes, to spread out the zone for penetration purposes, and to induce early fatigue by making the defense move continuously.

Principle of Replacement. This movement develops a situation where one defensive man must attempt to guard one offensive man leaving a specific area, and a second offensive man entering the same area at the same time.

Internal Attack. The mixer is designed to have two cutters breaking to the ball through the key area with each pass. This motion forces the defense to play the cutters man-for-man and tends to disorganize the defensive alignment.

External Attack. Due to the persistent inside attack, we find that the outside, particularly the weak side, players are often open for the short perimeter shot.

Passing Lanes. The continuity of player movement develops a minimum of three alternative passing lanes for each player with the ball. This situation develops judgment and confidence in the players and reduces turnovers.

The mixer's initial formation is a 2-1-2 (Diagram 15-1). This setup is designed to reduce the pressure, particularly against teams that employ a two-man front, on the designated guard as he attempts to put the mixer into motion. After the lead pass has been made, the defense is forced to spread out, and the mixer converts to a 1-3-1 pattern.

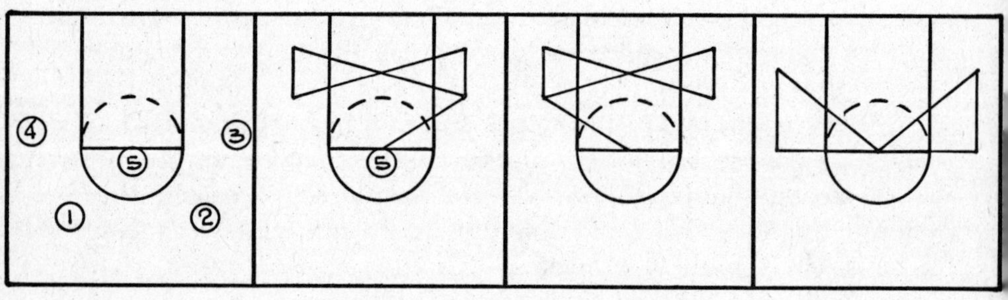

Diagram 15-1 **Diagram 15-1A** **Diagram 15-1B** **Diagram 15-1C**

This offense incorporates three areas of player specialization. The first concerns the point man. After the initial pass has been made, the point man remains at the top of the key. His major responsibilities are to move the ball, take the shot from the top of the key, and act as a defensive safety valve when a shot is taken (Diagrams 15-3 and 15-4).

The second area involves the center. He begins the offense at the high post with his back to the basket. If he receives the lead pass, he may shoot or become a feeder (Diagram 15-2). 01 passes to 05. Then 05 may shoot, pass to 02, 03, or 04, or return the ball to the point man. If 02 starts the offense, all players rotate in the same manner.

Diagram 15-3 shows 01 passing to 04 to his left. Then 04 looks for 03 cutting first and 05 cutting second. He looks *across the street* to see if 02 is open for a pass before returning the ball to the point man, 01.

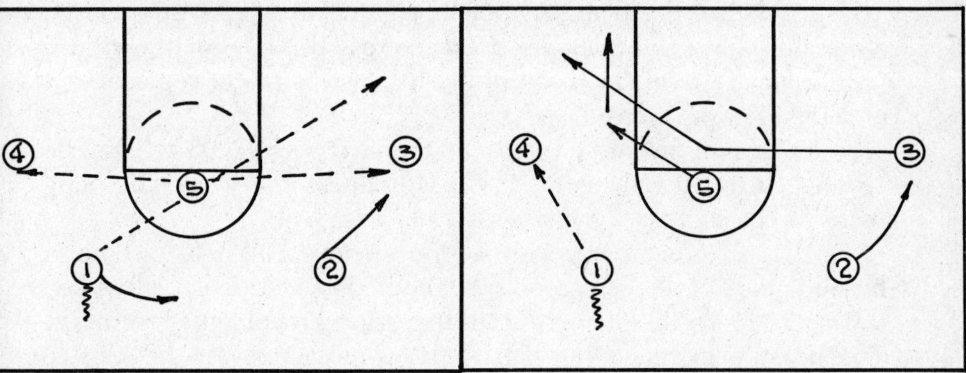

Diagram 15-2

Diagram 15-3

Offensively speaking, the center is known as the second cutter. His movement is from the high post to the medium post, after the wing man has cleared the key area. On a two count, he drops to the low post (Diagrams 15-1A and 15-1B). This movement is used to clear the post area of player congestion and open the passing lanes for the weak-side wing man. During his entire movement, the center must be trying actively to receive a penetrating pass (Diagram 15-1C).

The third area of specialization centers around 02, 03, and 04. 02 helps initiate the offense and then becomes a wing man (Diagram 15-4). 01 cannot make the lead pass to 04 and elects to pass to 02. Then 02 starts the offense. He passes to 03 and then makes a diagonal cut replacing 04, who has vacated his spot. 03 looks for the first cutter, second cutter, 05, and *across the street* for 02.

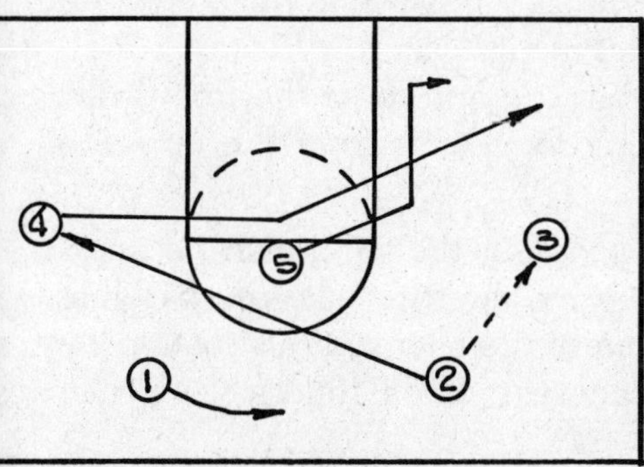

Diagram 15-4

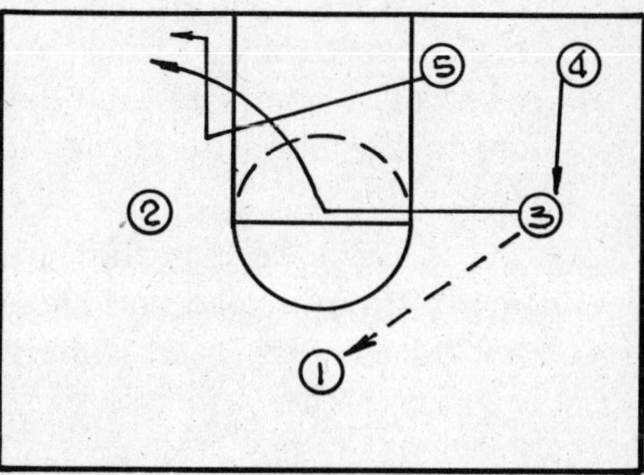

Diagram 15-5

03 checks the overload before passing to 01 (Diagram 15-5). After he makes the pass, he breaks across the key for the return pass from the point man. 04 utilizes the principle of replacement and fills 03's position.

02 cannot make the pass to the first cutter, 03, or to the second cutter, 05 (Diagram 15-6). He checks the weak-side wing man, for the *across the street* pass.

After 02 checks the overload for a penetrating pass to 05 or a baseline pass to 03, he passes to 01 and begins his cut across the key (Diagram 15-7). 03 fills his vacated spot for a reverse pass from 01. The point man relays the ball to 04, who cannot get the pass to cutters 02 or 05.

Diagram 15-6

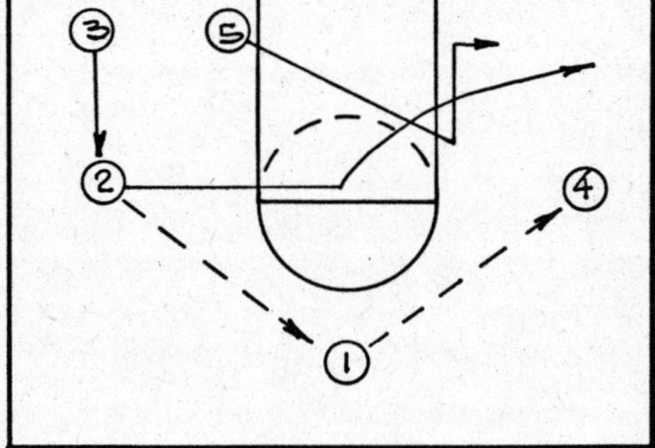

Diagram 15-7

The continuity of the wing men is shown in Diagram 15-1C. They have three basic responsibilities:

1. Each time a wing man passes to the point man he becomes the first cutter. He breaks across the free throw line in an effort to receive a return pass from the point man (Diagrams 15-7 and 15-8). If he is not open, he then cuts from the middle of the free throw line to the opposite corner looking for a pass from the opposite wing man.

2. Once he is in the corner position, the wing man becomes part of the overload and should be prepared to take the baseline shot if it is open. A basic ingredient of the offense is a situation we refer to as the principle of replacement. Each time a wing man

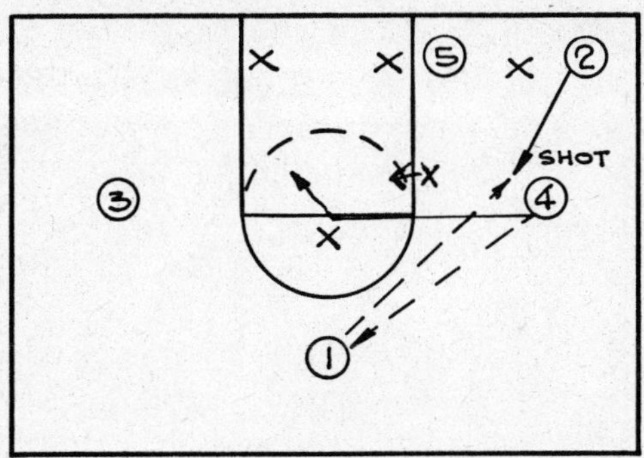

Diagram 15-8

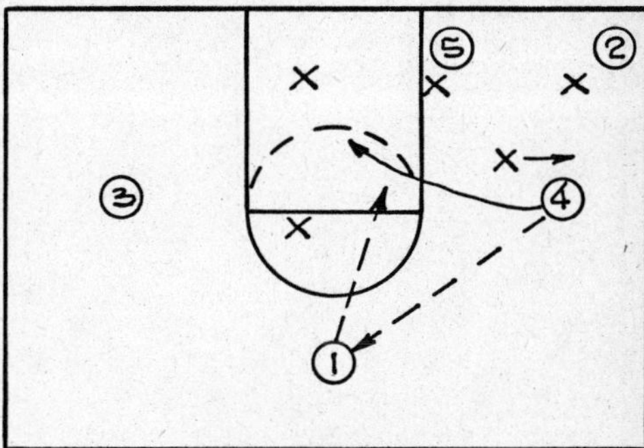

Diagram 15-8A

passes to the point man and makes a cut into the key area, the corner man must replace him at the wing position to receive a return pass from the point man (Diagram 15-8). Most defensive players are coached to follow a penetrating cutter for a few feet before releasing him to a teammate in another area. The principle of replacement attempts to exploit this principle of zone defense by forcing one defensive player to guard two offensive men at the same time.

In Diagram 15-8, 04 passes to 01 and breaks across the key for the return pass. His defensive man has followed him a few feet into the key area to prevent the pass. 02 breaks into 04's vacated position, receives the return pass from 01, and takes an open shot.

Diagram 15-8A shows how the defense usually reacts after being hurt by following the first cutter for a few feet into the middle. Most of the time they forget the cutter and look for the corner man. This opens up another avenue for scoring. 01 is now free to pass to 04 at the free throw line for an open shot.

3. The weak-side wing man, away from the overload, should position himself parallel to the free throw line. The majority of zone defenders are coached to protect the weak side of the basket and will seldom venture as high as the free throw line lest they weaken their internal defense. When the wing man in the overload has the ball, he must look *across-the-street* to take advantage of the situation (Diagram 15-9). Actually, the defensive point man will more often than not dictate the pass, i.e., if he is playing normal sag in the top of the key area, the passing lane will open.

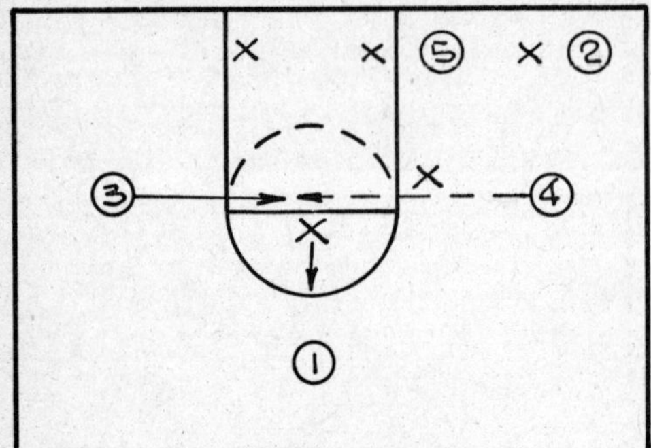

Diagram 15-9

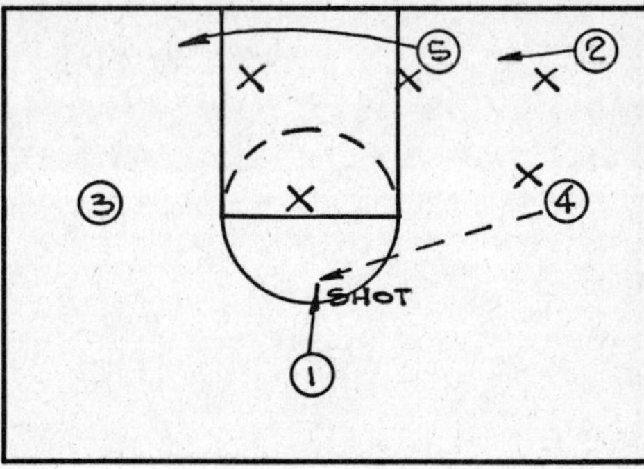

Diagram 15-9A

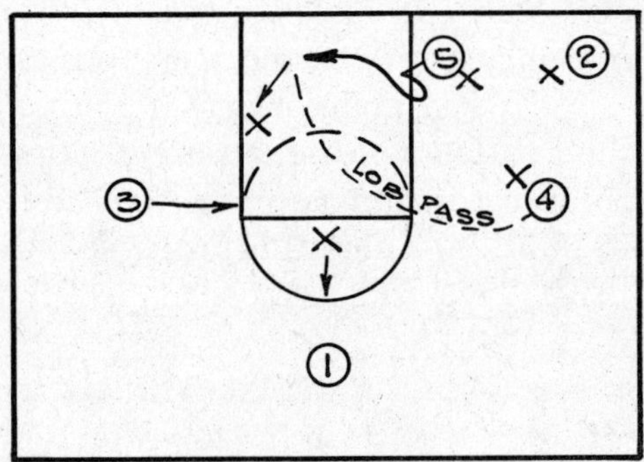

Diagram 15-9B

Diagram 15-9A shows a typical reaction by the defensive man after the *across-the-street* option has been successful. As the defensive man on top drops to plug up the passing lane to the weak side, 01 penetrates for the 17-foot unguarded shot. When this option is being used, 05 covers the weak side rebounding area and 02 goes for the offensive boards from his corner.

A secondary defensive reaction to the *across-the-street* option is for the weak-side defensive man to play higher in an effort to prevent the pass (Diagram 15-9B). This will open up the inside and allow 05 to operate. 05 will make a backdoor move and force his defender to front him. If he is being fronted, he can receive a lob pass from 04 as the weak side has been cleared. If the defense uses the half front he can receive the pass from 04 and have a good deal of room to develop a one-on-one situation.

Chapter 16

THE PASSING GAME

by Allen Svenningson

Using the 1-2-2 alignment as the basic set, the passing game alignment and numbering system are shown in Diagrams 16-1 and 16-2. The spots on the floor are numbered, not the players. We will usually start the offense from the #1 spot (point). It is, however, desirable to encourage the players to occasionally initiate the offense from either the #2 or #5 spots (wings). All players must vary floor position with defensive pressure.

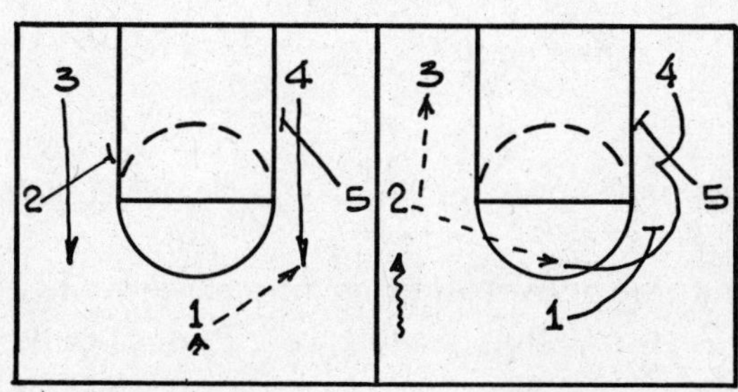

Diagram 16-1 Diagram 16-2

Terminology

Flare: A screener backs off a screening action to receive the ball (Diagram 16-3). This is most effective following a flash and is a good counter to a switch or a sagging defense.

Flash: A hard, straight line cut to the basket with or without the aid of a screen. It is used most effectively as a give-and-go (Diagram 16-4) or by a player away from the ball (Diagram 16-5).

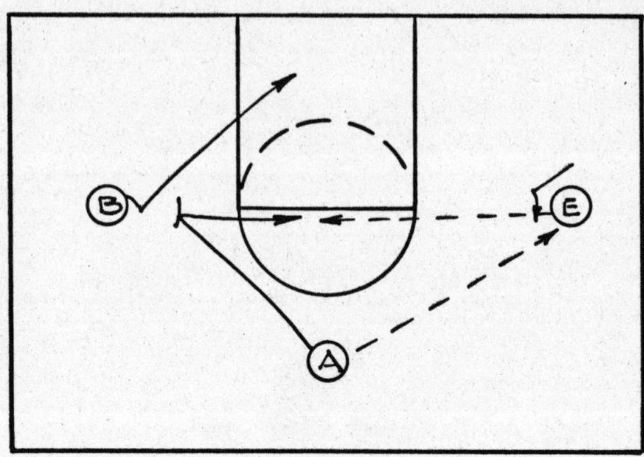

Diagram 16-3

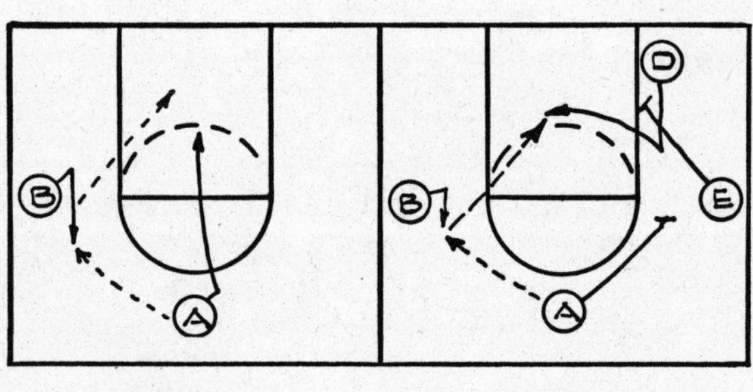

Diagram 16-4 Diagram 16-5

Fill: Any player moving to an open spot (Diagrams 16-6 and 16-7).

Continuation Screen: Setting one screen and then a second screen. The continuation screen is initiated only from the #1

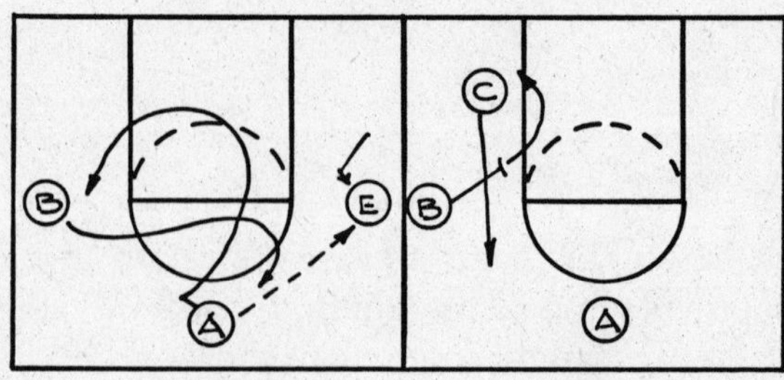

Diagram 16-6 Diagram 16-7

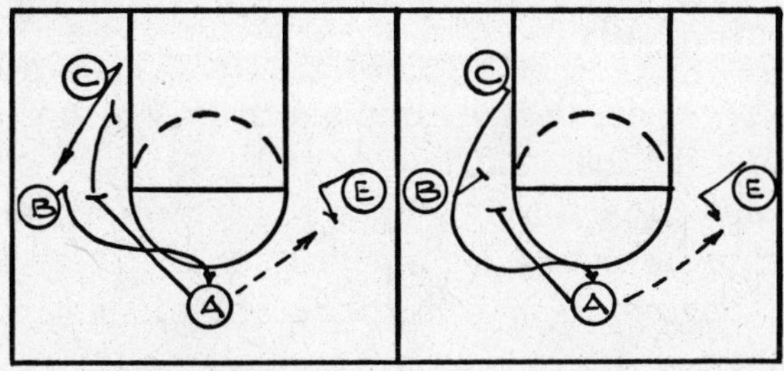

Diagram 16-8 Diagram 16-9

(point) position. As shown in Diagrams 16-8 and 16-9, A sets the screen for C, then for B coming, off the baseline.

Dribble to Balance: To maintain balance one may dribble to an adjacent spot (Diagrams 16-10 and 16-11). Howcvcr, we discourage this action for it is easy to misuse the dribble.

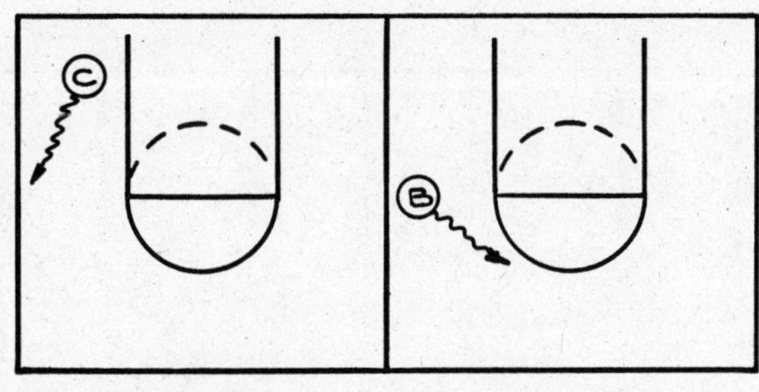

Diagram 16-10 Diagram 16-11

Passing Game Rules

1. After passing the ball: screen away; flash (effective against overplays and switching defenses); fill.

2. After setting a screen: continuation screen (used only when leaving the point); slip screen (effective against a switch or a head turner—replaces the pick-and-roll); flare (effective against a switch or sagging defense); fill.

3. After receiving a screen: accept the screen with a flash or fill; reject the screen with a flash (effective against a switching defense or head turner).

4. Maintain balance by: following a flash, clear to the side away from the ball; filling to an open spot; dribbling to balance.

Passing Game Drills

There are a number of one-man drills which can be used to teach creating the lead and the V cut.

Diagrams 16-12 through 16-16 show two-man drills with the coach feeding the ball. Diagram 16-12 shows the reject with the flash while Diagram 16-13 drills the accept principle with the flash.

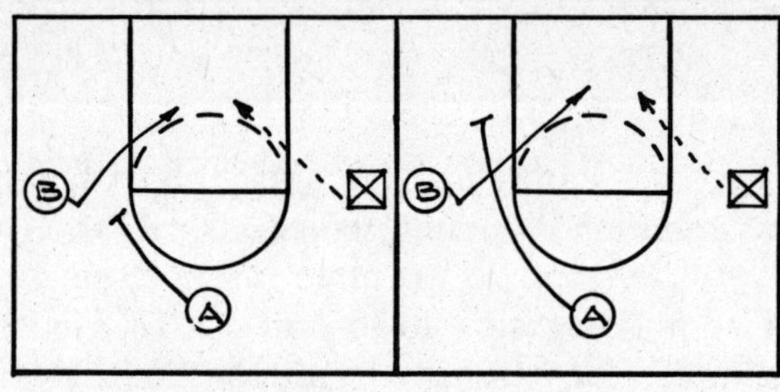

Diagram 16-12 Diagram 16-13

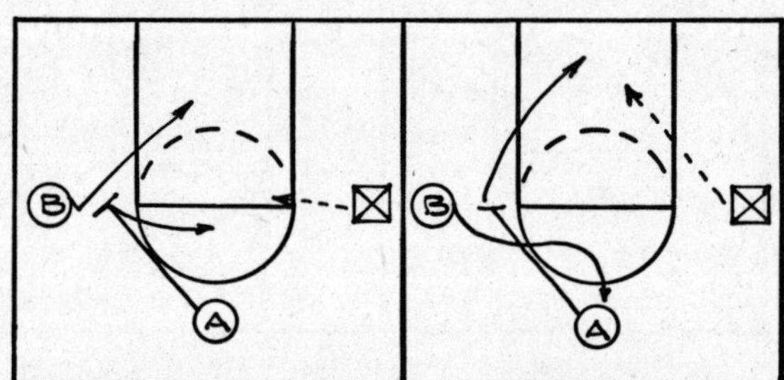

Diagram 16-14 Diagram 16-15

Diagram 16-16

Diagram 16-14 shows the drill to teach the flare action. Diagram 16-15 is the slip screen principle. The drill progression culminates in the jump shot, as shown in Diagram 16-16.

Diagrams 16-17 and 16-18 illustrate the two-man fill drill. We repeat the action until the coach yells *shot*; a player may then flash, flare, etc.

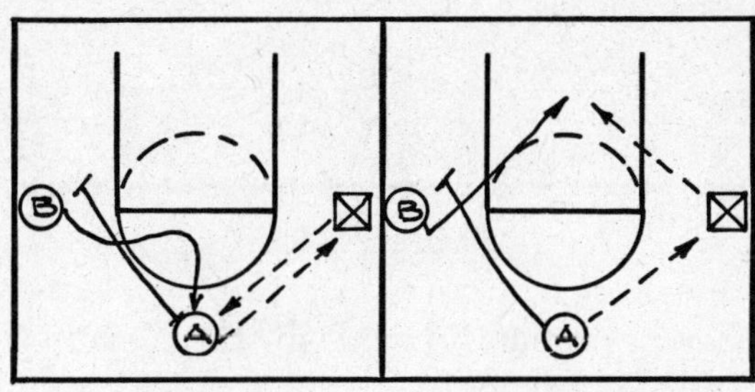

Diagram 16-17 **Diagram 16-18**

Drills for the players in the #2 and #3 positions are: reject—duck under (Diagram 16-19); accept with the flash (Diagram 16-20); flare (Diagram 16-21); slip screen (Diagram 16-22); and jump shot (Diagram 16-23).

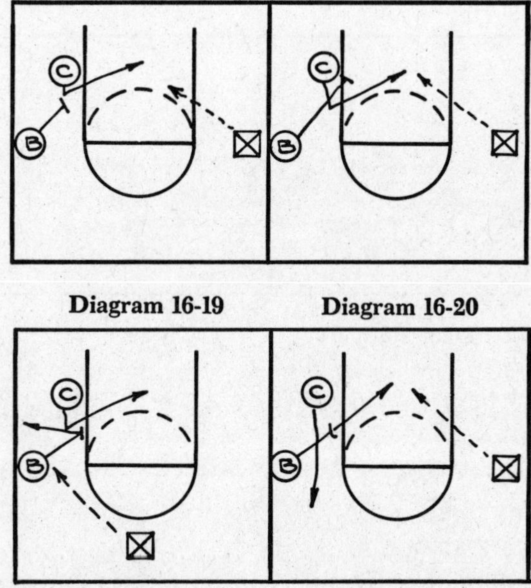

Diagram 16-19 **Diagram 16-20**

Diagram 16-21 **Diagram 16-22**

Diagram 16-23

We also have two-man fill drills for the players in the #2 and #3 positions and these would be similar in nature to the fill drills for the #2 and #1 positions (Diagrams 16-17 and 16-18). The action is repeated until the coach indicates *shot*, and a player may then flash, flare, etc.

We then bring in two defensive players and run a 2-on-2 fill drill (Diagrams 16-24 and 16-25). We repeat the fill several times before exercising an option.

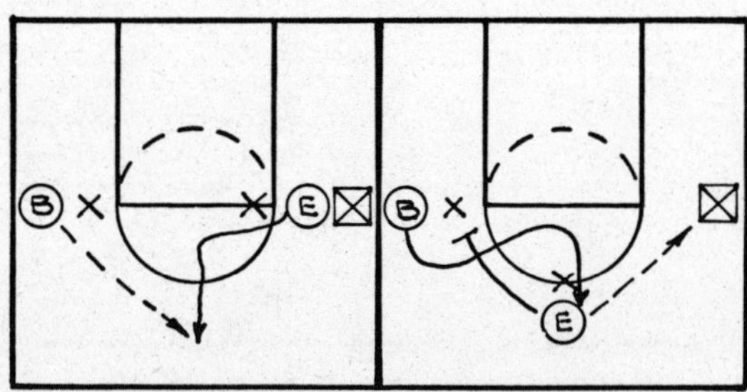

Diagram 16-24 Diagram 16-25

Diagrams 16-26 and 16-27 show the 2-on-2 fill drill when it is executed to the side.

Next we go to the 3-on-3 fill drill when executed from the front (Diagrams 16-28 and 16-29. The drill is repeated several times before exercising an option.

The 3-on-3 fill drill executed on the side is shown in Diagrams

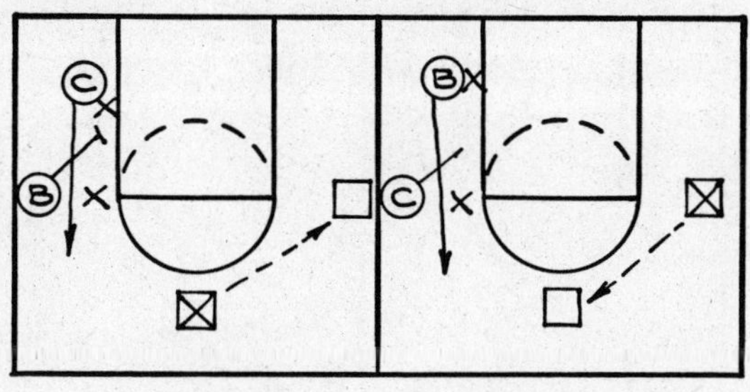

Diagram 16-26 Diagram 16-27

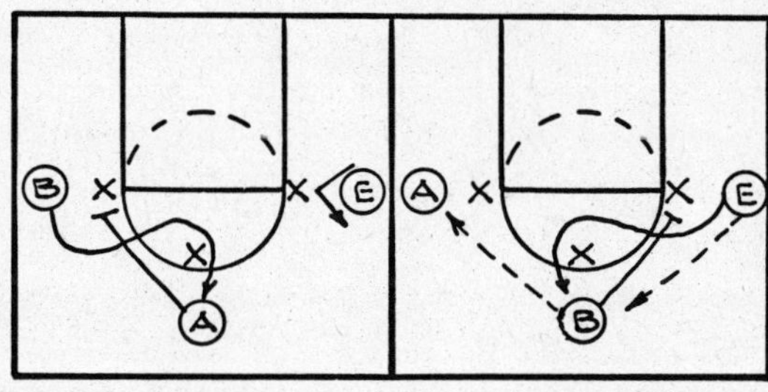

Diagram 16-28 Diagram 16-29

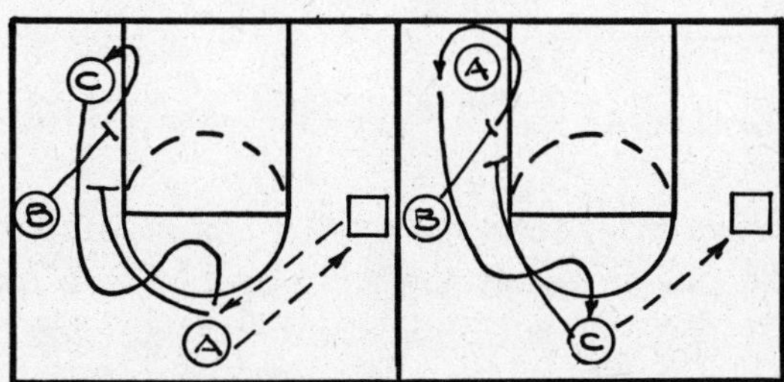

Diagram 16-30 Diagram 16-31

16-30 and 16-31. Again we repeat the drill several times before executing an option.

Next we bring in the fourth player (Diagrams 16-32 and 16-33) and run the fill drill. Finally, we are ready to practice our five-man passing game (Diagram 16-34). We continue this for 15 passes or 30 seconds, making certain that the players are exercising a variety of

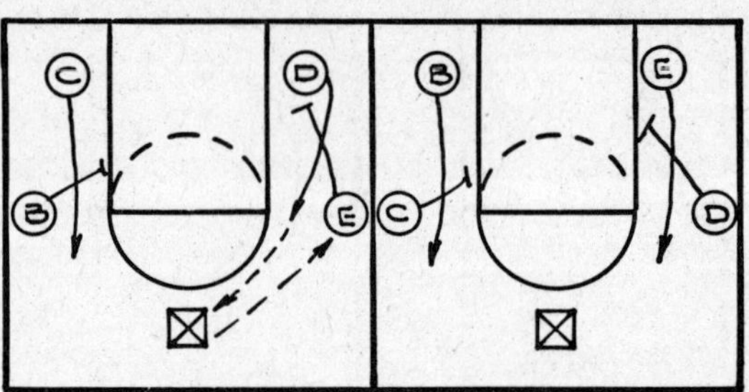

Diagram 16-32 Diagram 16-33

Diagram 16-34

options; otherwise, the drill becomes an exercise in perimeter offense.

It is not necessary to spend a great deal of time on some of the options. If the players know the rules and how to read a defense, then the passing game can be learned very quickly.

Coaching Hints

1. Emphasize penetrating passes more than perimeter passes.

2. Come hard to the wings. If the pass is being contested, go *at least* one step beyond the free throw line extended and then flash or screen down. The passer should not give the player coming to the wing the ball before he reaches the free throw line extended unless the wing is creating a perimeter shot. This principle will help to maintain desirable spacing.

3. Come hard to the point. Use the same V cut in creating a lead at the point as would be used at the wings. If a player receives the ball inside the circle, he should be creating a shot. If he is not creating a shot, he should be receiving the ball at the head of the circle. This principle will assist in keeping desirable spacing and will enhance the reverse court action.

4. There should always be a player leaving and coming to the point. If not, it will be difficult to reverse the court and give variety to the offense.

5. If the defense switches when a player is screening, he should slip screen or flare.

6. A flare is most effective following a flash by a teammate off the screen.

7. The screener is often the most likely player to be open.

8. Emphasize rejecting and accepting screens preceding a flash.

9. Always use sharp V cuts cutting off screens and when creating leads—no rounded cuts.

10. If a player is attempting to flash and his defensive opponent has position, the player should cut behind him and not make a banana cut.

11. A player should vacate a position within three counts if he does not receive the ball. The one-count theory is too fast and does not allow for things to happen.

12. Remember: If a team has the greatest motion possible, it will have a limited screen game. If a team has the most effective screening game, it will have limited motion. Strive for a happy medium.

13. If there is a breakdown in the screening game, consider the following: Check to see if the player being screened for is waiting for the screener to come to him. Is the screener making contact with the defensive player? Is the screener holding contact on all screens?

14. Baseline players will often reject the screen with a duck under but they should never go beyond the width of the lane on a duck under. If a baseline player does not receive the ball, he should return to the spot he came from.

15. Players screening to the baseline should consider slip screening frequently.

16. Never accept more than two screens. Reject the third screen with a flash.

17. A team must have good movement if it is to rebound well.

18. Assign rebounding responsibilities; thus, when the shot is taken, regardless of where these players are, they will rebound.

19. Assign a player the responsibility for defensing the fast break. No matter where he is when the shot is put up, this safety man will defense the break.

20. If posting low, fill the baseline position on the posting side.

21. When flashing from the point, a player should come out the weak side opposite the ball. Quite frequently it makes little difference as to which side he comes out.

22. Baseline players in the #3 and #4 positions may cross under the basket when making the transition from defense to offense. However, once the offense is in motion, do not cross the lane from #3 and #4 positions. To do so would jam the middle and take away the effectiveness of back cuts, flashes, and duck unders.

23. How a player arrives at the shot is of great importance to the success not only of the shot, but of the total offense as well (balance, rebounding, defensive safety).

24. The shot can come too early. A team must set the tempo of its offense by using at least six to eight passes before shooting. This (tempo) is a very important factor in the early stages of each half.

25. Do not become too rule conscious. The defense will determine the option.

26. Coaches should remember that the passing game is a difficult offense to diagram because of the many options available to the players. However, it is because of these concepts that the offense is effective and relatively easy to teach.

Chapter 17

ATTACKING THE ZONE DEFENSES

by Franklin A. Lindeburg

There are many different offenses designed to combat zone defenses, but they can be reduced to four basic methods. The first is to deploy the offensive men in various positions on the floor in a 1-3-1, a 2-1-2 or similar pattern, and rely primarily upon outnumbering (overload principle) the opponents in a particular area of the floor 2 to 1, 3 to 2 or 4 to 3, using fast, accurate passing to score. The second is to place the players in advantageous positions, combining passing with short well-timed cuts into unguarded areas of the zone or toward the basket for scoring shots. The third is to employ a rotation or movement of players in a prescribed pattern, combined with good ball-handling, to combat the zone. Finally, the defensive players are screened so that an unguarded shot can be obtained at a predetermined place on the floor inside the zone.

This article will point out examples of these four basic types of methods of attacking zone defenses: the set, cuts, rotation, and screens.

In order to have a continuity of thought, all offenses in this chapter start from the 1-3-1 setup. It should be understood that these four basic methods could start from a 2-1-2, a 3-2, a 2-3, or some similar arrangement.

The set zone offense is concerned with fast, accurate ball-handling and relatively little movement of the players. The original deployment of the offensive men in a particular area of the floor so that they outnumber the defensive men 2 to 1, 3 to 2, or 4 to 3 is important. The overloading of an area, plus good ball-handling, pulls a defensive man out of position in the zone and results in an opportunity to score.

This overload principle, as shown in Diagram 17-1, shows the offense lined up in a 1-3-1 set zone offense against a 2-3 zone defense. Examples of this overloading show that offensive players, 03 and 04, outnumber X5. 01, 03, and 04 outnumber X2 and X5, while 01, 03, 04 and 05 outnumber X2, X4, and X5.

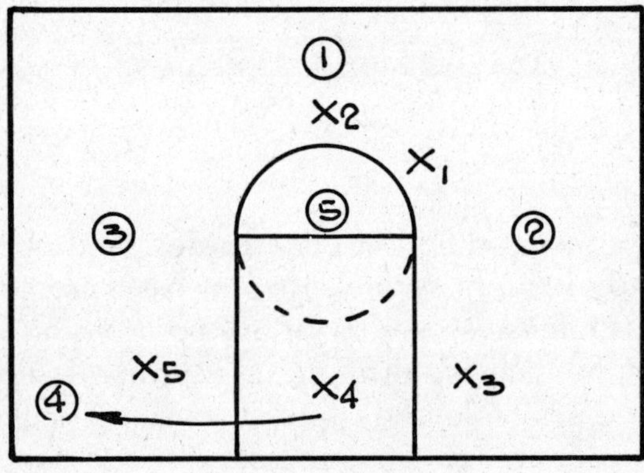

Diagram 17-1

Diagrams 17-2 and 17-3 show passing lanes between the offensive players, who outnumber the defensive men on that portion of the court. Good ball-handling between those players, who move only a step or two in and out or back and forth as the

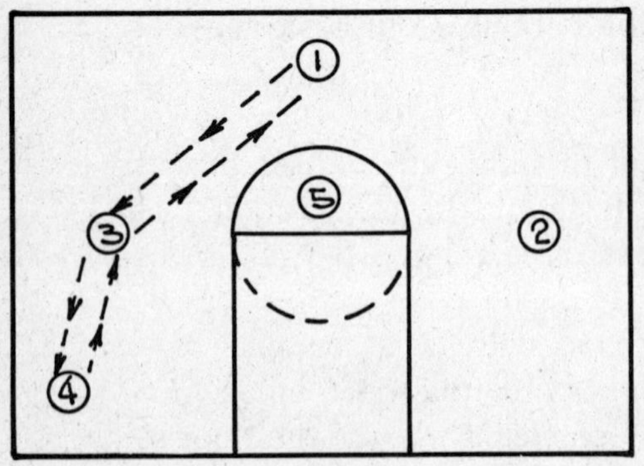

Diagram 17-2

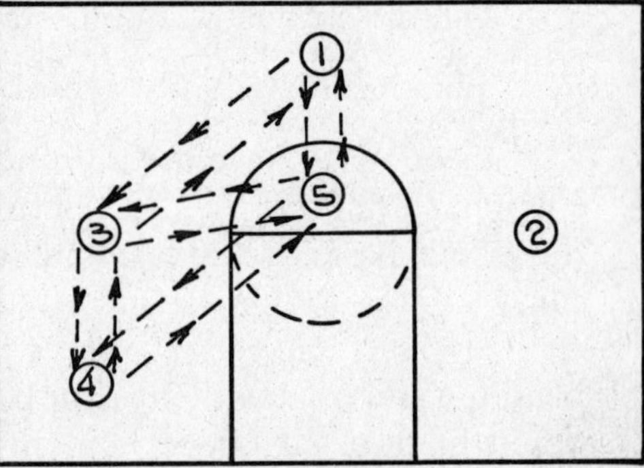

Diagram 17-3

situation dictates, produces excellent opportunities for good shots. Move the ball faster than the defense can shift in this method of beating the zone.

The use of cuts when operating against the zone is a means of putting an offensive man into an open area or presenting the defensive man the difficult choice of guarding one of two men in his area of responsibility.

Diagram 17-4 shows the various effective cuts which each player can make.

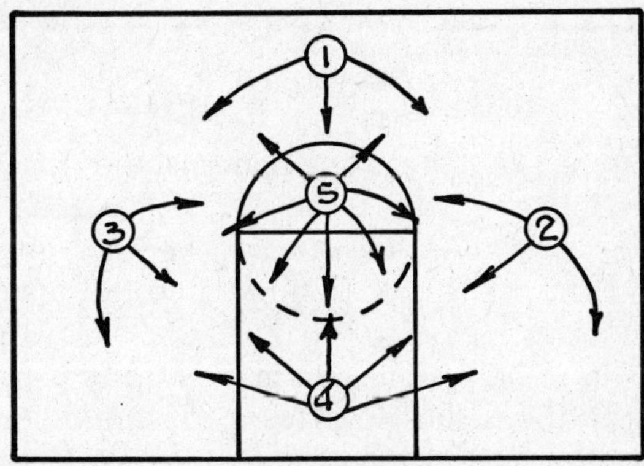

Diagram 17-4

A play with a cut to the basket is shown in Diagram 17-5. 01 passes to 03, and when 03 passes on to 04, then 05 cuts between X4 and X5 toward the basket for a pass and a shot.

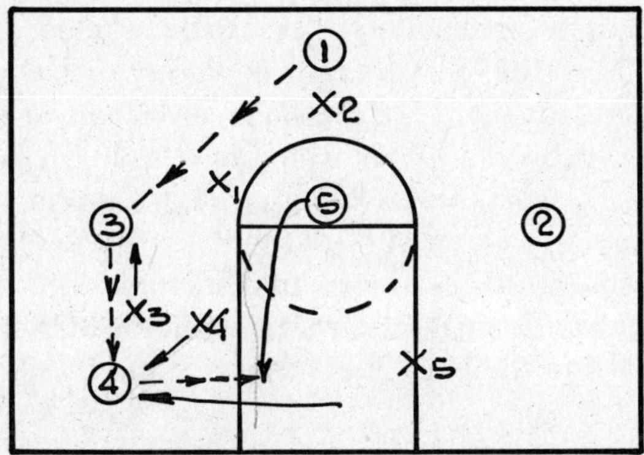

Diagram 17-5

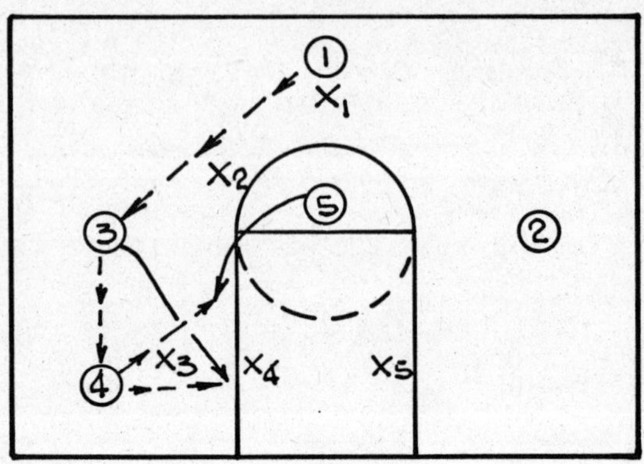

Diagram 17-6

Another example of a cutting play is shown in Diagram 17-6. 01 passes to 03 to start the maneuver. 03 gives to 04 and cuts directly for the basket. X4 must decide whether to pick up 03 or stay with 05. If he takes 03, 05 moves into the open area and is open, or vice versa.

The cuts in some systems are made by any player into a free area or between the defensive players. On the other hand, some teams will use the man in the post position as the one-man zone breaker. This player cuts into open areas for shots, or obtains the ball and feeds off to teammates who are open. Other coaches will seek to have their players cut into open spaces or avenues in the zone. The object is to get the defense shifting, get a strategic cut, a pass, and then a shot.

A rotation or revolving type of offense against the zone defense presents overloading with cuts, and gives the players a pattern to follow that offers defensive balance plus offensive strength. While the players move through the pattern, they attempt to take advantage of the defense whenever it fails to shift quickly, when it overshifts, or when an opening is observed.

Diagram 17-7 shows an example of a rotation offense where there is a circular pattern of movement by players 02, 03 and 05.

An alternate play is shown in Diagram 17-8. The ball goes from 01 to 03 to 04, and 03 starts the rotation. Of course, if 03 is clear, 04 gives him the ball, but if he is not and 05 sees an opening, he can cut for it.

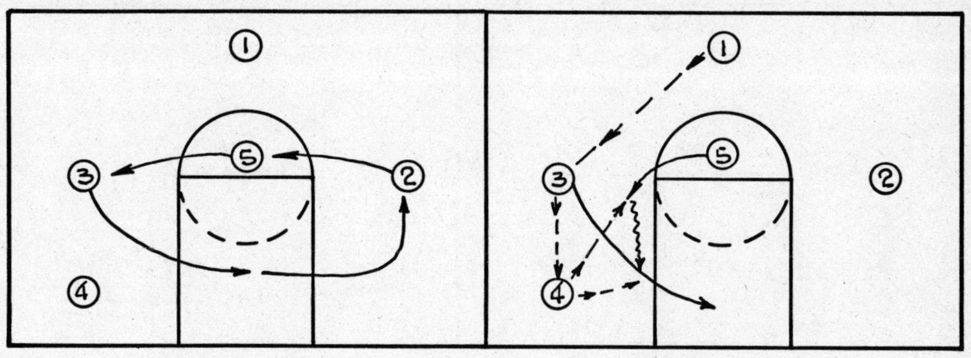

Diagram 17-7 **Diagram 17-8**

Diagram 17-9 shows how 05 can get a jump shot just off the corner of the free throw linc. 03 cuts and 04, not being able to pass to 03, does so to 05 for a short jump shot. If 05 does not have the opportunity to get off a shot, he can pass to 01, 04 or 02 and continue the rotation.

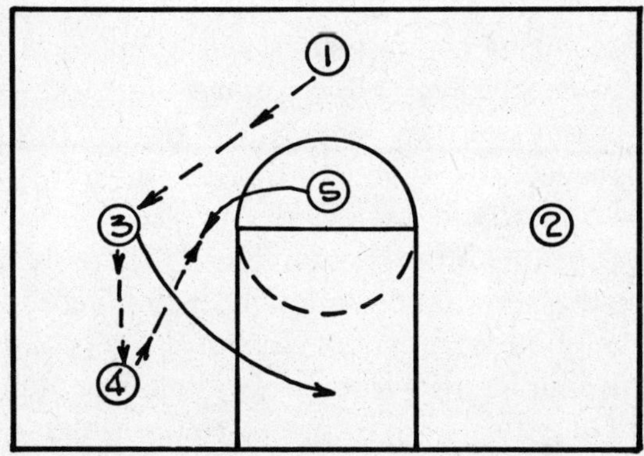

Diagram 17-9

This continuity is shown in Diagram 17-10, where 04 passes to 05, who looks for 02 to cut into the free throw line area for a pass. As 05 passes to 02, he cuts, giving 02 the choice of a shot or a return pass.

Diagram 17-11 shows the pattern necessary to reverse to the other side of the court. If a play does not materialize, 04 passes to 05, and 05 to 01. 01 dribbles to the left, while 04 moves across the

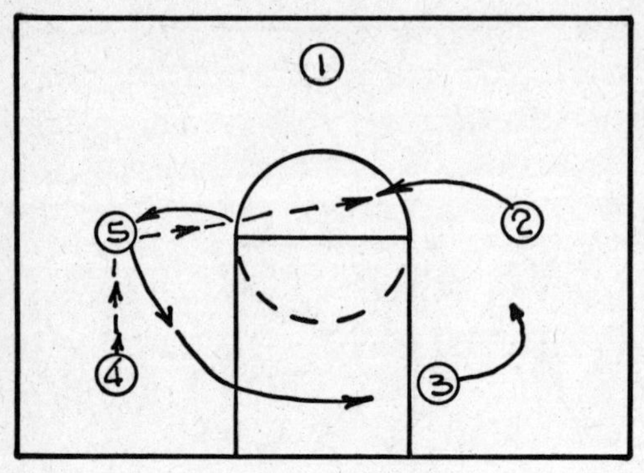

Diagram 17-10

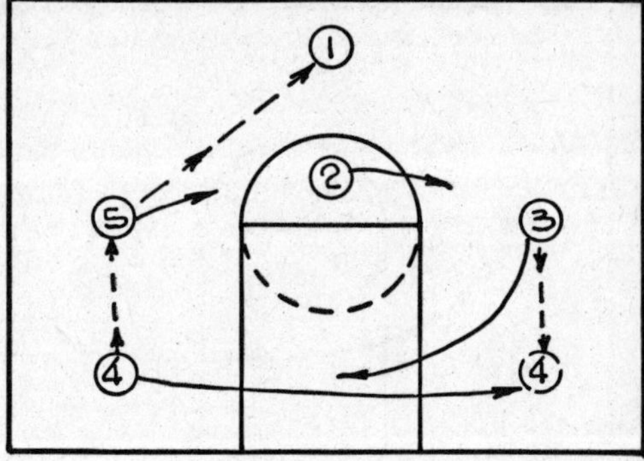

Diagram 17-11

baseline to the other side of the court. Then 01 starts the new play by passing to 03. 03 gives the ball to 04 and cuts for the basket, with 02 and 05 continuing the rotation in reverse of the original maneuver.

The use of screens against the zone is becoming more popular as the players in the zone offense become more aggressive, more determined to cut off passing lanes, and in general, more troublesome. Screens can be very effective and are used to cut off a man who is away from the ball. The ball is moved to one side of the court, which causes the zone to adjust to this new position. As the ball is moved back to the weak side, the screen is set on a defensive man, which prevents him from moving to his assigned position. It is at this time that a shot is obtained in that open or free area against which the screened man cannot defend.

A jump shot at the free throw line is obtained by 01, as indicated in Diagram 17-12. 01 passes to 03, which causes the zone to shift to that side of the floor. 02 sets a screen on X1 as 03 returns the ball to 01. Then 01 dribbles behind the screen for a shot.

The play can be carried further if X5 tries to stop the shot (Diagram 17-13), in which case 01 has the option of passing off to 04 for a lay-up.

Another screen play is shown in Diagram 17-14. 01 works the ball to 02, who in turn gives it to 04. The ball is then returned from 04 to 02 to 01. As 02 return passes to 01, he cuts toward the basket and around 05, who has screened X3. At this time, 03 screens X2 and 01 passes to 02 for a short shot. 05, 04, and 02 rebound, while 03 and 01 balance.

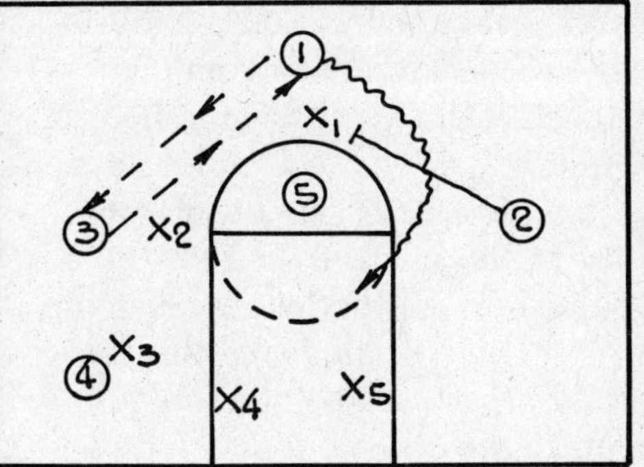

Diagram 17-12

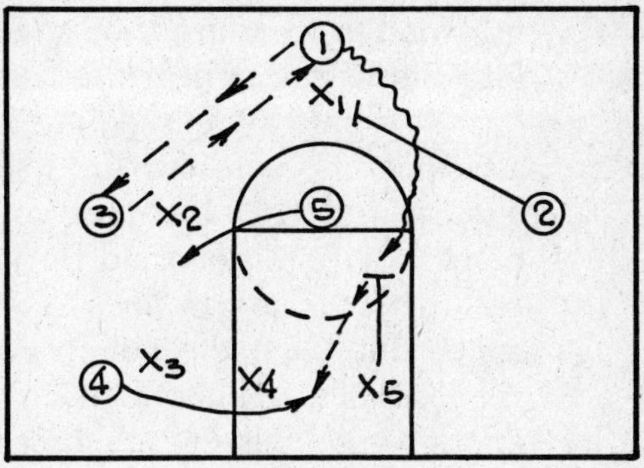

Diagram 17-13

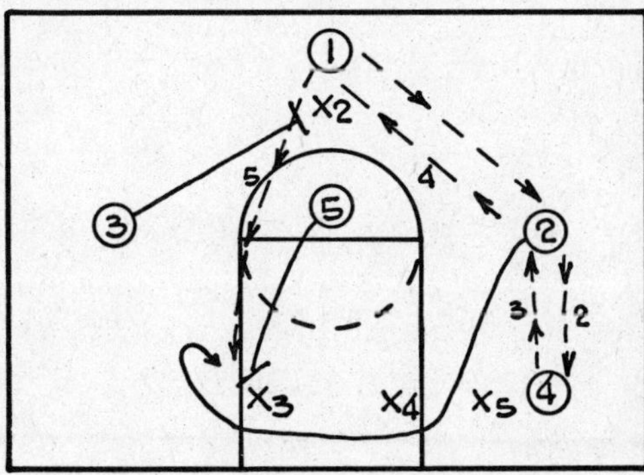

Diagram 17-14

Diagram 17-15 shows how quick passing and a screen break 02 free for a jump shot in the vicinity of the free throw line. The ball is moved quickly from 01 to 03 to 04 and back to 03. As the ball is

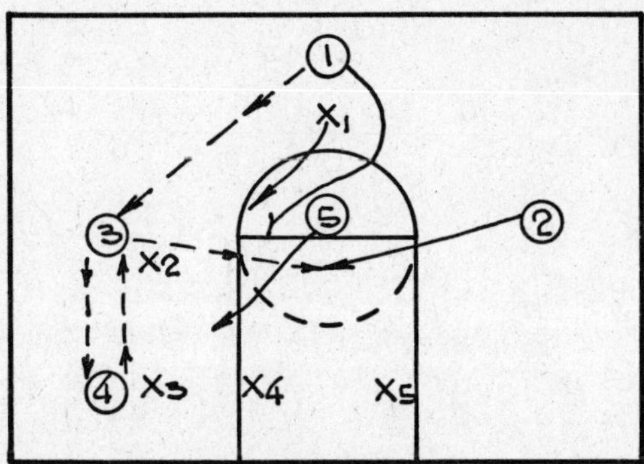

Diagram 17-15

returned to 03 from 04, 01 screens X1, enabling 02 to cut behind X1 into the free area near the free throw line for a pass from 03.

It should be pointed out that each of the four basic methods of attacking the zone can be used individually as a complete zone offense, but it is not uncommon to use a combination of two or more to give variety and flexibility to the offense. The fast break before the zone can form is still the best method to combat the zone, but once the zone is formed, one or more of the basic methods of attacking the zone should prove successful in obtaining enough good percentage shots to make the opponent wonder if the zone defense was the correct one to use.

Chapter 18

THE 1-3-1 INSIDE-OUTSIDE ZONE ATTACK

by Dennis L. Smith

When a team with a reputation for a tough, aggressive zone defense can force the opponent to be so concerned about attacking the zone that other important pre-game preparation suffers, then the defense has gained an advantage once enjoyed by the offense. It remains a defensive axiom that the offense must not be permitted to do what it wants to do when it wants to do it—or the game is in danger of being lost. Conversely, the offense must have the freedom to develop scoring opportunities from any area at any time if it is to capitalize on the advantage of having the ball.

Use of the 1-3-1 inside-outside attack returns the edge to the offense by forcing the defense to cover predetermined areas of attack. This slows the zone down, by restricting the scrambling pressure techniques employed in a successful defense.

The 1-3-1 utilizes the most successful coaching points of a sound zone offense—screening within the zone, overloading the zone, and movement within the zone. The success of the offense requires exercising these attack principles against the zone when and where the zone is least able to cope with them. One of the most common problems which occurs in using a type of total movement zone offense is that the man, the ball, and the open shot rarely arrive at the same place at the same time. The 1-3-1 prevents this type of error because it allows all offensive players to recognize and anticipate the next offensive maneuver, thereby, reducing the number of good shot opportunities usually lost due to a momentary break in timing.

The offense revolves around three basic attack patterns that are mirrored and work equally well to either side. The patterns are: *gut it*, *outside* and *wheel it*.

In the basic offensive alignment (Diagram 18-1), the position of the players appears to be rather static, but 04 is constantly on the move. He breaks back and forth across the top of the free throw line and holds a high post position on each side of the lane a few moments before breaking again. He tries to time his movement so he will be cutting to the ball as soon as possible. At the same time 05 breaks back and forth across the free throw lane at the low post position always staying on the opposite side of the free throw lane from 04.

04's position requires the best big man, and preferably a player who can shoot in a crowd. The position assigned to 05 is not limited to the next tallest man, by any means. It is a position that can be filled quite rewardingly by any shorter player who is aggressive and hustles. Desire and quickness work wonders at this position.

01 must be the best ball-handler, and must also be able to read the moves of the other four players, because they will move in response to his actions.

Positions 02 and 03 are best for the forwards who have the best scoring punch. Their responsibilities are the same for either side, and they can exchange positions at will.

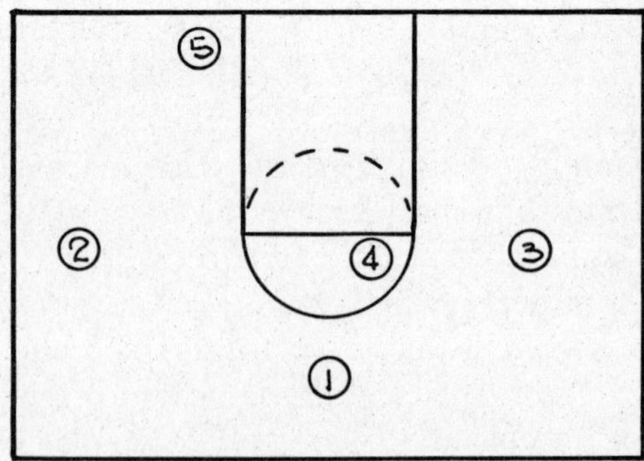

Diagram 18-1

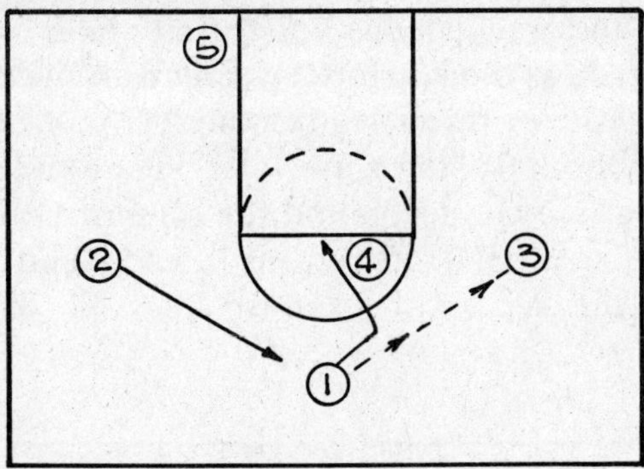

Diagram 18-2

The first pattern run by the point man is *gut it* (Diagram 18-2). The choice of sides on which to run the play is dictated by the position of 04 at the time the play is called. The ball may or may not be on that particular side at the time the play is called, but everyone on the team knows on which side the play will be run, because 04 holds his position, and the play will be run to his side. This cuts down on the confusion that occurs in many offenses because one man is out of position when the play starts.

As shown in Diagram 18-3, 04 has keyed the side of the play due to his position. 01 has passed the ball to 03 and has started to run his *gut it* route through the *gut* of the defense. 02 has replaced 01 and now several things occur simultaneously. As 01 passes 04 on his route, the ball is passed back to 02 who has replaced 01. The instant 01 passes 04's position, 04 breaks to the opposite side of the

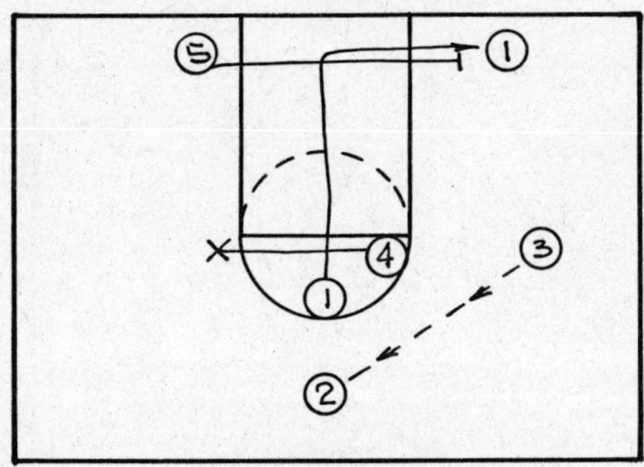

Diagram 18-3

free throw line and waits for his opportunity to break to the ball, while 05 breaks across the key to set a screen on the defensive man on that side of the free throw lane at the low post position. As 02 receives the ball from 03, the zone will adjust to it, allowing 01 to cut to the strong side corner behind the screen set by 05. As soon as 02 receives a pass from 03 he returns it, and 03 hits 01 free in the corner behind the screen to exercise any one of four options (Diagram 18-4).

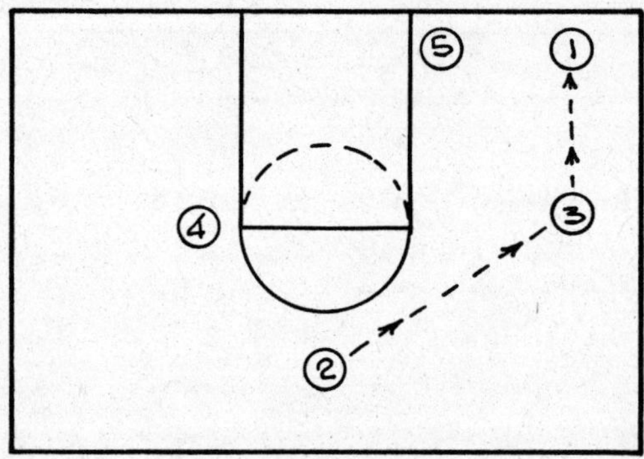

Diagram 18-4

The first option is the shot by 01 from the corner. Second, he can drop the bounce pass along the baseline to 05 for the power lay-up if the defensive man fights through the screen to cover 01 (Diagram 18-5). The third option is the bread-and-butter play for attacking the zone from the inside. After the zone has adjusted to cover the corner pass and has covered the inside pass to 05, an open

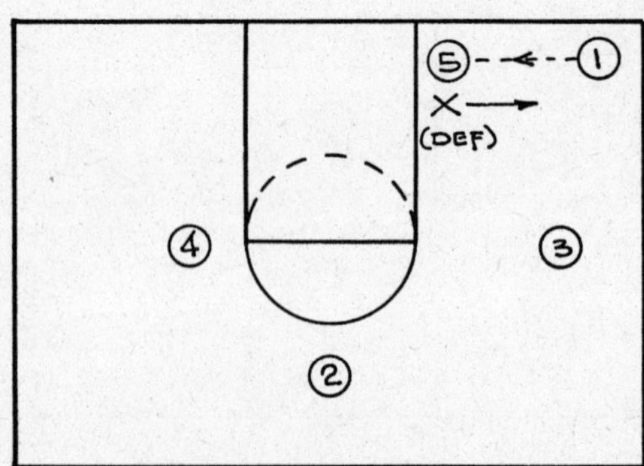

Diagram 18-5

lane remains for the cut of 04 toward the ball and the open shot six feet from the basket (Diagram 18-6). The major advantage of this option is two-fold: first, the cut lane is wide-open; and second, the defensive players have their backs to 04 allowing him to cut high or low down the open lane, whichever he chooses. The fourth option is a reversal of positions initiated by a pass back out of the corner by 01 to 03 after the other options appear not to be open. After the pass, 01 cuts along the baseline to the opposite corner, and at the same time 05 moves to a new screening position on the opposite side of the key (Diagram 18-7). 04 returns to a high post position opposite the screen set by 05 and awaits his break down the open lane. 02 and 03 move the ball as rapidly as possible around the top of the zone to 01 in the opposite corner and the options are again available (Diagram 18-8).

The *outside* play calls for a slight change in pre-cut maneuvers

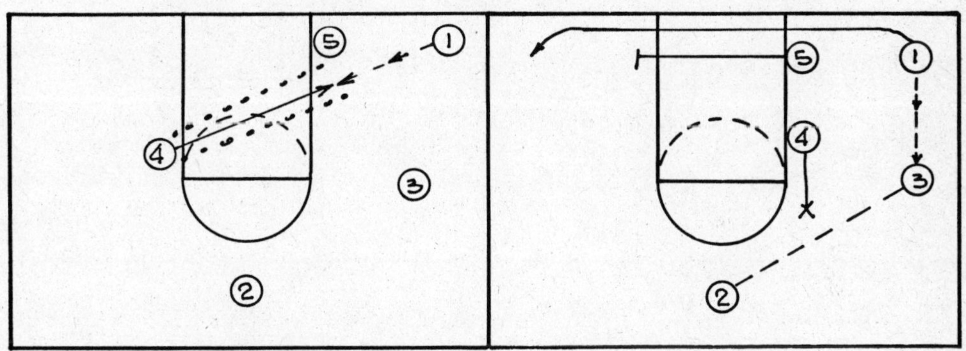

Diagram 18-6 **Diagram 18-7**

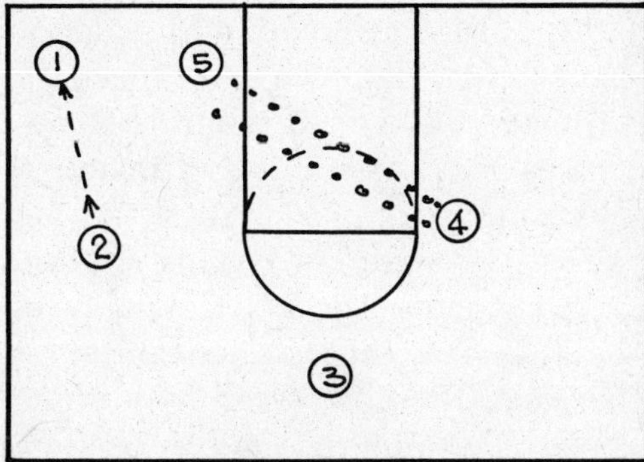

Diagram 18-8

to present the same shot option to the forwards, but all other options remain the same. On the call of *outside* the play is again run to the side of the 04 position. The point man starts by passing to either 02 or 03, but instead of running the *gut it* route, he moves to the player to whom he passed and receives a return hand-off pass (Diagram 18-9).

As shown in Diagram 18-10, 03 now runs the cut as 01 ran it in the *gut it* play, and everyone performs the same moves the instant he passes the 04 position. It is important that the ball be passed back to the point man to force the zone to adjust to the ball's position. 03 is now presented the corner shot with the other scoring options available to his teammates.

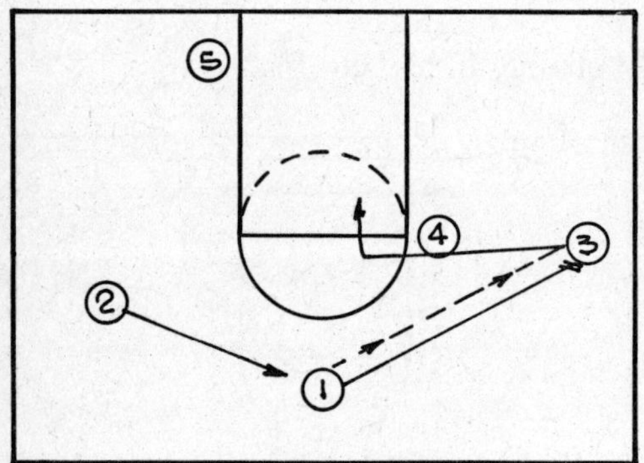

Diagram 18-9

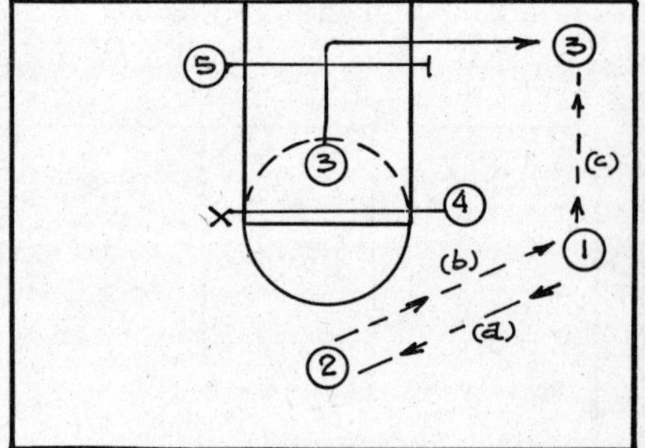

Diagram 18-10

The third attack pattern, *wheel it*, is used to attack the zone inside, especially when the defense becomes corner-conscious. The constant cutting of 04 and 05 generates considerable rapid internal movement, but is movement with a definite purpose and occurs in a set pattern that is known and expected by the offensive players. The cutting of 04 and 05 is initiated by the point man calling *wheel it*, takes place around the perimeter of the free throw lane, and is always counterclockwise, unless the point man reverses the cutting by calling a reverse. The cutting of 04 and 05 to the high post position, shuffling across the free throw line and fading down the opposite side of the key, causes the defense to become alert to passes within the zone, thereby releasing outside defensive pressure. The patterned movement of the two post men establishes a moving triangle attack on either side of the zone involving either 02 or 03. Many times the defense will concentrate on picking up the next cutter and becomes lax in covering the post man who is fading down the free throw lane. When the ball is on one wing, the opposite wing man can option to cut to the corner for the zone overload (Diagrams 18-11 and 18-12).

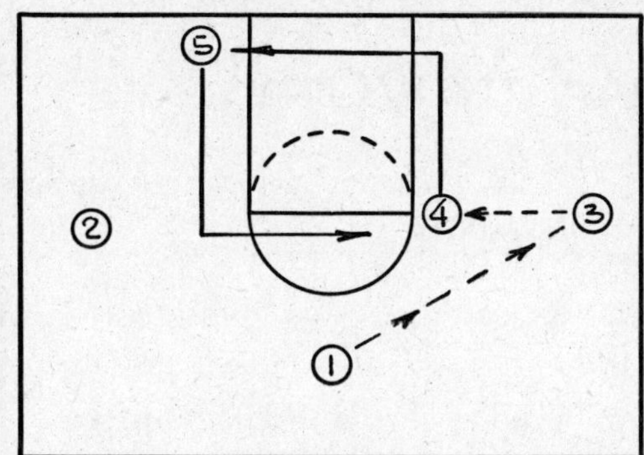

Diagram 18-11

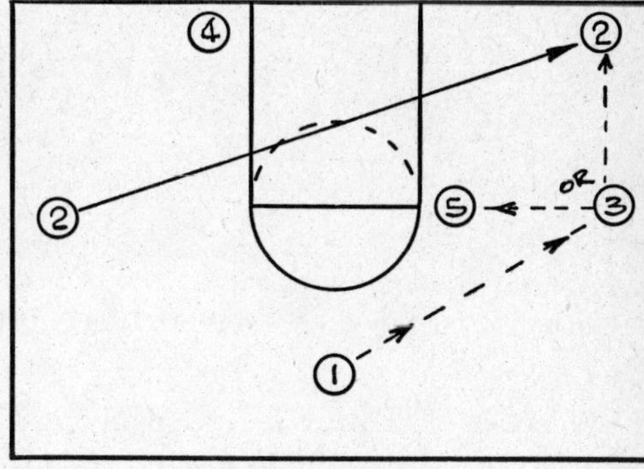

Diagram 18-12

Chapter 19

THE 1-3-1 OFFENSE VS. THE MAN-FOR-MAN AND ZONE

by Paul D. Lockhart

The 1-3-1 positions are numbered as shown in Diagram 19-1. Each player is given considerable one-on-one drill in these spots, and all players are expected to be able to handle a one-on-one situation in each one of them.

Against the man-for-man defense, the ball is brought down the floor using three men. 02 and 03 are instructed to set up in their spots. Then 01, 04, and 05 bring the ball down the floor. This method is used to prevent the quick two-time by the defense, which often results in the dribbler trying to make a long and hurried, or high lob, pass to a teammate.

Diagram 19-1

Our players are instructed to go down the floor fast with the ball. They go right in for the lay-up in the event the defense is slow in getting back, or is caught out of position. Two or three quick passes may be made in getting the ball across the center line, or one or two passes and a quick dribble may be made to get the ball down the floor. In either case three players should be coming down the floor with the ball for protection, and should be on the alert for a two-time on the ball-handler.

After they get across the ten-second line with the ball, and if no quick pass can be made to a teammate who is breaking under the basket for a lay-up, they go into the 1-3-1 offense and start play. Although our plays are diagrammed to the right side, we run them to both sides.

The player who has the ball is called the playmaker. He takes the ball over to the side of the floor where we plan to attack. The playmaker will do one of three things with the ball: 1. He will pass to 05 and cut around him. 2. He will pass to 05 and hold. 3. He will pass to 05 and go away.

As shown in Diagram 19-2, the playmaker brings the ball over to the side of the floor to make his pass to 05 and cut around him for a return pass. If there is difficulty getting the ball to 05, he turns and cuts hard for the basket, then comes back quickly to get the pass. Then, if the difficulty persists, 05 should go over and set a screen for 02 on the free throw line. 02 comes off the screen and cuts for the basket, getting a pass from the playmaker, 01, or he comes out to 05's spot to take the pass. Once the pass is made to

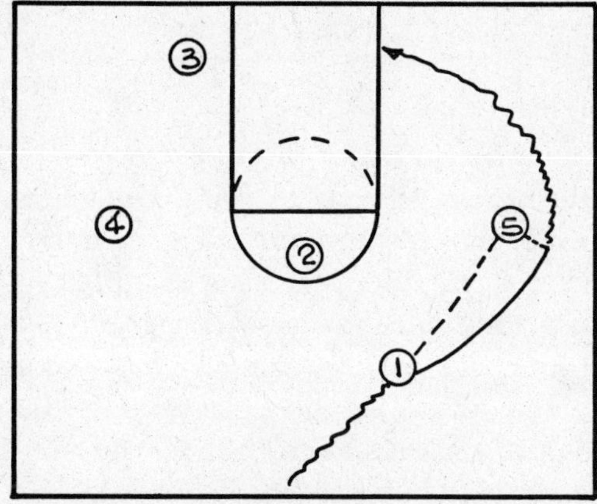

Diagram 19-2

05's spot, 05 faces out toward the cutter, with his back to the basket. 05 sets up this way in feeding the cutter, because he can give the cutter a little flip pass right straight in front, which the defensive player cannot see, thus preventing 05's defense from switching in time. If the pass is made out to one side before the cutter gets to 05, then the defensive player on 05 switches in plenty of time. The cutter simply picks the ball out of the air and drives in for the shot. If the ball is not flipped up, then the cutter continues on around under the basket.

After the playmaker cuts by, 05 turns, faces the basket, and looks the situation over. First, he looks to see if he can give the cutter a delayed pass, as shown in Diagram 19-3. Many defensive players feel that the danger is over after they cut over 05, and they slow down and look back up at 05, who has the ball.

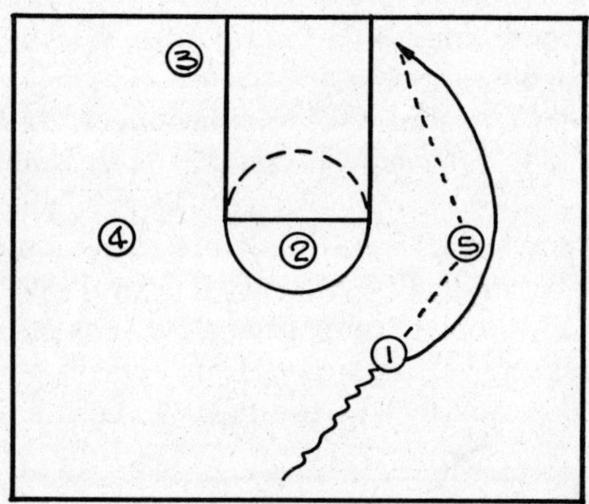

Diagram 19-3

If it is impossible to make the delayed pass, 05 looks for 03, who is breaking across the lane, using the cutter for a screen (Diagram 19-4). 05 may hit him and hold, or cut.

If this option is not open, 05 tries to hit 02 on the free throw line, which starts the high-low game (Diagram 19-5).

As shown in Diagram 19-4, the playmaker made his cut and did not receive the return or the delayed pass. 03 cut across the lane, using the cutter for a screen, but he did not get the ball, so the pass was made to 02 on the free throw line.

When 02 gets the ball, he should turn around, face the

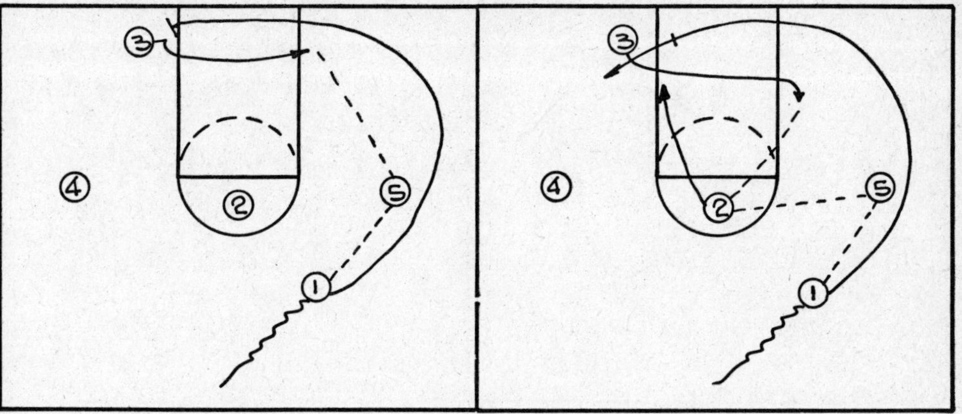

Diagram 19-4 **Diagram 19-5**

basket, and see what the conditions are. 04 and 05 should widen when the ball is passed to 02. If the defense has loosened, 02 may take the jump shot. If the defense charges, he may fake the shot and drive. Then 02 may pass the ball down to 03 and cut (Diagram 19-5).

02 should cut for the opposite side of the board every time the ball is passed to 03. 02 may pass to 03 as he breaks across the lane, and again 02 should break for the board. Then 03 has the option of making a bounce pass back to 02 as he cuts for the board. This play is shown in Diagram 19-6. 02 may want to pass out to 04 or 05 and come over and set a screen for him.

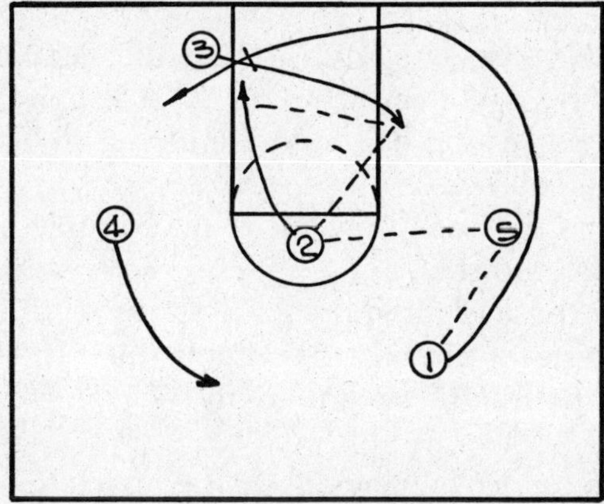

Diagram 19-6

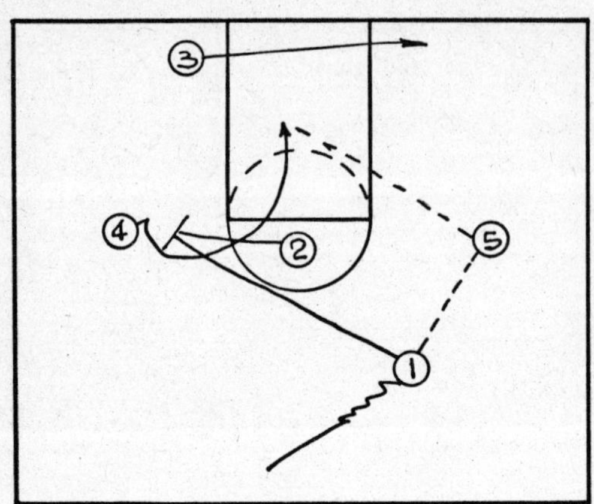

Diagram 19-7

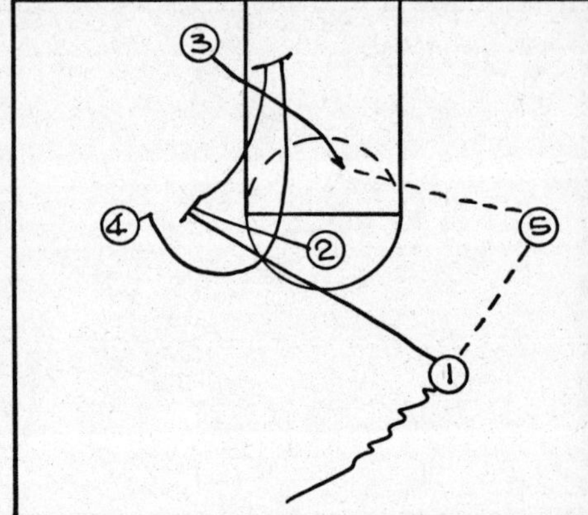

Diagram 19-8

When the playmaker passes to 05 and goes away, 02 should go with him and set a double screen for 04 (Diagram 19-7). 02 always comes off the screen for the rebound. If 04 cannot get the ball, then 02 and 04 should set a screen for 03.

The ball is passed to 03 as he comes up the lane for the jump shot (Diagram 19-8).

Against the Zone

Against the zone, the offense prevents the players from ganging up and provides movement and balance. If the players have patience and keep running the pattern, the good shots will come.

Our zone offense is started from either side. As shown in Diagram 19-9, the pass is made to 04. If 04 is open, he takes the shot: if not, he passes the ball in to the corner to 03. After 04 has passed to 03, he cuts across the lane, looking for a pass from 03. 02 comes down from the free throw line to the baseline. A pass may be made to him, for the shot.

If none of these is attempted, 03 passes the ball back to 01, who has moved down near the free throw line. Then 01 (Diagram 19-10) looks to the free throw line to hit 05, who is breaking in for the jump shot.

If the pass cannot be made to 05, he jumps out and takes the pass from 01, and helps get the ball around to the other side of the

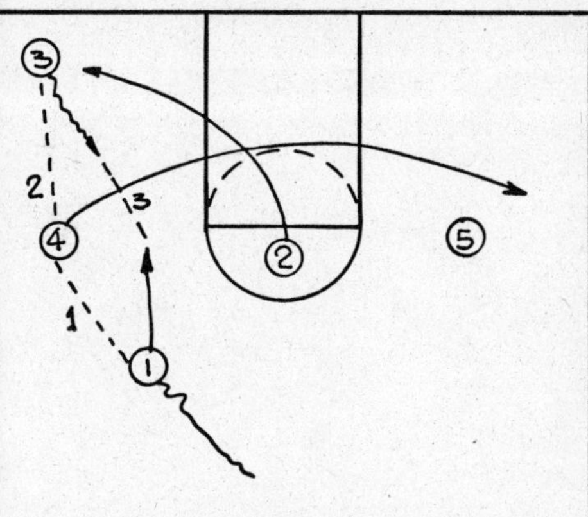

Diagram 19-9

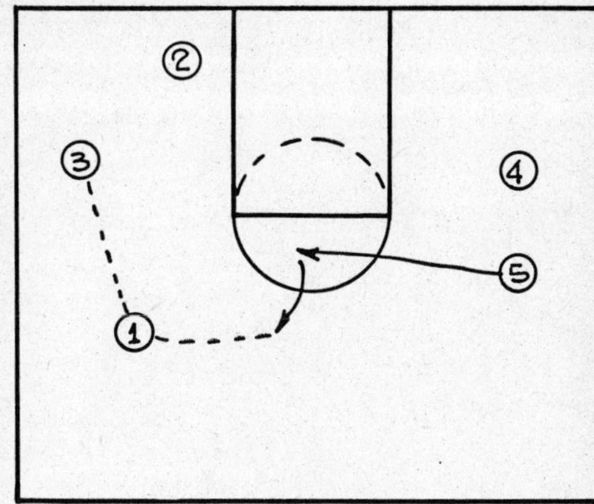

Diagram 19-10

floor (Diagram 19-11). The ball is passed to 04, and 02 moves across the baseline to the opposite corner, and takes the pass from 04. Then 03 comes to the free throw line. 04 breaks across the lane again, and 03 drops down from the free throw line to the baseline and looks for a pass from 03.

If this pass cannot be made, the ball is passed back up the floor to 05, who has moved over, and he looks to the free throw line for 01, who breaks in for a jump shot (Diagram 19-12). If the pass cannot be made to 01, he jumps out and helps get the ball back around the court again. Then the play is run over.

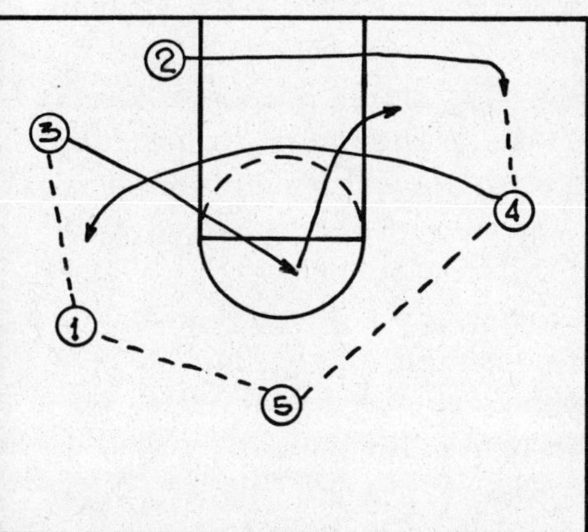

Diagram 19-11

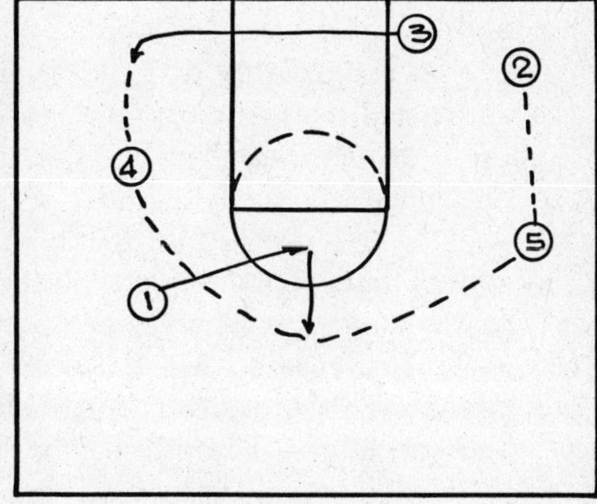

Diagram 19-12

Chapter 20

THE FOUR CORNER DELAY

by Jan. S. Bennett

Regardless of whether it is called the stall game, ball control game, lead protection game or delay game, this phase of offense is probably the most important, and exasperating to coach. The delay offensive game is centered around the basic idea of keeping the pressure on, and working to secure an uncontested high-percentage shot, or the free throw.

The delay game is an offensive phase not enjoyed by all players. Therefore, it is necessary to cultivate interest in it and develop a desire to learn more about the delay. Teaching this game requires daily motivation and practice.

The delay game must be practiced at least 10 minutes a day with drills being used, as is the case with the regular offense and defenses. We do considerable half-court work, utilizing the clock and ball possession.

It is necessary that all players be conscious of the score, time, and the defense the opponents are using. They must realize that these three items predicate the purpose of the delay game. Reasons for using the delay game are: a) lead protection; b) to protect players who are in foul trouble; c) to bring opponents out of the zone; d) to change the tempo of the game; and e) to secure a psychological advantage for upcoming games.

Most coaches use the delay game solely as a lead protection offense. This purpose is relatively easy to cultivate among players and spectators. The other four purposes may require daily selling to the players. Because few people fully understand the delay game, it is a phase of offensive basketball where a coach may be second-guessed.

The four corner delay game can be used as a stall, as a delay, and as a complete scoring offense. The defense, score, and time indicate what will be done. The offense is a 3-out, 3-under set (Diagram 20-1).

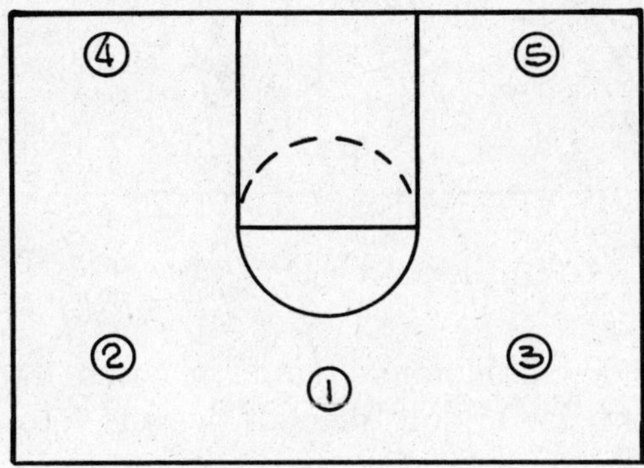

Diagram 20-1

The best ball-handler is placed in the center and instructed to penetrate down the middle as far as he can go (Diagram 20-2). He turns the ball loose before the double team occurs, and never penetrates into the lane. When he moves down the middle, the following opportunities occur: a) He can beat his man for the lay-up (Diagram 20-3); b) He can beat his man, and if the low defensive man switches, he can pass the ball off to his baseline teammate (Diagram 20-4); c) He can penetrate and hit one of the two baseline men who are cutting backdoor (Diagram 20-5).

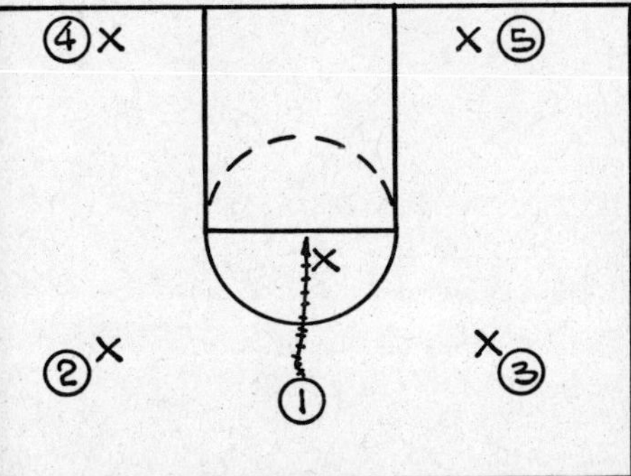

Diagram 20-2

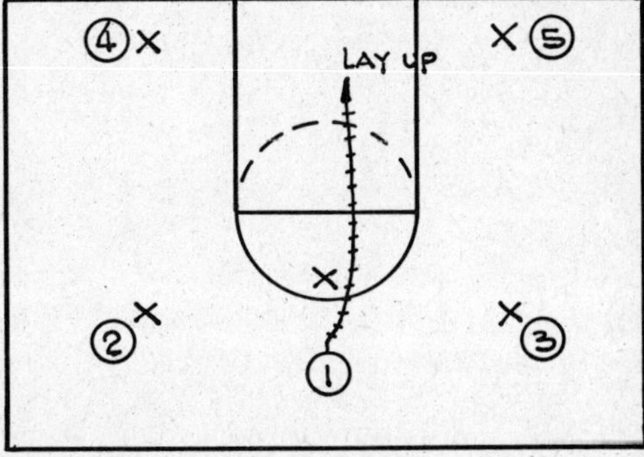

Diagram 20-3

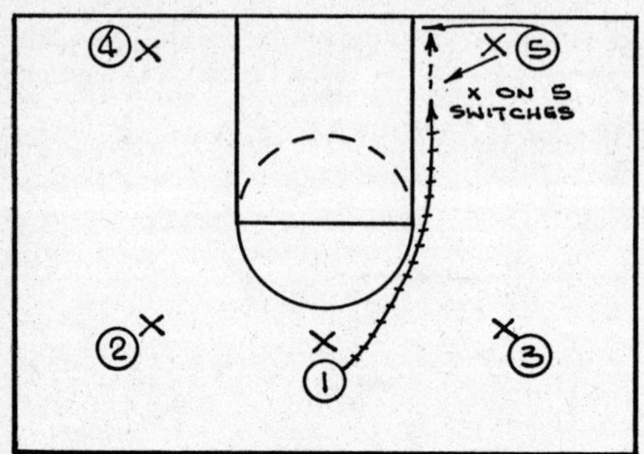

Diagram 20-4

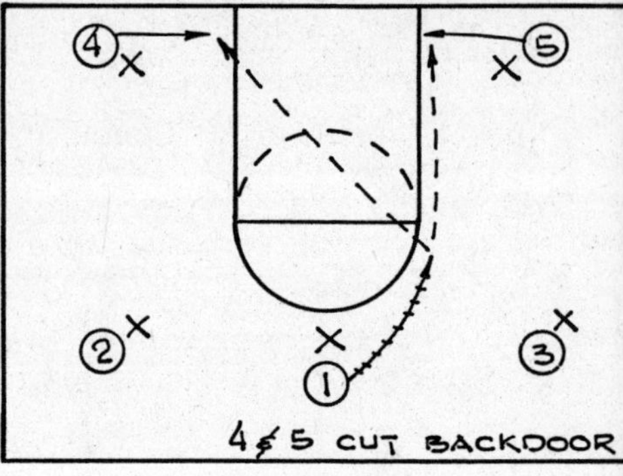

Diagram 20-5

Other outside ball-handlers should be coached to circle out to get the ball from the middle man, if he gets into trouble or is double-teamed (Diagram 20-6).

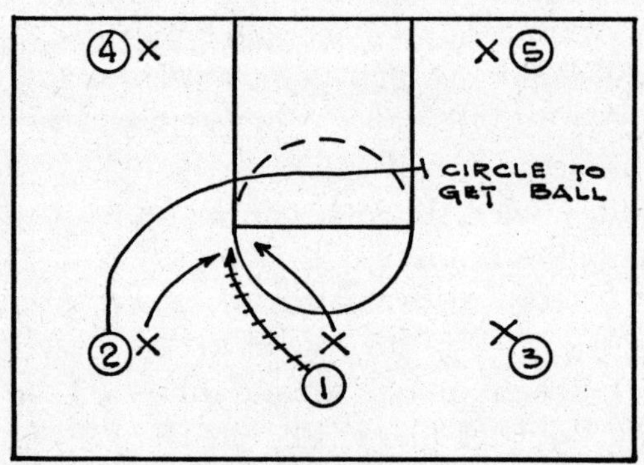

Diagram 20-6

Chapter 21

ATTACKING THE MATCH-UP ZONE

by Gene Keady

The special zone attack against a match-up zone commences with the basic set (Diagram 21-1). 04 and 05 start behind the defense. The point guard, 01, has the option of making the first pass to either wing. After the pass, 01 executes the cut to either corner. 02 then fills the point guard's spot and 04 may flash to the medium post (Diagram 21-2).

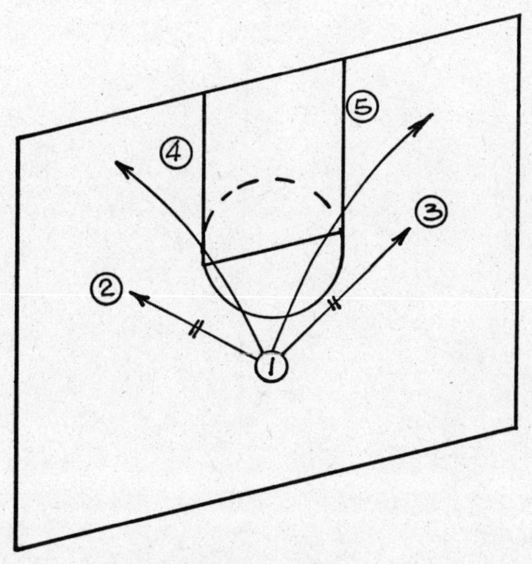

Diagram 21-1

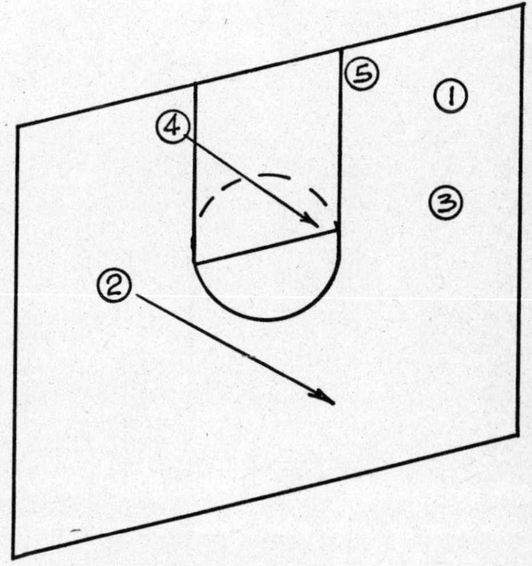

Diagram 21-2

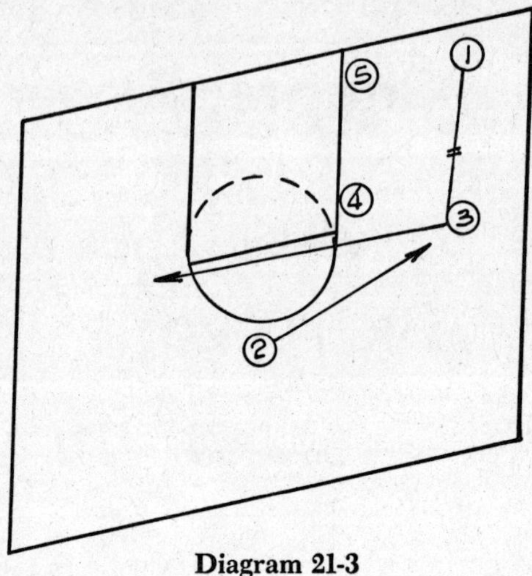

Diagram 21-3

Continuing the action (Diagram 21-3), 03 looks to either 04 or 01. If 03 passes to 01, 03 will then make a cut away from the ball. 02 fills the opening.

01's objective is get the ball inside; however, he should not force it (Diagram 21-4). 05 may cut away and 04 will then slide down the lane to the low post position.

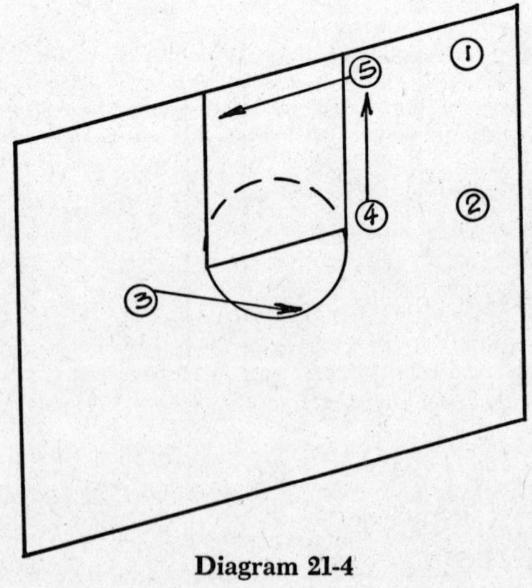

Diagram 21-4

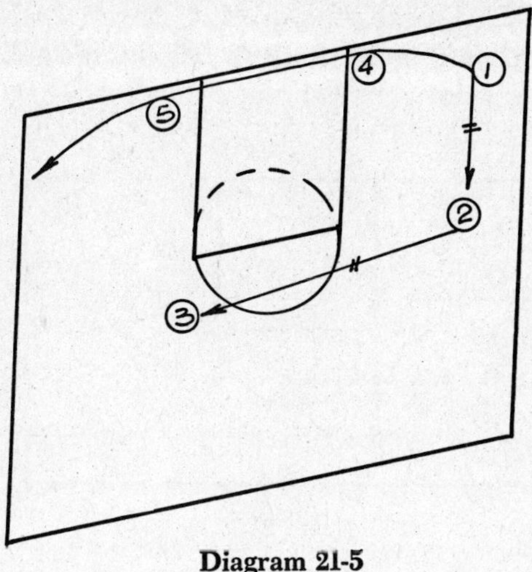

Diagram 21-5

If nothing presents itself (Diagram 21-5), the ball is reversed to the weak side. After his pass, 01 runs baseline to the weak side. The movement progresses with continued reversal of the ball until we are able to move the ball inside or find an open jump shot (Diagram 21-6).

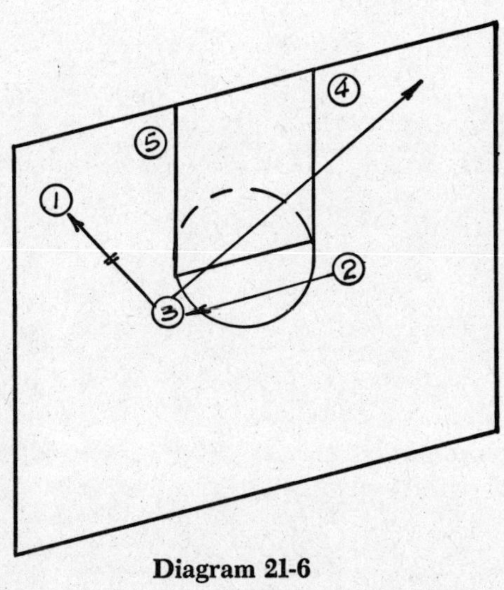

Diagram 21-6

Finally, if 03 is successful in getting the ball to 04 at the medium post position (Diagram 21-7), 04 should look weak side to 05 or to 02 stepping into the 3-hole.

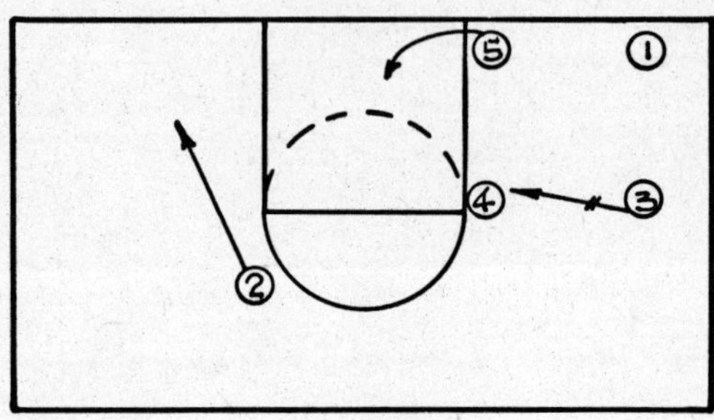

Diagram 21-7

part THREE

Defense

Chapter 22

BUILDING A SOUND DEFENSE

by James Dutcher

With the continued improvement of team and individual offensive skills, the tasks of the defensive player have become increasingly difficult. Even the average offensive player will shoot a good percentage unless he is closely guarded. We realize that a team cannot be held scoreless, but this is our goal. Cheap points that come as a result of defensive errors must not be given up. These consist of failure to box out on defensive rebounds, lack of communication on screens, unnecessary fouling, giving up the baseline, and failing to convert to the defensive end of the court quickly.

Our game is based primarily on defense due to three factors:

1. Offensive performance varies greatly from game to game. Variables such as crowd noise, shooting background, lighting, condition of the floor, and type of backboards can affect shooting percentages. The defense should not be affected by these factors and is much more consistent.

2. Defense can dictate the tempo of the game. A full-court press automatically speeds up the game; a sagging zone tends to slow down the pace. A team's offensive game plan can be destroyed by changing defensive tactics at the proper time.

3. Players who do not have great ability can play adequate defense. Physical attributes such as size, speed, and agility are important in playing good defense, but desire is probably more important.

One of the most difficult tasks a coach has is to sell his team on the value of good defense. A good defensive player gains little recognition and is appreciated primarily by his coach and his teammates. Following are a few things we do to try to motivate our players defensively:

1. Give adequate practice time to defense. Preaching good defense and not giving adequate time to it is self-defeating.

2. Praise good defensive performance. Too many coaches take good defense for granted. A pat on the back lets the player know the coach is aware of his defensive performance.

3. Encourage the press and radio to give recognition to defensive play. We select a defensive player of the game and his picture always appears in the local newspaper.

4. Keep defensive charts and statistics. A record of defensive credits such as steals, blocked shots, interceptions, recoveries, closing baseline, and screening off the board should be kept and exhibited on the team bulletin board, and given to the news media.

5. Stress the team aspect of good defense. Let every player know his job is important to the total team defensive performance.

Once the players are aware of the importance of good defense, a great deal of hard work and repetition are required to make them fundamentally sound on defense. We try to emphasize these coaching points:

1. Begin with fundamental drills such as one-on-one. Assume that everyone needs work on stance, footwork, proper vision, etc. Return to fundamental drills frequently.

2. Explain the objective of each defensive drill and tell how it will contribute to success. Each drill should serve a definite purpose.

3. Do not stay with any drill too long. About ten minutes will be long enough for most drills.

4. Careless or lazy defensive errors should be corrected as soon as they occur. Do not wait for a convenient break in the play.

5. Stress *do not foul* in all defensive work. Containing an offensive player by fouling him is not good defense. Permitting fouling to go unchallenged in defensive drill work leads to bad defensive habits.

6. Have all players use the same terminology. Words such as *switch, slide,* and *pick* should mean the same to all the players on the squad.

Chapter 23

ADVANTAGES OF THE MAN-FOR-MAN OVER THE ZONE DEFENSE

by Robert L. Stevens

Undoubtedly, the most controversial of the defenses in basketball today is the zone defense. Whenever basketball is discussed, there is usually a debate about the zone defense. Certainly the zone has many advantages and, as is true in any defense, it has disadvantages. We would not like to see the zone defense abolished, because it has an important place in the overall basketball picture.

Very few college and university teams use the zone as a basic defense. This practice indicates the finer qualities of the man-for-man and the switching defenses. Because of the swing to even more pressurized defenses, we feel the zone will be used only as a surprise element to cause a definite change-up in the style or tempo of the defense employed.

We believe that defense, regardless of the type used, will always revert back to man-for-man fundamentals. Therefore, we would like to list several points that are emphasized in the man-for-man defense.

1. With today's great jump shooters, the ability of the defense to match size for size, speed for speed, and cleverness for cleverness certainly increases the overall power of a defense. The man-for-man defense is the only one that is able to maintain an equal situation at all times, because the individual offensive moves that are taught today create many defensive problems. In order to combat individual offense, a man-for-man defense is indicated.

2. Man-for-man defense gives responsibility to the individual player, thus building enthusiasm and desire. Naturally, the man-for-man is only as strong as the individual who is employing it, but a team effort is developed as each man helps his teammates. Every player enjoys responsibility, and each one likes to be given the responsibility of carrying out a definite assignment. When the players have developed a sense of responsibility, it is easy to give individual assignments which will provide the defense with additional strength. Regardless of the type of zone defense employed, responsibility is never given to a player regarding another player's ability.

3. In our present-day world, psychological warfare is being emphasized by the various countries. The same is true in the psychological advantage of the man-for-man defense, in which a man or a team is keyed to certain situations such as trying to stop a team's high scorer, staying with their fastest man, or playing the number-one team in the conference. The ability of a coach to use psychology in his man-for-man assignments, both on an individual and team basis, will often produce an exceptionally fine performance. Again, we revert to the advantage of individual responsibility, a point that is not found in any of the zone defenses.

4. Motivation is one of a coach's greatest teaching weapons. Therefore, we believe it is easier to teach the man-for-man defense than the zone defense due to the presence of a motivation influence which helps a player's pride and sense of responsibility. Since every player is endowed with personal pride, and motivating individual responsibility, these qualities will spur him to unusual heights in outstanding performances.

5. Zone defenses have a tendency to be more passive because of the lack of individual responsibility. Therefore, the man-for-man defense encourages a much more aggressive type of play.

6. If an offensive team has started stalling tactics or ball control, the zone defense does not have the aggressiveness or individual responsibility necessary to place enough pressure on the ball to regain possession. Usually, when teams revert to stalling tactics they have a lead and the defensive team is trailing. Thus, in order to score and regain the lead, the defensive team must be more aggressive in regaining the basketball for an offensive scoring opportunity.

7. The aggressive man-for-man defense with its many trapping or double-teaming tactics, provides the coach with an added weapon to use against an opposing team's scoring star. Overload tactics which are used against zone defenses make it very vulnerable by having two offensive men with only one defensive man in that zone or area.

8. The man-for-man defense enables the coach and the players to detect the strong or weak aspects of an opponent's offense. Many times a player will come to the sidelines during a time-out, and because he has had individual responsibility assignments, he will be able to detect immediately his assigned man's weaknesses. Also, through pressurized tactics, he will be able to notice glaring weaknesses in the entire offensive team. Therefore, since the coach has added opportunity to the player's ability to detect weaknesses, this may be the key which can be the difference between a game won or lost.

It is very difficult to inspire good individual performances in both individuals and teams without motivation for individual responsibility and pride of performance. Zone defenses are not very effective on large courts, but the man-for-man defenses can be effective on all types and sizes of playing areas. Aggressive and pressure tactics of the man-for-man defense, when compared to the zones, will enable a team to place pressure on outside shooters, combat the slow delay tactics, and control fast-breaking ball clubs. One of the greatest weaknesses of the zone defense is its inability to combat the fast-break tactics which are so popular today.

A player who is able to play man-for-man defense can play any defense. If his team has been playing any type of a zone defense, the basic and fundamental rules of individual man-for-man defense apply immediately when the ball and the player are in his defensive zone. A player who has been taught to use zone defenses usually has a very difficult time adjusting to man-for-man tactics.

Chapter 24

ONE-ON-ONE DEFENSE

by John H. Harvey

When the opponent has the ball, the defensive man who has full command of the fundamentals and employs them in personal strategy can neutralize and eliminate certain moves of the offensive player. The confident defender should become the aggressor. A game of cat-and-mouse develops—the defensive man being the cat who plays with his victim.

The customary defensive stance, playing 1-on-1 against the ball-handler, is shown in Diagram 24-1. The defensive player's inside foot is forward and his outside foot back. If the defensive man is on the left side of the court, his right foot must be in front—on the right side, the opposite foot is up. In this stance, the player is

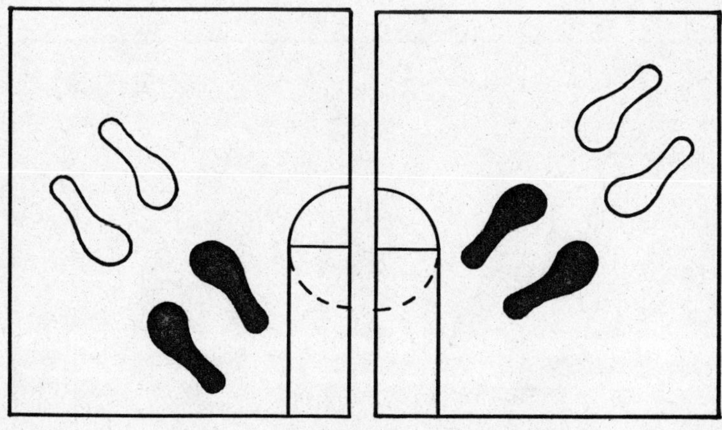

Diagram 24-1

strongest to the side of his rear foot. He has already opened up on that side in order to be prepared to handle the offensive drive in that direction. He is weaker to the inside, since he would have to withdraw his front leg in order to begin a retreat to handle a drive in that direction.

The choice of placing the inside foot forward is predicated upon the knowledge that help can be obtained from teammates should the offensive player drive over this lead leg and gain a one-half step advantage. With this basic understanding of his strong and weak sides, the defensive player can make certain adjustments to conditions in order to make the best use of his knowledge and try to control the offensive man's movements. These adjustments can mean the difference between victory and defeat in the personal 1-on-1 battle.

The defensive man should make the offensive player go the way he wants him to go—force him to the strong side.

As shown in Diagram 24-2, this is toward the left or rear leg. The move of retreat with the drive can be made best in that direction. To accomplish this, the defensive position can be moved to the right, as shown in Diagram 24-3. This means opening the gate wide to the offensive player, but almost completely closing off the possibility of a drive over the right leg. Thus, the defensive man eliminates one choice for the offense and can expect a move toward his strong side. Then he must be prepared to ride the offensive player hard to the outside once the inital move has been made.

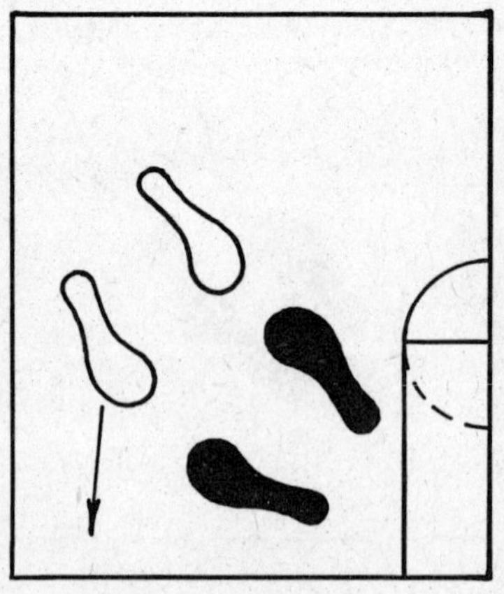

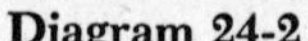

Diagram 24-2

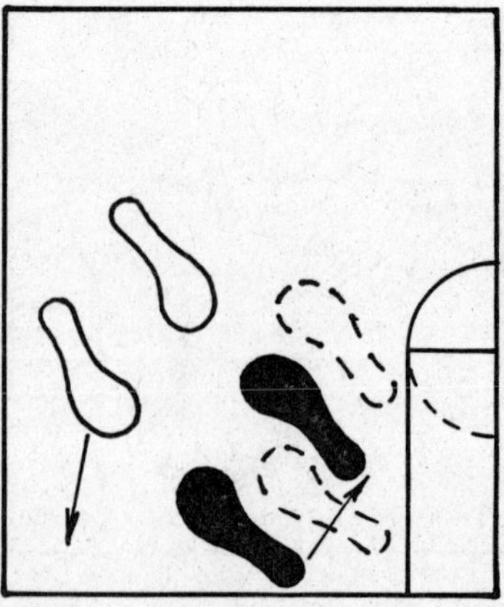

Diagram 24-3

This position adjustment is more important to a big man than to a very quick guard. The tall defensive player cannot handle a drive over his front leg as quickly, because he is presumably less agile. The big man should also play a little farther away from his offensive opponent for the same reason. He cannot retreat as quickly as a smaller man. Naturally, the proximity to the offensive man also depends upon the size and known quickness of the opponent.

Conversely, a good defensive back-court player can stay closer to his man in order to bother him more. He may also position himself nearer to the direct line between his man and the basket. He has the agility to go either way almost equally with the movement of the man who has the ball.

A smaller player should do everything in his power to prevent his larger opponent from driving either side. His best bet is to force the shot from outside, since the closer the bigger man gets to the basket, the greater his advantage over a smaller defensive player.

The defender must remember that preventing a drive to the basket is his most important job, since that offensive move has a better chance of scoring success than a 20-foot jump shot. Thus, he must always be ready to retreat to prevent the drive. It is very satisfying for the defender to see his offensive man with the ball try several fakes and eventually realize that he cannot drive either way. Frustrated, he finally decides to take the long jumper or pass back out to a teammate who is farther from the basket.

Chapter 25

THE SHELL DRILL

by Lynn Nance

Our teams utilize both the man-for-man and zone defenses. However, the major emphasis is directed toward an aggressive, pressure defense. This defense is a helping man-for-man, which denies all penetrating passes. The center fronts or sides his man either high or low to prevent the ball from reaching the key area.

The guards pick up at mid-court and force the dribbler to the hash mark where they square off to the sideline and attempt to prevent further penetration. Influencing guards to the sideline develops a poor passing angle for the guard to pass forward, utilizes the sideline as a defense tool, and makes pressure on the guard easier. Forwards influence their men to the baseline, squaring off at a position approximately 15 feet from the basket. This places the offensive player in a very poor shooting position behind the backboard, with difficult passes required for further penetration.

One of our drills which provides a variety of important defensive manuevers in a short period of time is the defensive shell drill. This drill is run daily in practice sessions.

The Shell Drill

The shell drill is an all-important drill which allows game-like practice in defensing six crucial game situations. The shell emphasizes shifting in the direction of the pass, defensing the dribble penetration, defensing the cutter, the flash post, sealing the baseline when a defensive breakdown has occurred, and executing the 4-on-4 block out situation.

Shift in the Direction of the Pass

This drill is set up with four offensive players at the guard and forward positions. Four defensive men are added and take up changing positions as the ball is passed from one offensive player to another.

The defensive players are instructed to allow all passes, and emphasis is placed on proper ball-man relationships.

As the ball is passed from player to player around the shell, the defensive players are required to shift, maintaining sight of their man and the ball.

The defensive man who is covering the player with the ball should be attempting to influence the player to the sideline with the outside foot approximately in line with the midpoint of the ball-handler. He should be within arms' reach of the offensive man to prevent a cross-over dribble and to maintain pressure on the ball.

The weak-side guard should sag one step toward the ball and one step off the line of the ball, but still be in a position to deny if the passer should decide to pass to his man. He must realize that should the ball-handler penetrate the middle, he is required to drop off and help stop further penetration.

The strong-side forward (forward on the side of the ball) should be in a deny position on top with his rear foot in the midpoint position allowing the offensive forward no alternative but to go baseline. When the offensive player receives the ball, the defensive forward must adjust to a position of influencing baseline by placing his front foot in the midpoint.

The weak-side forward (forward away from the ball) should have both feet in the lane and be in a position in which he can see his man and the ball without turning his head.

Emphasis should be placed on the shift in the direction of the pass by all four defensive men on the pass and not at the completion of the pass.

Dribble Penetration

Using the same defensive and offensive set, the offensive player with the ball is allowed to beat his man either right or left and penetrate into the lane with the dribble. When this takes place, the closest defensive man should give help by making a lateral move from his man. It is important to emphasize that the helper should keep the line of the ball (imaginary line between the defensive man and the ball) in front of him, not allowing his man to cut behind and receive the ball. The helper must understand that he is required to maintain a position allowing him to get back to his man should he receive the ball or cut and leave the play.

When penetration is stopped by the helper, the offensive player passes to the helper's man who immediatley attempts to penetrate until he is stopped. The helper must react quickly and recover under control realizing he is in the most vulnerable of defensive positions. His goal should be to prevent penetration and still put defensive pressure on the outside shot.

Defensing the Cutter

Utilizing the same basic set, we drill on defensing the cutter by means of an automatic shift in the direction of the pass by the defensive man who is guarding the passer. This quick shift prevents the passer from getting ball side (between the defense and the ball) and executing the give-and-go. Since we are influencing the sideline, a guard-forward pass makes the shift toward the ball more difficult. Considerable emphasis is placed on this move in our drill work.

When the cutter starts his cut, the defensive player should attempt to body check him if the angle of the pass is such that it does not take him out of defensive position.

As the cutter is now forced to make the back-side cut, the defensive man should close over the top preventing the pass, getting his hands into the passing lane until such time as he can again see the ball over his shoulder.

Emphasis is on preventing the cutter from going ball-side by body checking and closing over the top stopping the back-side pass.

Defensing the Flash Post

This drill emphasizes proper defense away from the ball. The cut is made from the weak side to the strong side. It is essential that the weak side is initially in the proper position as the offensive player begins his cut to the ball. The defensive man's first move is to cut off the offensive man in such a manner that he cannot cut in a straight line to the ball. The defensive player must body check him to slow down the cutter's move and must deny the ball utilizing the close-out on the back-side cut. Should the offensive player continue his cut, the defensive man should deny to the perimeter.

Emphasis should be placed on preventing the pass into the area of the key. The defensive player on the passer should also make every pass as difficult as possible by crowding his man and playing the passing lane.

Sealing the Baseline

Sealing the bseline is a term we use to describe the defensive rotation which must take place immediately whenever a defensive breakdown occurs requiring the center or weak-side forward to help. Two major situations that are being defensed are the successful backdoor cut by the forward or the dribble penetration into the key. In both situations, the weak-side forward (or in a game situation, the center) is called upon to seal off the baseline from any further penetration and secure proper defensive position. This is an excellent opportunity to gain position to take the charge.

After the baseline has been sealed off by the forward (or possibly the center), it becomes the responsibility of the weak-side guard to sag down into the lane and prevent or intercept any pass to the helper's man. We call this situation helping the helper and in games when the center helps, the weak-side forward has the responsibility of helping on the center's man while the guard must drop and cover the forward's man.

4-on-4 Block Out

This drill utilizes the same shell set and incorporates basic fundamentals of the defense. The four offensive players are allowed to maneuver in a limited range before the shot is taken. The offense is required to pass and cut, screen and so forth making defensive adjustments necessary.

As the shot is taken, a live block-out drill is executed with the defensive men being told to allow the ball to hit the floor before touching it. The offense attempts to rebound the ball and score.

We emphasize the importance of the weak side and require our players to go to the offensive man and set the block.

Almost any type of defensive situation can be incorporated into the shell concept, such as screens on the ball and post defense. The key to good defense is constant drill on the fundamentals until they become as instinctive to the player as his offensive skills are.

Chapter 26

THE ABC ZONE DEFENSE

by Norman Held

The 1-2-2 zone, using the ABC principle, applies equally well to any zone, whether it is a drop-back or pressure zone. Diagram 26-1 shows how the ABC principle divides the court. Zone A is always to the defensive player's left as he faces the offense, and it includes the area from the left sideline to the left free throw lane line extended. Zone B is the area between the two free throw lanes

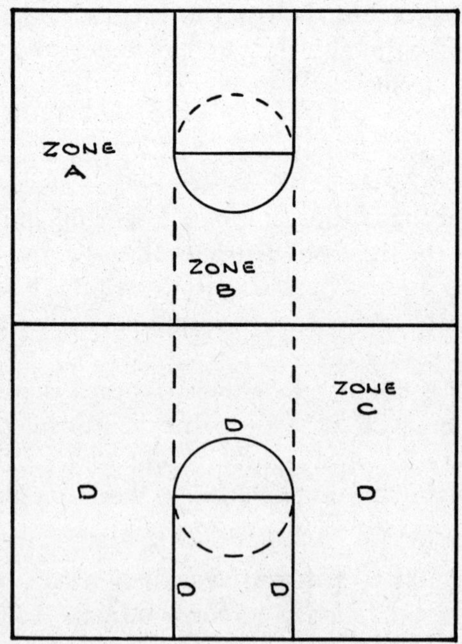

Diagram 26-1

extended. Zone C covers the same area as Zone A except that it is on the other side of the court.

There is only one basic guideline for the operation of the ABC principle. When the ball is some two passes away from a zone (Diagram 26-2), the defensive man in that zone is allowed to leave his zone and free-lance defensively. For example, as shown in Diagram 26-2, D3 has become the free-lance man as the result of a pass into zone A to 02. After the defense switches, D3 is left with the weak-side assignment. Since only the 1-2-2 zone is used, we are able to place our best defensive thinkers at the most likely free-lance positions which are D2 and D3 according to our defensive shifts. If a situation should occur where zone A or C would become void of offensive players, all five of the defensive men are permitted to move into the two occupied zones.

It is our hope that the offense will let us defend them on two-thirds of the floor, either in zones A or B or in B and C. When the zone defense is used, the players try to force the opponent to make his first pass into zone C, which we feel is the weaker shooting side and the poorer driving side for a right-hander, and then cut off any return pass around the horn and back to the weak side. If this works successfully, the area the players must defend has been reduced.

This same principle is applied to the zone press. In fact, it is probably employed more here than in the drop-back defense, because the zone press is used more frequently. The ABC principle simplifies the teaching of the press. A version of the 1-2-2 zone press makes the job of the anticipators a little easier.

Diagram 26-3 shows how the defense is set up for the zone

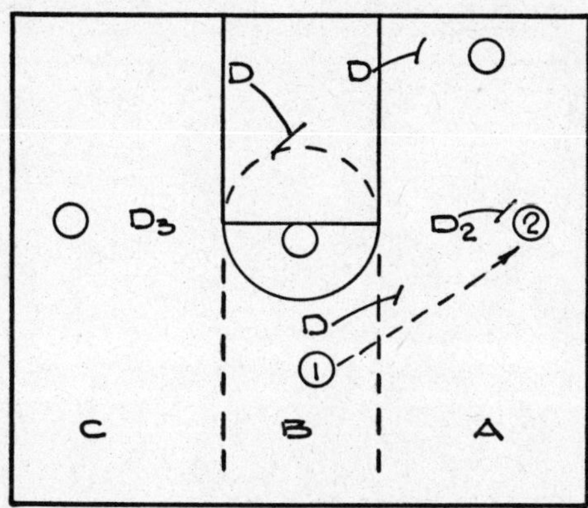

Diagram 26-2

press. The offense is in a box setup, so we play the box man-for-man until the ball is in bounds. Even if the offense should tandem (Diagram 26-4) these front two men are still played man-for-man. After the ball is in bounds, then the zone press is used. Since the players try never to let the ball come in bounds in zone A or B, we are permitted to use the ABC principle quite a bit. If the ball does come into zone C (Diagram 26-5) as desired, then D3 and D1 trap, and D2 leaves zone A to defend against the pass into that area. D5 plays his man tight man-for-man while D4 drops off his man into zone B. D4 must be able to move in any direction as an anticipator after reading the offensive man in the trap. If D4 anticipates toward his own basket, then D5 must release and get back as a safety. This is just one situation, but most adjustments are fairly simple.

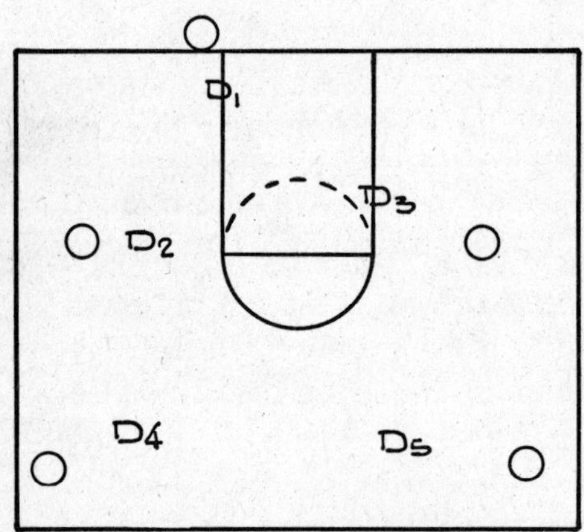

Diagram 26-3

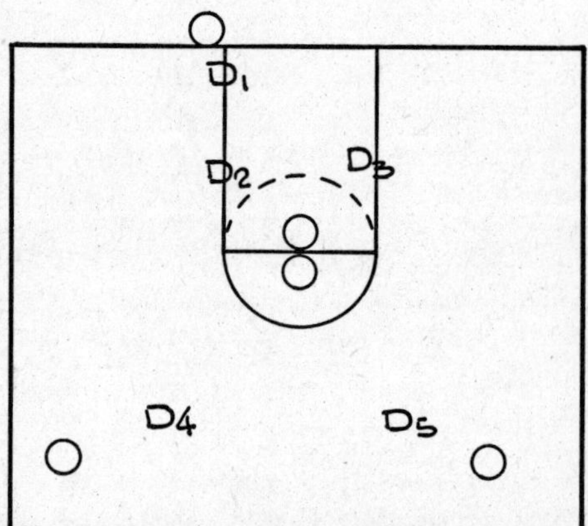

Diagram 26-4

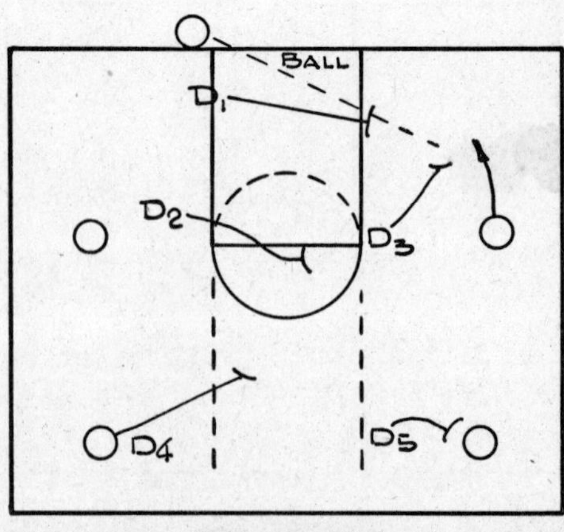

Diagram 26-5

Chapter 27

1-2-1-1 FULL-COURT ZONE PRESS

by William Lopez

The popularity of the full-court press has become widespread because of its many positive results. It is an excellent surprise weapon. It can bring about a desired change in the tempo of the game. It can prevent an opponent from using an offense that has been effective. It can compensate for lack of size, lack of shooting ability and lack of rebounding ability. It is an excellent *offensive* weapon that forces a great deal of turnovers which lead to easy baskets.

Diagram 27-1 shows the basic set of the 1-2-1-1. G1 is usually the taller of the two guards. Since he will be putting pressure on

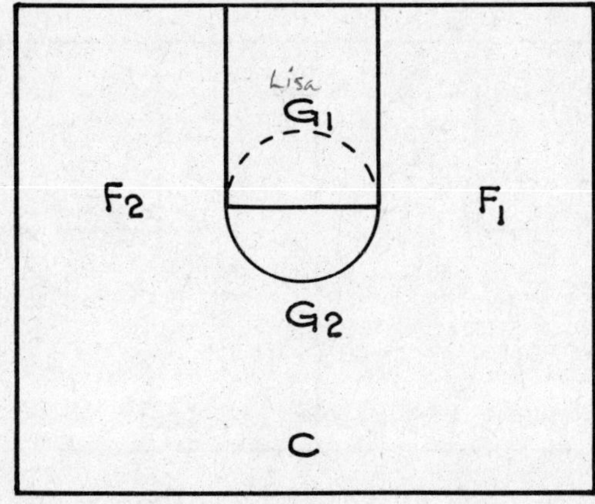

Diagram 27-1

the ball, we want to present a taller object to throw over. At the same time we want somebody quick to play this position. We allow the first pass to be made in front of G1, F1 and F2. G1 must follow the ball and attack at the right time. The pass receiver's movement will determine what G1 should do. G1 should look for three things that his opponent can do with the ball: 1) If the opponent has not dribbled, G1 must stay approximately five feet from him with his hands up and knees bent, ready to react to any movement. G1 must never allow the player to drive by him. 2) If the opponent starts his dribble, G1 must keep his distance and force the opponent to the sideline towards one of his forwards for help and the double team. 3) When the opponent stops his dribble, G1 must get as close to him as possible without fouling him. He should have his hands up in order to obscure the opponent's vision. This will also keep the defensive player from reaching for the ball. A player who reaches for the ball will more often than not be called for a foul.

What is the forward's responsibility in this position? When the ball is passed to his side of the court, the forward must also attack the opponent in the same manner G1 did.

F1 must never allow the dribbler to beat him along the sideline, as shown in Diagram 27-2, but instead must force the dribbler back toward G1, trapping him. Both G1 and F1 must try to get the dribbler to pick up his dribble. If this happens, both defenders attack as close as possible with hands up, trying to create a turnover (Diagram 27-3).

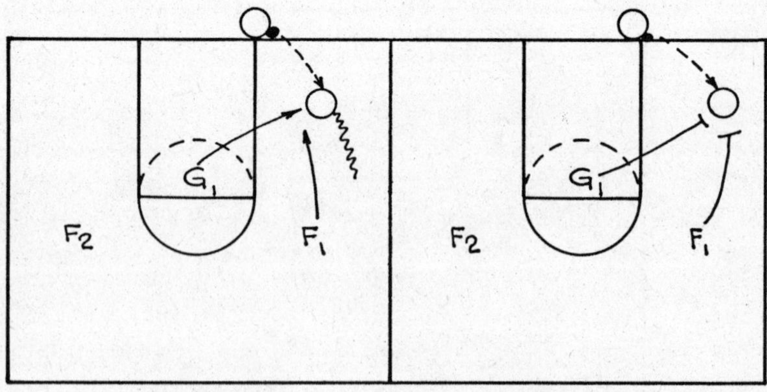

Diagram 27-2 Diagram 27-3

As soon as the trap is made, the opposite forward, F2, goes to the top of the key or free throw line anticipating a pass (Diagram 27-3). His movement is dictated by the opponent.

We are not concerned about F2 leaving his side of the court. A pass in that area cannot really hurt since it is not a penetrating pass. We are primarily concerned about movement of the ball forward, not across the court or back toward the basket.

What happens when the ball is passed back into that vacant area to the guard who was taking the ball out (Diagram 27-4)? G1 must follow the ball and F2 returns to his side of the court. G1 and F2 try to trap the ball in the same manner that G1 and F2 did. F1 falls back, and as soon as the trap is made, he moves to the free throw line or the top of the key (Diagram 27-5).

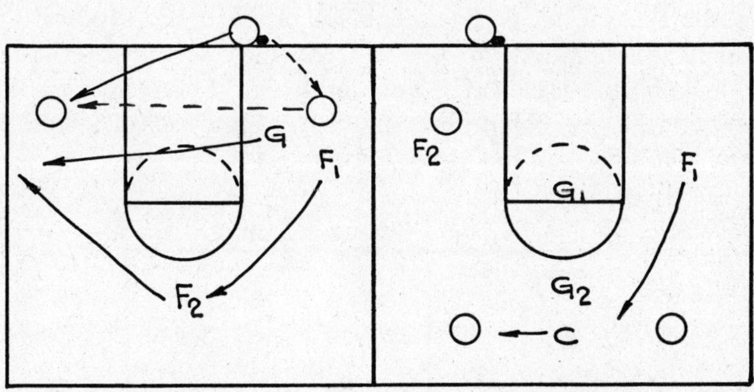

Diagram 27-4 Diagram 27-5

It is important for F1 and F2 to remember that if the ball is being taken out on the opposite side and there is no opponent in front of them, they must fall back to the middle of the court to prevent the long pass which would immediately break the press. If the ball is returned to his side of the court, F1 moves up and attacks (Diagram 27-6).

G2 must be extremely quick in his position. He is responsible for any opponent coming up on the ball side of the court. Diagram 27-6 shows G2 moving to cover the opponent on the ball side and F2 moving to the top of the key. G2 must anticipate and try to steal or deflect the pass. It is extremely important for G2 to learn that if he

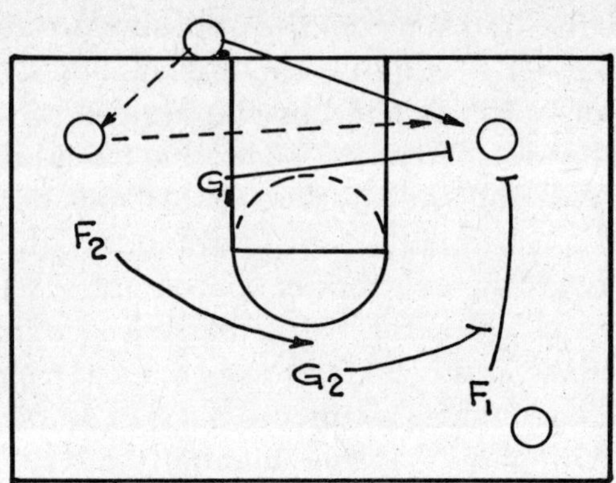

Diagram 27-6

cannot make the steal, he is not out of the game. Too often the player in this position misses the steal and then turns around and watches a 5 on 4 attack. G1 must learn that if he cannot make the steal he must prevent the opponent from making an uncontested pass or dribbling up the court toward the basket.

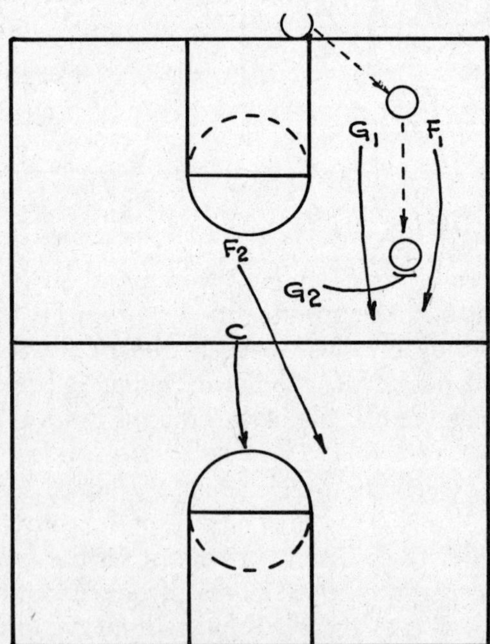

Diagram 27-7

C's responsibility is to protect the basket against easy lay-ups and to protect against the long pass.

Diagram 27-7 shows what happens if the second pass up the sidelines is completed. G2 tries to prevent the ball from penetrating any farther. C falls back to protect the basket. G1 and F1 hustle back and swipe at the ball; an F1 and G2 trap is possible. F2 hustles back to help protect the basket and the sideline.

Chapter 28

DEFENDING THE FOUR CORNER DELAY

by Bill Gappy and Mike Moran

The purpose of the delay game is to: 1) obtain an easy lay-up; 2) get the big player away from the basket; 3) maintain ball possession; 4) take time off the clock (stall in the last minutes of the game); and 5) attempt to increase the lead through ball possession and a defensive mistake.

The purpose of defensing against the delay game is to: 1) *not* give up the lay-up; 2) utilize various defensive techniques to gain possession of the ball; 3) challenge teams to take the pull-up short jump shots; and 4) force the ball away from the basket.

The rules of defensing the delay game are as follows:

X5, the big post player, must maintain control of the basket. He leaves the lane area only when the ball is in the fore-court area. He does not contest jump shots upon penetration. His primary responsibility is to discourage and stop the lay-up attempt and then to rebound if a jumper (pull-up) is taken. X5 must look to take the charge and *never* stop ball penetration by moving up the lane to meet the ball.

X1, X2, X3 and X4 match up with offensive players. They pressure the ball and force the dribble. Using the jump-and-run technique or double teams whenever possible, they attempt to force the dribbler toward one of their teammates. They must maintain poise and not foul. These four players must be willing to go all-out on defense for up to one-and-a-half to two minutes. If the open player, usually 05, is found, the closest defensive player must pressure him into a dribble. The other three defensive players rotate into the passing lanes. They must force the best ball-handler to give up the ball and then they must deny him the ball.

Unless there are just a few remaining seconds, most teams are neither experienced nor disciplined enough to hold onto the ball without making a mistake or taking a shot (other than a lay-up). We play the percentages. Although we do not want to give up an uncontested short jump shot, we would rather a team take one than get a lay-up.

By keeping our big player in the lane with basket responsibilities and matching up man-for-man (except when an unguarded player, usually X5's opponent when he leaves the lane area), an unorthodox situation exists that most teams have not prepared for.

With constant pressure on the ball, jump-and-run tactics, plus occasional double-teaming, the ball handlers look to penetrate quickly only to find the defensive big player waiting at the basket.

Quite often X5's opponent will be wide open in either corner or at the top of the key and in possession of the ball; but again, we feel that this is an unnatural position for him, especially in the scope of a delay game ideology. Most teams want their best handlers to control the ball.

Depending upon 01's movement, you can force either way, double team or jump-and-run (Diagram 28-1).

In the event that the ball handler penetrates and passes off to X5's opponent, X1 will follow the pass and pressure X5's opponent.

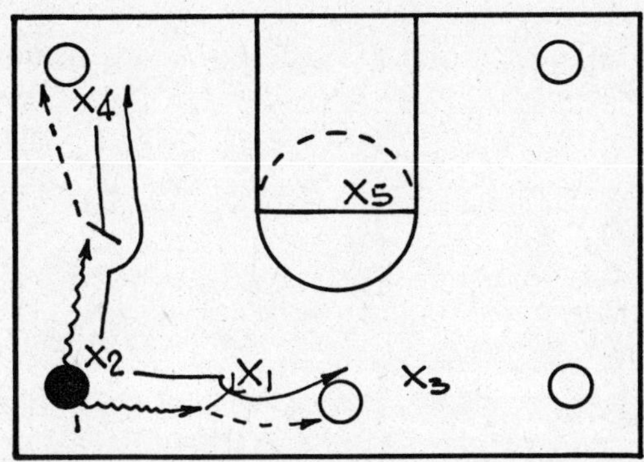

Diagram 28-1

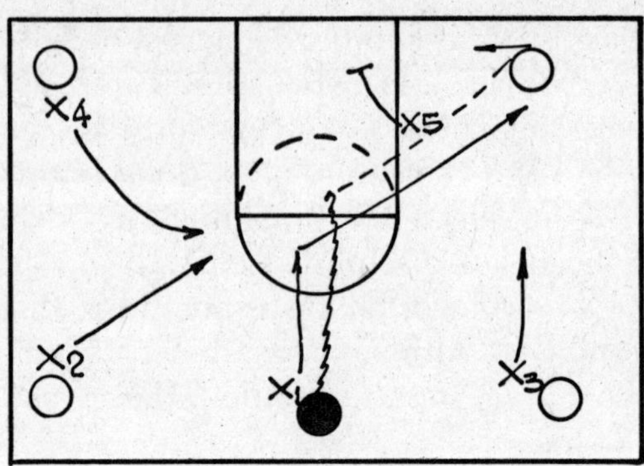

Diagram 28-2

X2 rotates to the middle and picks up X1's opponent. X3 rotates toward the ball, while X4 rotates toward the key area, but is on the lookout for a lob pass to either X2's opponent or his own (Diagram 28-2).

If X5's opponent does pass the ball back out, we match up the best we can and put extreme pressure on the ball-handlers. With the offensive players out of position, the jump-and-run or double teams will be most effective in forcing a mistake.

part FOUR

Fast Break

Chapter 29

THE ROLE OF QUICKNESS IN BASKETBALL

by Jerry Tarkanian and William Warren

In the absence of height, quickness is the greatest attribute a team can have. No matter how tall a player is, if he cannot get back on defense to stop the opponents from taking high-percentage shots, his height will not help his team. Quick, mobile, small players can often keep the ball away from taller, relatively immobile opponents, and quick players can make life miserable for ball-handlers outside. Speed can tire opponents physically, force them into mental errors when they are not accustomed to playing high-speed basketball, confuse them by taking away vital aspects of their offensive game plan, and wear them down mentally by forcing them to play cautiously in order to avoid turnovers and the resultant, ever-present threat of the fast break.

It is not necessary to be faster than the opponents in order to fast-break against them. The success of any given fast break is determined largely during the first two to three seconds after transition. Training defensive players to anticipate and react to transitions improves the fast break, obviously, but factors other than those most commonly cited also act in favor of the defensive team:

1. In the case of steals, the defenders, facing the ball or their own basket are in better position to take advantage of the first second or two after the steal. The player stealing the ball is either facing his own basket, or at least is closer to facing his basket than

the player from whom he stole the ball. Many times he will already be in motion toward his own basket and moving at top speed when he steals the ball. Also, the players on the offensive team, particularly the ball-handler, generally will have to turn around before starting downcourt to stop the fast break. These factors definitely place the attacking advantage with the fast-breaking team.

2. Offensive teams are generally basket-oriented; that is, they are trained to take the ball to the basket and attack the defense rather than worrying about the defenders stealing the ball and fast-breaking. When a shot is taken, for example, certain offensive players will move to the basket to rebound offensively, but in order to rebound effectively they will have to get *inside* the defenders near the basket. Their momentum, then, will be toward their own basket and it will involve movement that is necessarily more aggressive than that of the defenders already stationed near the basket. The offensive team's basket orientation can work against them in terms of their vulnerability to fast-breaking. Only, however, when the defenders can anticipate transition and begin moving downcourt before the opponents can react will the fast break reach its ultimate effectiveness.

3. Most teams are not accustomed to playing high-speed basketball. We are often told that players cannot realistically be expected to give 100 percent effort on defense, and then turn around and give the same effort on offense. *They have to rest sometime,* is the argument usually given. But after working so hard to get the ball why would the players want to rest when they have the opponents at a disadvantage? Do they really want to slow down and wait for the opponents to get back and set up in their half-court defense, thereby surrendering all hope of penetrating on offense, just because they are not supposed to be able to give 100 percent at both ends of the court? Why work them hard at all on defense if they are not going to reap the full rewards of their efforts at the other end of the court?

Players should be drilled constantly in transition basketball. Fast-breaking requires a certain amount of quickness but the mental factor is also important: the faster a player is able to anticipate and react to transition, the less he will have to rely on speed to be a part of the fast break. Even relatively slow players can become involved in fast-breaking when their anticipation on defense gives them a step-and-a-half start on the opponents.

The running game depends primarily upon speed and quickness, but it is also habitual; that is, the tendency to run at every opportunity is a voluntary, learned skill. If players do not practice high-speed ball-handling drills and fast-breaking, they will not be able to perform the skills involved without committing ball-handling errors and turnovers. But more important, they will be unable to play high-speed basketball effectively against teams that are accustomed to the running game and transition basketball.

Quickness can help teams in other ways. Full-court pressing defenses can take advantage of ball-handling weaknesses, and aggressive defenses such as pressure man-for-man or the run-and-jump defense can further enhance a team's defensive effectiveness. Individual and team speed never hurt a team's overall chances. You can always slow down a fast team if need be, but you'll never speed up a slow team without practicing fast-breaking and transition basketball.

Chapter 30

ORGANIZING THE FAST BREAK

by Billy Key

Nothing is more satisfying to a coach than seeing his team hook the ball out at the beginning of a fast break, fill the lanes properly, and then score a driving shot before the opponents are able to get back on defense. In order to perfect this phase of the game, hours of hard practice are necessary. Even if the team does not use the fast break, the drills which have been practiced will help develop skills in ball-handling, dribbling, shooting on the move, rebounding, and conditioning.

The most important factors of the fast break are rebounding, moving the ball out quickly, filling the lanes, staying spread, and being able to score after gaining an advantage. With these points in mind, we have developed drills which will provide player perfection in these different fundamentals. The whole-to-the-part method is used in developing the drills.

The basic principle of our fast break is to move the ball to the player on the side where the rebound has come off the backboard. In turn, he passes it to a teammate who is moving into the center lane. We want our center to carry the ball down on a fast dribble until he is challenged by the defense. From this point the team will react according to the defense. However, if the center is jammed, the side man will dribble the ball down into a scoring position, or until he is challenged by the defense. One important point should be stressed. When the player who is carrying the ball down on a fast dribble reaches a point approximately three steps past the center line, he should slow down a little. This slowing down will give him much better control of the entire situation. We have our players walk through this basic movement, so that as the drills are inserted they will be able to see the purpose of each drill.

Our basic fast-break pattern is shown in Diagram 30-1. 05 rebounds and passes the ball to 02, who in turn passes it to 01 filling the center lane. 03 will fill the third lane, and 04 and 05 will be the trailers.

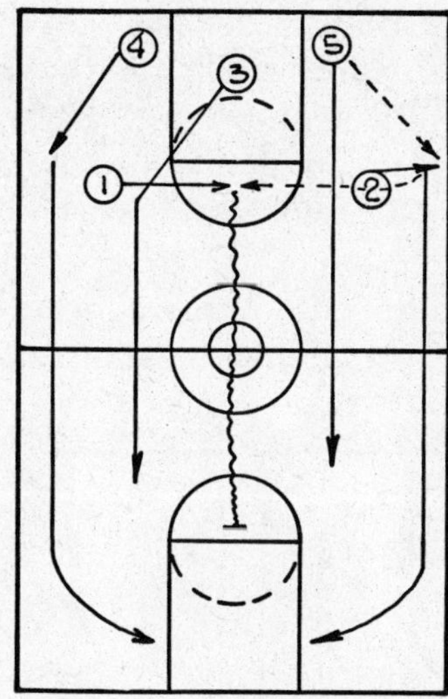

Diagram 30-1

Our fast break is organized in early practice sessions, and during that time a number of ball-handling drills are used. An example would be the simple drill of two or three players moving the ball back and forth in a spread position while moving up and down the court.

We are as much interested in giving the player a general idea of what we mean by lanes and staying spread as we are in the ball-handling aspect of the drill. If the coach is not careful, the players will have a tendency to move too close together while moving down the floor. This will hinder the development of the break. If the players are grouped together too closely it will be much easier for the defense to cover them.

From these simple ball-handling drills the players move into a simple two-on-one drill, starting at the mid-court line and then moving the length of the floor. It is advisable to run through this drill slowly at first. Diagrams 30-2 and 30-3 show the proper movements in this drill.

As shown in Diagram 30-2, the center dribbles the ball directly at the defensive man with the idea that he must take him. If the defensive man challenges the dribbler, 01, which he must do sooner or later, 01 swings a couple of steps in the direction opposite 02. Our players hope to pull the defense with them so that it will be easier to pass off to 02, who is angling in toward the basket. If the defensive man follows 01, as shown in Diagram 30-2, he will pass the ball off to 02. Attention should be given to the flanker (or flankers). In this case, 02 should stay fairly close to the sideline until he is even with the top of the circle, at which time he should start angling in toward the goal. This will bring him in to the basket without having the players bunch together too soon.

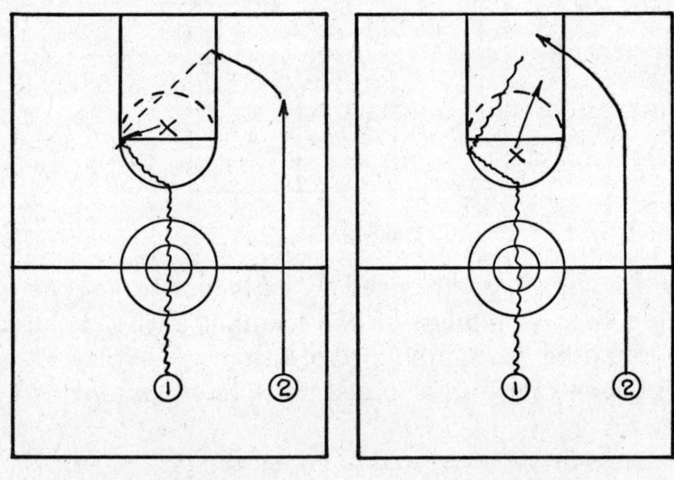

Diagram 30-2 **Diagram 30-3**

As shown in Diagram 30-3, 01 again comes down the court and angles a couple of steps, but this time the defensive man fails to move with the dribbler. Then 01 will angle back on the dribble and drive for the basket. Due to the weakness of most players in using their left hands, it is important that both sides of the floor be worked in order to give them practice with both hands.

From the two-on-one situation, work is started on a three-on-two. Our players start at half-court and move back the length of the

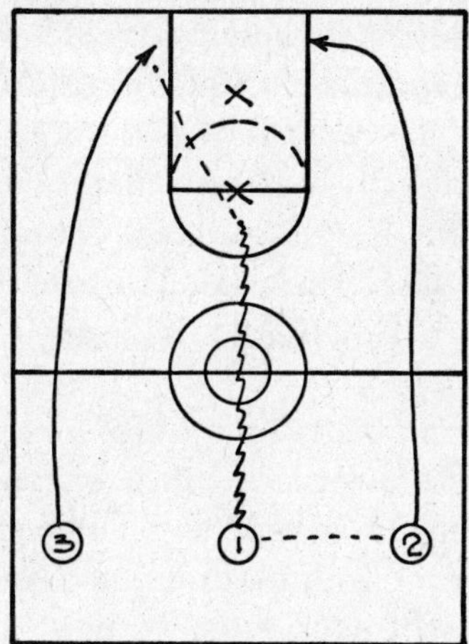

Diagram 30-4

floor. Diagram 30-4 shows the basic principles of this drill. 02 starts by passing the ball to 01, the center man. Then 01 dribbles the ball directly down the center of the floor, making the defensive man take him. When the defensive man takes him, he passes off to one of his flankers, in this case 03, who drives for the lay-up. If 03 is unable to shoot, he may be able to move the ball to 02. When the center man passes the ball, we like to have him take a couple of steps in the direction in which he has thrown the ball.

The drill shown in Diagram 30-5 is the same as that shown in Diagram 30-4, except that 01 passes to 03, who is unable to shoot

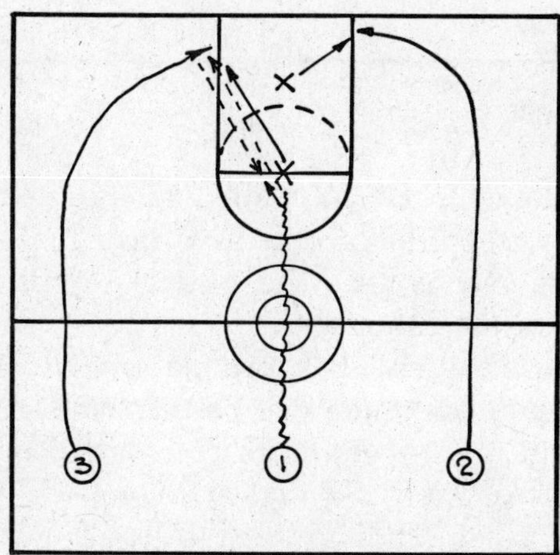

Diagram 30-5

and 02 is also covered. Consequently, 03 moves the ball back quickly to 01 who has moved a couple of steps in that direction for a quick jump shot.

From this situation the team drills on getting the ball off the backboard and out to an outlet man. This is one of the most important phases of fast-breaking. The different types of outlet passes are covered in ball-handling drills such as the baseball pass, hook pass, etc.

In the drill shown in Diagram 30-6, a rebounder, 01, and two outlet men, 02 and 03, are placed in a set position. From a close position the ball is put up against the backboard. 01 rebounds the ball, using the proper techniques and passes out quickly to 02, who in turn passes to 03 who is moving straight, and not at an angle, into the center lane. The rebounder should practice making the outlet pass either before or after the dribble. The players should work both sides of the floor so they will be able to use both hands in throwing the ball out. Various types of passes should be used. Also, we like to have our outlet man get the ball, facing to the inside of the court, because then he can see what is developing.

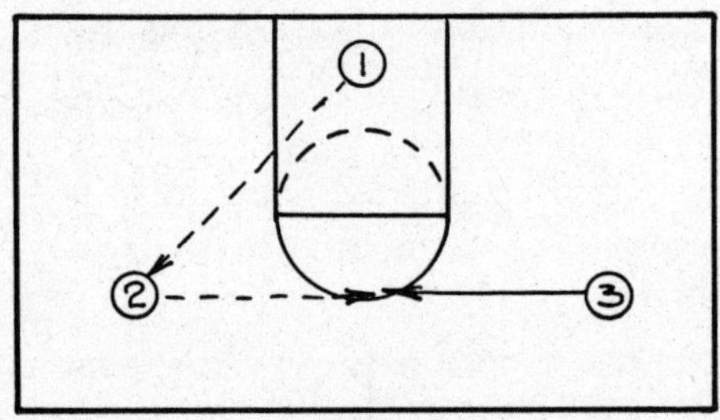

Diagram 30-6

Diagram 30-7

The drill shown in Diagram 30-7 is the same as that shown in Diagram 30-6, except that a defensive man is placed on 01, the rebounder. This means that the outlet pass is thrown with a defensive man on the rebounder.

As shown in Diagram 30-8, two players, No. 4 and No. 5, are placed on 01. The outlet men will be the same. After rebounding the ball, 01 will try to get it to the outlet man while he is surrounded by two men. So that everyone will get the idea of moving, as well as conditioning, this drill is run as follows: 01, the

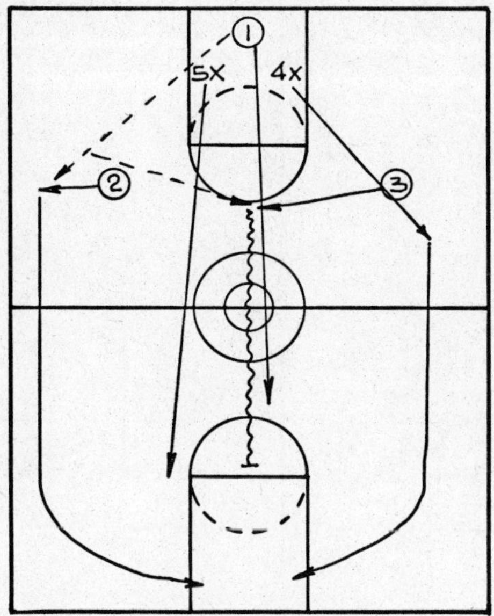

Diagram 30-8

rebounder, passes to 02. Then 02 passes to 03 who is moving into the center. No. 4, who was trying to stop the outlet pass, is the closest man to the unfilled lane and fills that lane. No. 5 and 01 will be the trailers on a team fast break. Once the outlet pass is made, No. 5 and No. 4 move over on offense to complete a five-man fast break. As a general rule, no defense is used on this drill other than for the original rebound.

Now the players are ready for our continuous three-on-two drill, which has been very successful. In this drill, all of our players are used.

The drill shown in Diagram 30-9 is started from a three-on-two situation with the other players, except for two defensive men, lined up outside the court. Their positions are somewhat similar to that of outlet men. 01, 02, and 03 start the drill. Notice that on each end of the court there are two defensive men (No. 4 and No. 5), and at the other end No. 6 and No. 7. The balance of the players are lined up outside of the court in the positions as designated in the diagram. In this drill, three situations will probably arise which involve something different. They are shown in Diagrams 30-9, 30-10, and 30-11.

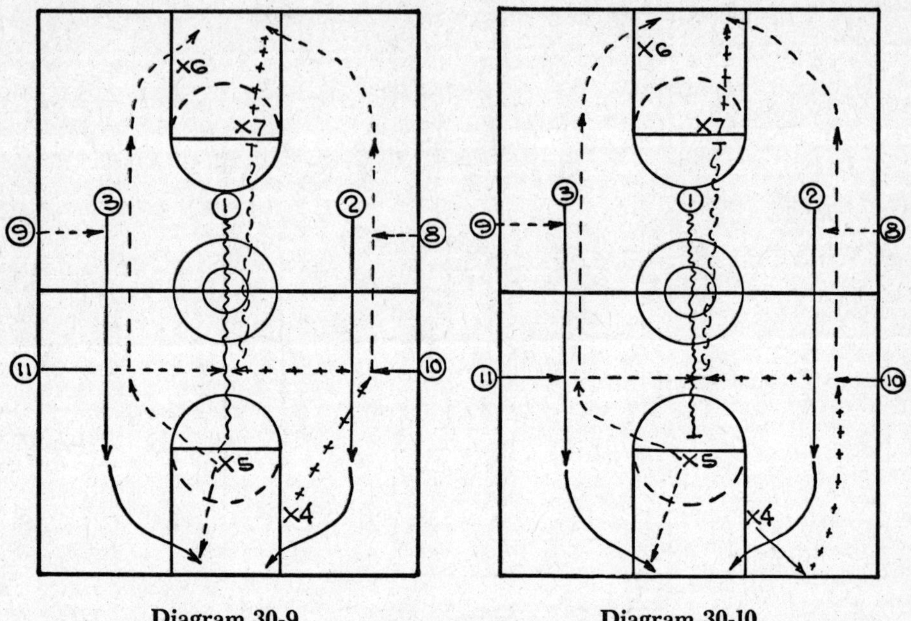

Diagram 30-9

Diagram 30-10

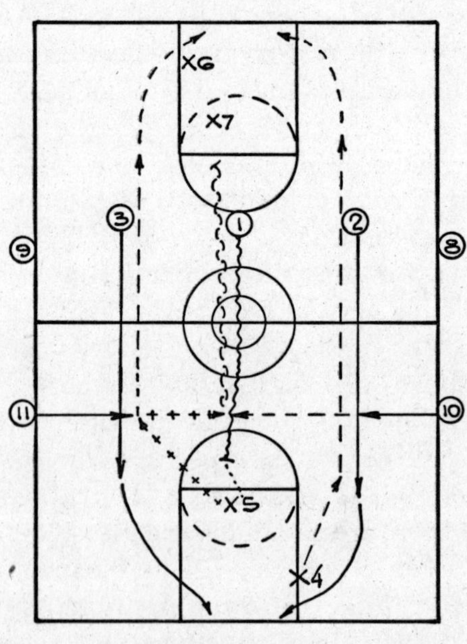

Diagram 30-11

In the drill shown in Diagram 30-9, the offensive unit consisting of 01, 02, and 03 moves down on the fast break using the principles learned in the other drills. 01 dribbles the ball down, flanked by 02 and 03. As they pass No. 10 and No. 11, who have been outside the court, these players step in and assume positions where we would like to have our outlet men. 01, 02, and 03 continue down the court and attempt to score. However, in this particular situation they missed the shot and the defensive man, No. 4, rebounded the missed shot and passed the ball by way of an outlet to No. 10. No. 10 moves the ball to No. 11 who has moved in to fill the center lane. The other defensive man, No. 5, who did not rebound, will then fill the unfilled third lane. Now the players are going the other way with our three-lane fast break. No. 11 is in the center flanked by No. 10 and No. 5. They will continue on down and attempt to score. As they pass No. 9 and No. 8, they will move in to an outlet position. From this basic formation they keep going. In order to maintain two defensive men, the man who rebounds will stay on defense along with the man who was in the center lane.

If the offensive group scores a basket, the second situation arises in this drill (Diagram 30-10). 01, 02, and 03 come down again and this time they score a basket. As they passed, No. 10 and No. 11 stepped in. After the basket is scored, one of the defensive men, in this case No. 4, takes the ball, steps behind the end line, and passes to No. 10. Then No. 10 passes to No. 11 filling the center lane. The other defensive man, who did not throw the ball, fills the third lane, in this case No. 5. Again, the players are coming down the floor with our three-lane break.

The third situation which may arise is the interception of a pass (Diagram 30-11). 01, 02, and 03 come down the floor again. However, this time 01's pass is intercepted by No. 5. He will move the ball quickly to one of the outlet men and again use the man who did not intercept the ball to fill the third lane. 01, 02, and 03 are again coming back down with a three-lane break; however, sometimes it might be feasible for the man who intercepts the ball to take the center lane, in which case the two other players would stay in their respective lanes. If the front man intercepts the ball, he will take the center lane, with No. 10 and No. 11 taking the outside lanes.

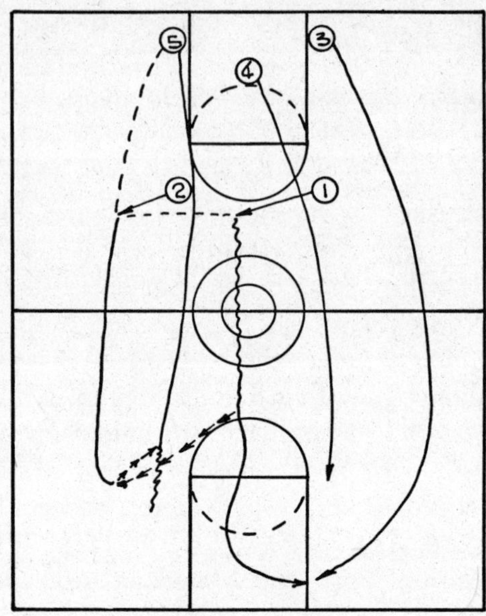

Diagram 30-12

The five-on-three drill (Diagram 30-12) is shown without a defense. 05 rebounds and passes out to 02. Then 02 passes to 01 filling the center lane. 01, 02, and 03 fill the lanes with 04 and 05 as trailers. 01 will drive until he is cut off and then he passes the ball to 02. 01 cuts through and moves to a rebounding position on the other side of the basket. If he is open going through, he should get the return pass. 01, in cutting to the basket, should pull the defensive man with him, at least a few steps. This means that 05, the trailer, who is coming down on this side, will cut through for a pass. If he cannot go all the way through, he will be able to stop for a jump shot. If neither one is open, the ball is held and then our continuity offense is started. 04 and 02 remain out for defensive balance.

Our fast-break drills are finished with a five-on-five situation.

We feel that once an offensive team manages to get down the floor, and has no advantage, it should have some kind of disciplined offense, because no team can depend entirely on only one type of offensive weapon.

Chapter 31

ORGANIZATION AND DRILLING FOR THE FAST BREAK

by Paul Lambert

To meet the needs of teaching the fast break, we found it necessary to incorporate our fast-break drills into one general category. To do so and not overlook any facet of the attack is very difficult. We found the best method to use is that of teaching in areas (Diagram 31-1). The following areas are used as a framework: 1. Possession 2. Outlet. 3. Organization. 4. Decision. 5. Scoring.

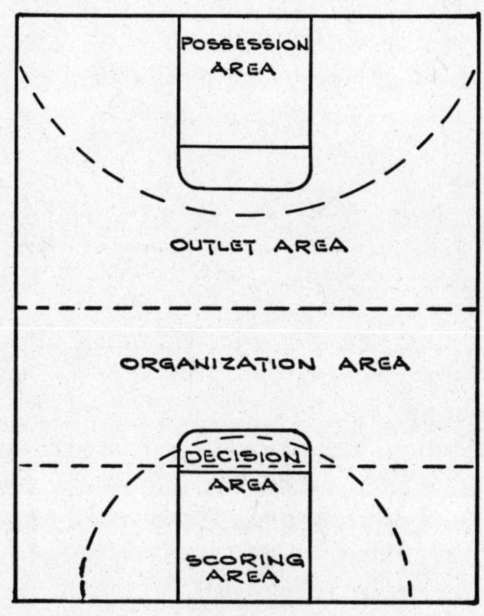

Diagram 31-1

Possession Area

Any team must have the ball before it can run. The steal, loose-ball situation, held ball, and the missed shot are possibilities leading to a fast-break situation. However, we shall only discuss the missed shot as a fast-break situation.

Many coaches feel their teams cannot run because the players lack size for rebounding. This is not true. The most important factor in many situations is position.

Getting to the spot where the ball is most likely to come is a simple way of explaining good rebounding. As a rule of thumb, the rebounder should be at least five to six feet from the edge of the backboard. This distance will allow for most long rebounds and at the same time give him room to compensate for pressure from the offensive rebounder.

Screening out, or failure to do so, has long been a very important topic. We feel that in order to block out the offensive rebounder, the defensive man must be aware of the position of the ball and the basket. The rules we use are as follows: 1. When the ball is shot, do not watch it. 2. Go to the rebounding rim, five or six feet from the backboard edge. An exception would be the long rebounder (guard should step into his man at the crossroads). Maintain ability to go with his pressure. 3. The defensive man should go after the ball, and have his hands and arms ready. Much of this may seem very elementary; however, we are sure that if a player will follow these simple steps and they become habit he will be a much better rebounder.

Outlet Area

Most of the time the next area will involve the second player. At this time the players become aware that this attack must have precision and timing.

The outlet man in the attack is the first man open nearest the ball, advancing the ball toward the offensive goal. Rules for the outlet man are: 1. Be a rebounder first, and then an outlet man. Protect for the long rebound. 2. Once the outlet man is sure the ball has been successfully rebounded, he should get to the sideline area quickly, and have his back to the sideline. 3. He should not run away from the outlet area.

Rules for the rebounder are as follows: 1. Once he has possession, he should determine whether or not he has pressure. 2. Try to hit the outlet man when he is open. 3. Do not force the pass.

Organization Area

This phase of the attack begins upon the successful completion of the outlet pass. Then the process of filling the lanes begins. We believe the best running team is the one that will organize the break in the back court. We do not mean to detract from the sleeper or the cherry-picker type of break, but do say the defense will cover this move with adjustments, perhaps using only one man.

Some terms in this phase are:

1. *Wing Man*. He is the player who received the outlet pass.

2. *Middle Man*. This position is filled by a player opposite the ball. Most of the time, use a guard as he might be a better ball-handler. One rule to follow is to force the middle man to come to the ball and not head up the court. He should be several steps behind the wing man.

3. *Weak-Side Wing Man*. This position will fill the third lane. He should be a step or two in front of the ball (middle man) when he reaches the scoring area. This is the most difficult position to fill. Many coaches feel that speed is all a player must have in order to fill this spot. However, a few rules might not improve his speed, but he will get to the third lane quicker. a) He should maintain good rebound position until he is sure the ball has been successfully rebounded. b) Release and get out from under the basket quickly. c) Once the mid-court is reached, he should get wide and stay wide until he reaches the free throw line extended, and then go for the basket.

Decision Area

This area is between mid-court and the top of the circle. However, it begins any time the man with the ball feels he has the advantage. We like the middle man to have the ball in the event the three lanes are full. The middle man with the ball and an advantage (three-on-one or three-on-two) can exert more offensive pressure than the wing man.

Rules for this area are as follows:

1. Any time the lay-up is available, give the ball to the man who is open. 2. Get the ball to the middle man and force the defense to commit. 3. When possible, pass the ball. Avoid the dribble.

Scoring Area

Not much explanation is needed for this area. On the lay-up, the short jumper, the trailer series, or when the defense has the advantage, set up the offense as the options are available.

For the rim drill (Diagram 31-2A, B, C) divide the square into the positions shown. Size and jumping ability are also factors to be considered. Begin with a one-on-one situation. As fundamentals improve, increase the number in the drill to two-on-two, three-on-three, etc. On a command given by the coach, a defensive player should make his move to the basket. The defense should cover the direction in which the player goes until the proper position is reached, five to six feet from the edge of the basket. Now the screening process should begin.

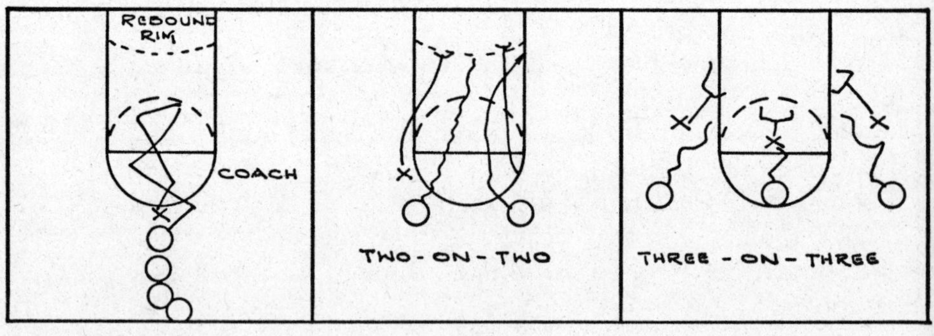

Diagram 31-2A **Diagram 31-2B** **Diagram 31-2C**

The figure-eight drill is shown in Diagram 31-3A, B, C. Divide the squad into groups of three's by position, size, etc. Place one group within the rebound rim.

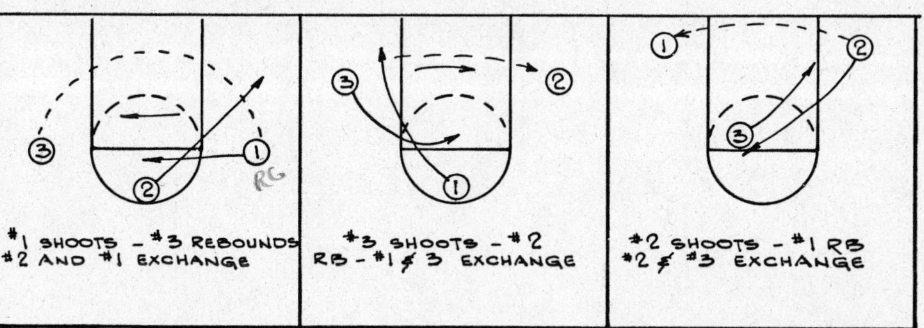

Diagram 31-3A Diagram 31-3B Diagram 31-3C

The drill begins with a wing man, 01, shooting the ball across the boards to the opposite wing man, 03. As 01 recovers, 02 moves to the rebound position held by 01. 03 returns the ball across the boards. As 03 recovers, 01 moves to 03's rebound position. The player going to the rebound position always goes inside.

Diagram 31-4 shows our off-the-boards drill, which can also be used as a warm-up drill. Organize the squad into a single file line. The first man begins the drill by laying the ball up against the boards. Then the next man rebounds the shot and places it up as high as possible. For variety, alternate the position of the sides. Watch for hands as the rebounder approaches the backboard area.

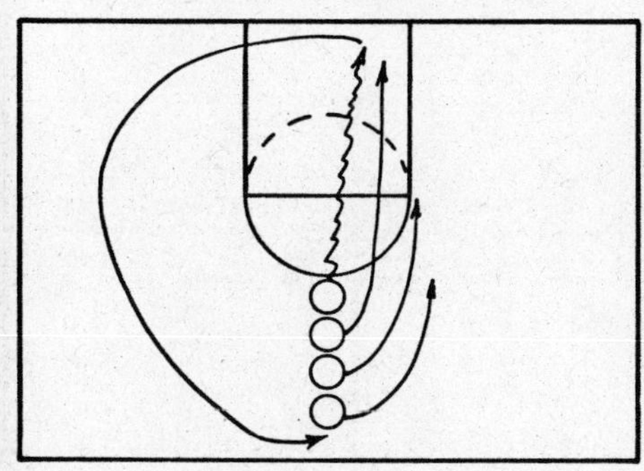

Diagram 31-4A

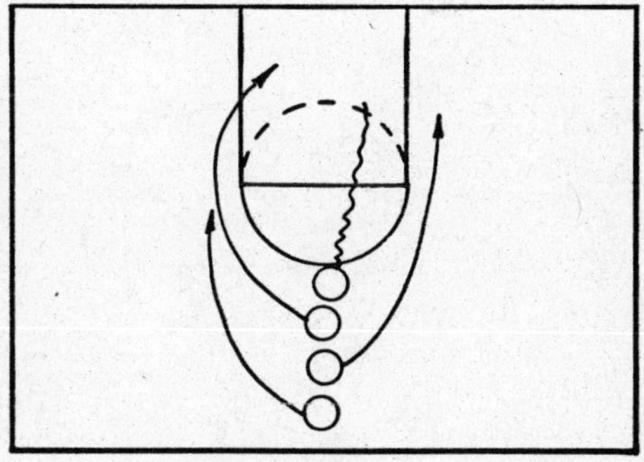

Diagram 31-4B

For the I drill (Diagram 31-5) organize the squad into groups of two's. Select a rebounder and a guard for size. Place the rebounder in the rim area and the guard in the outlet area. As the

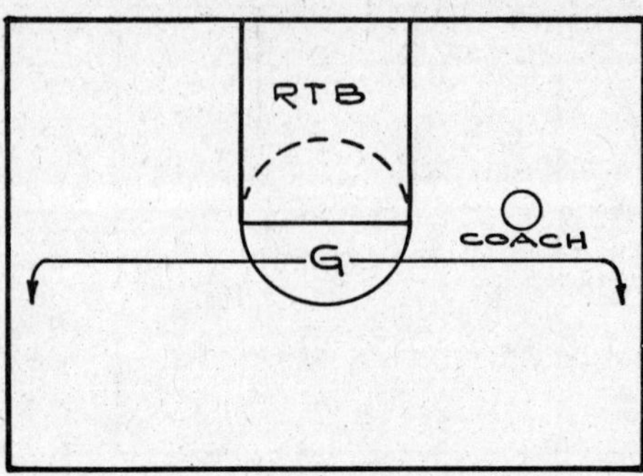

Diagram 31-5

coach shoots, the rebounder should go after the ball to either side. Then the rebounder should throw an outlet pass to the guard who goes to the ball side.

Divide the squad into groups as shown in Diagram 31-6 for the outlet pass drill. This drill begins with the rebounder throwing an outlet pass to the second man in line who goes to outlet the ball.

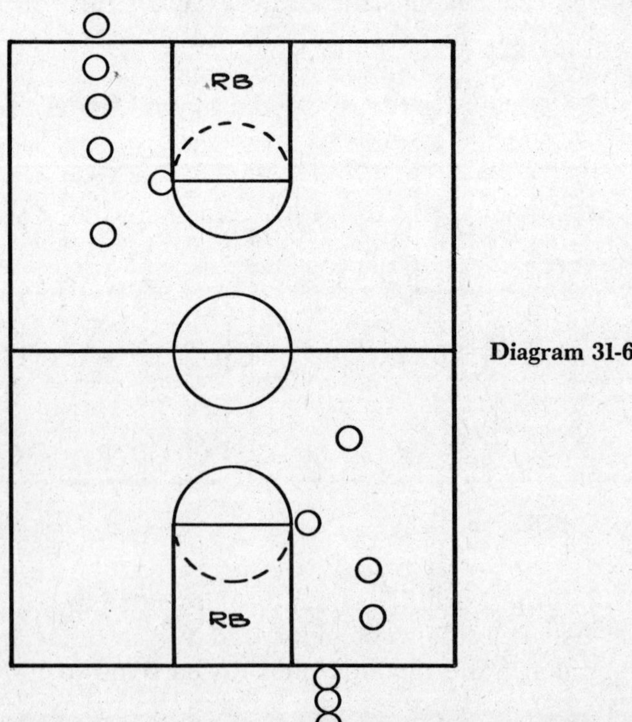

Diagram 31-6

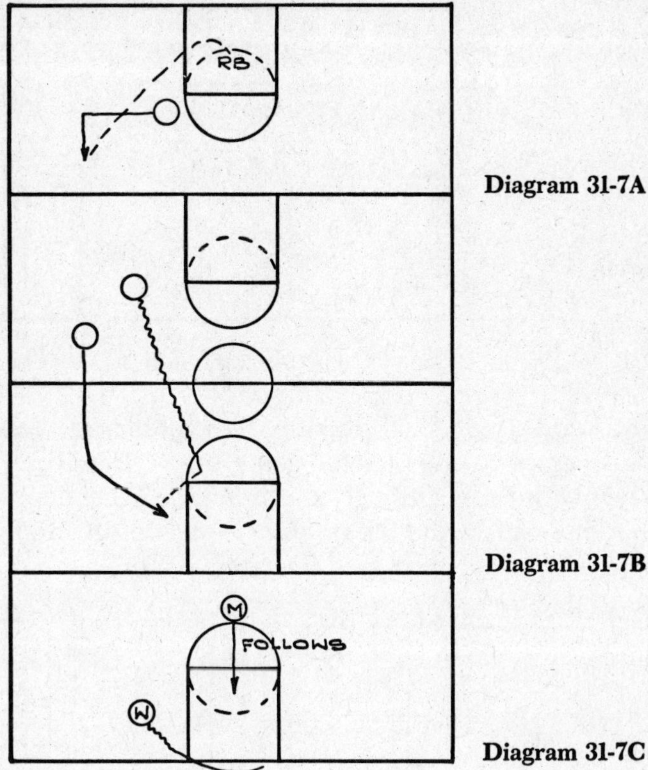

Diagram 31-7A

Diagram 31-7B

Diagram 31-7C

The first man starts his movement down the court until he reaches the proper wing position and then cuts for the basket. Meanwhile, the dribbler, keeping his head up and moving into the middle lane, passes the ball to the wing man, who lays the ball up. The middle man follows, rebounds, and passes to the next outlet man in line.

The drill shown in Diagram 31-7 teaches the proper path for the outside wing man, the position of the middle man, and also makes use of the proper outlet pass. Two balls should be used to start the drill at the end of the floor.

Organization Area Drills

Divide the squad as shown in Diagram 31-8 for the half-court wing man drill. This drill starts with an exchange of passes, and the middle man controls the ball from the top of the circle on. Then the wing man takes the proper path or angle and receives a pass from

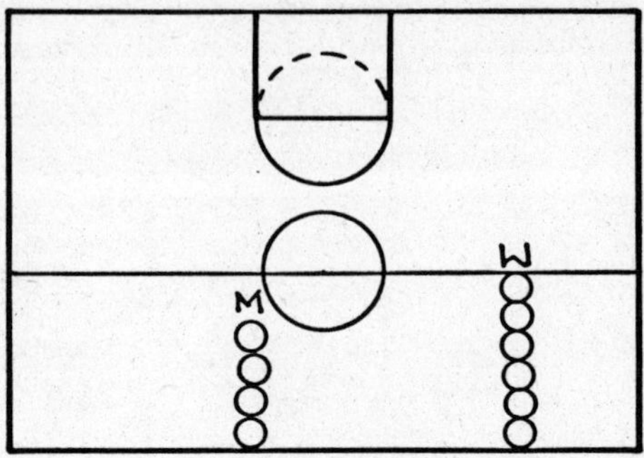

Diagram 31-8

the middle man for the lay-up. The middle man rebounds the shot, and passes to the shooter going out to the other side. Then the shooter returns through the middle of the floor and becomes a middle man, while the original feeder returns to the opposite side and becomes a wing man (Diagram 31-9).

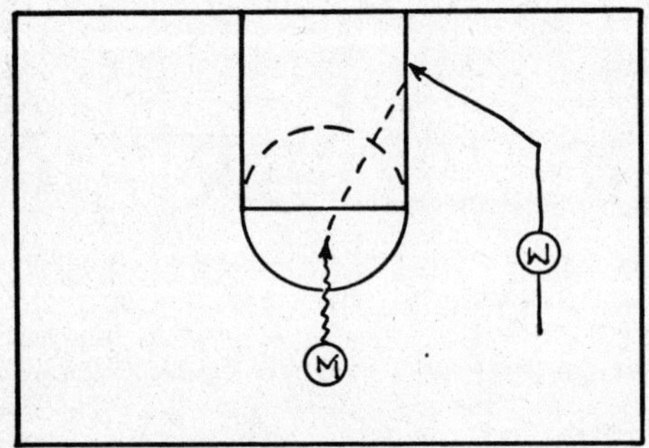

Diagram 31-9A

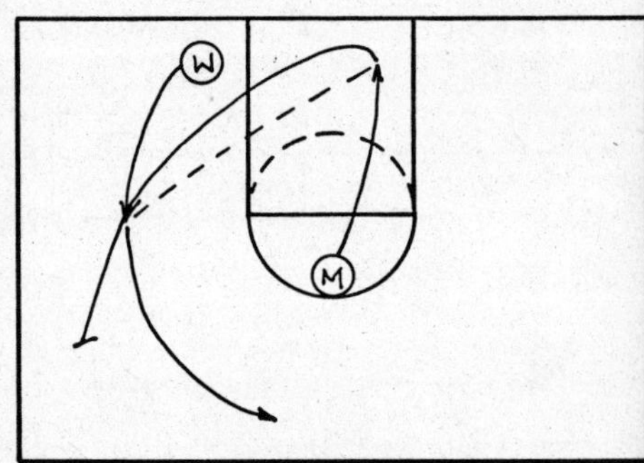

Diagram 31-9B

A variation of this drill is to have the middle man challenged by a defensive player and give him the option of shooting the jump shot from the free throw line or feeding the ball to the wing man.

Divide the squad as shown in Diagram 31-10 for the weak-side, third-lane drill. The rebounder assumes position. Then the outlet men assume their positions in case of a long rebound.

The rebounder outlets to the closest man and then hustles to fill the vacant lane (Diagram 31-11A). A variation of this drill is also shown in Diagram 31-11B. Let the rebounder fill the middle, and start the dribble break.

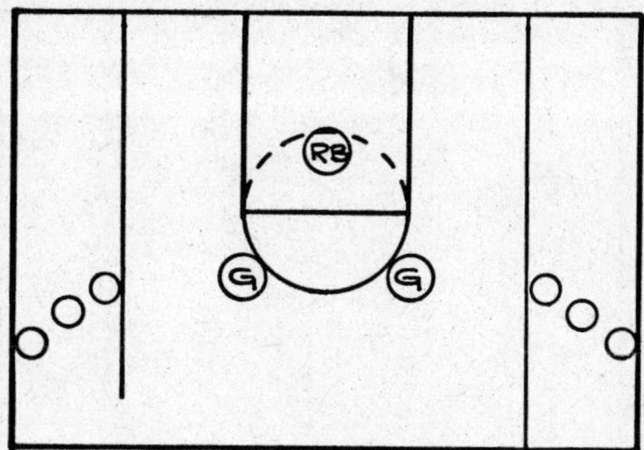

Diagram 31-10

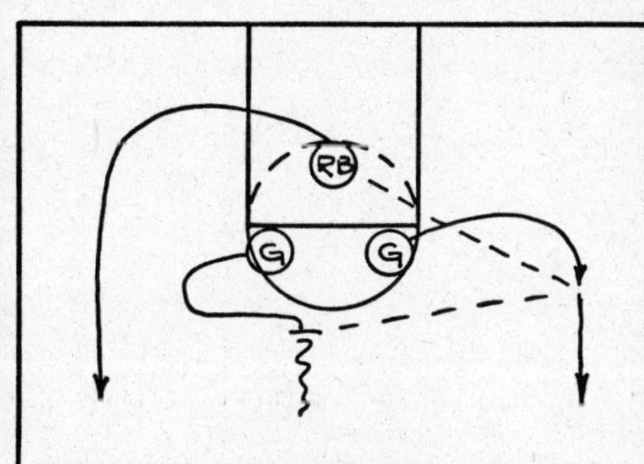

Diagram 31-11A

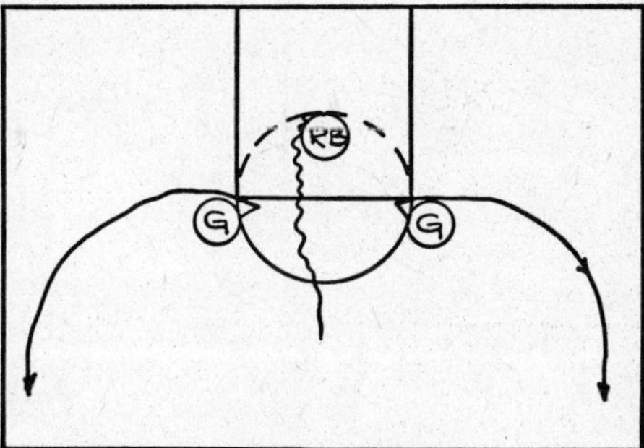

Diagram 31-11B

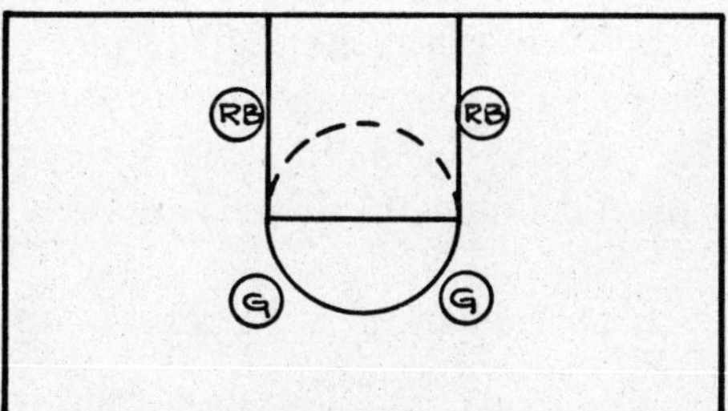

Diagram 31-12

Divide the squad as shown in Diagram 31-12 for the four-man fast-break drill. This drill is the same as the three-man drill, only the fourth man, usually the rebounder, becomes the trailer. It is an excellent drill to use in teaching the trailer position.

Diagram 31-13 shows the continuation of the four-man fast-break drill.

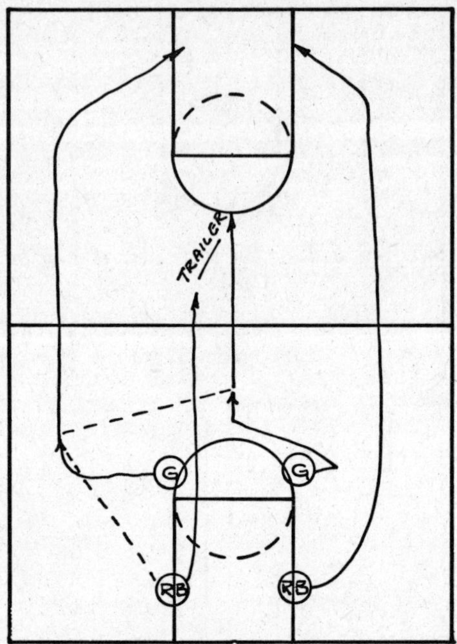

Diagram 31-13

Divide the squad into groups of three's (Diagram 31-14) for the three-lane fast-break drill. This division should be made according to size and speed. Try to place the players into groups they might be able to fill lanes with under game conditions. The drill starts with a rebounder passing the ball to one of the three players. The ball should be moved down the floor without a dribble until the decision area is reached.

The same three players should return up the floor in the manner shown in Diagram 31-15.

For the team break, divide the squad as shown in Diagram 31-16. In order to make the best possible use of the drill, start the break from various offensive positions. That is, where the defense will be on an overload, clear-out, and other offensive situations. The drill starts with the coach shooting the ball. Then the rebounders assume their positions, pass the ball to the nearest outlet, and fill the three lanes.

The last two men fill the trailer positions (Diagram 31-17).

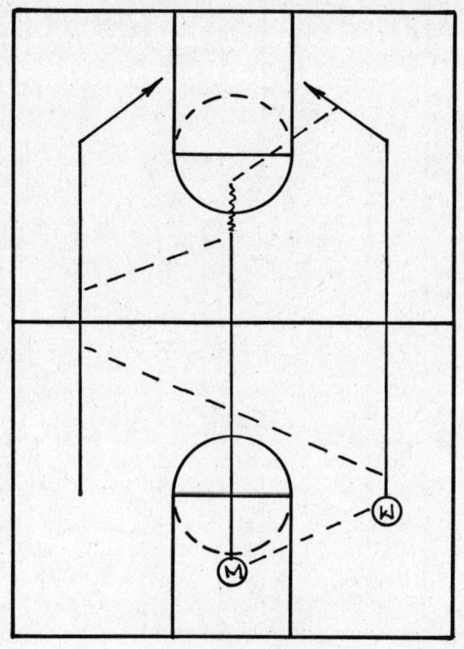

Diagram 31-14

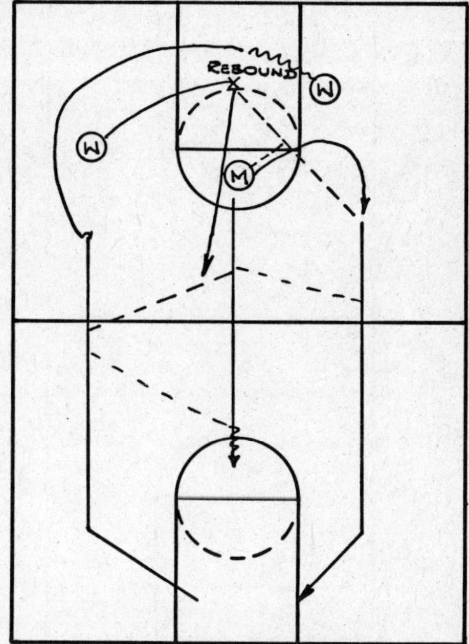

Diagram 31-15

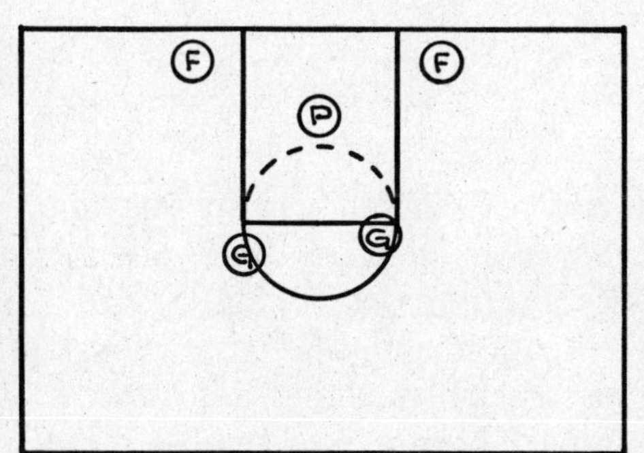

Diagram 31-16

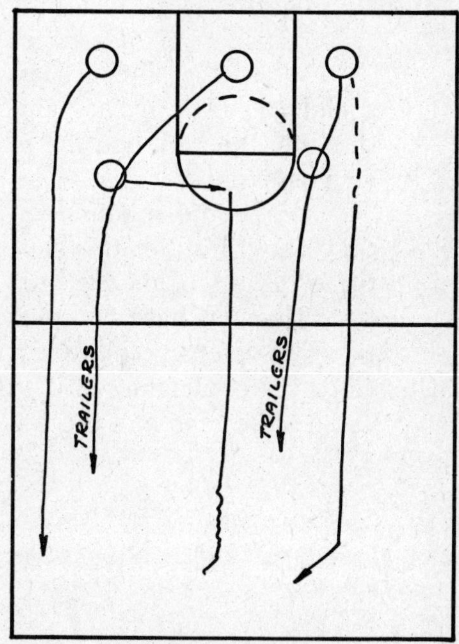

Diagram 31-17

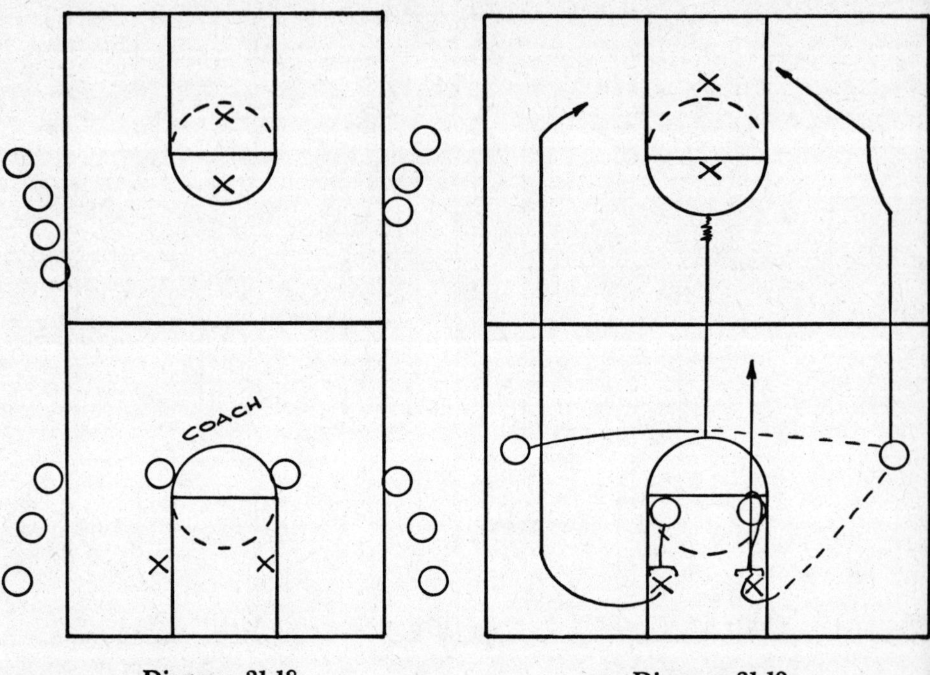

Diagram 31-18

Diagram 31-19

When the all-court fast break is to be practiced, divide the squad as shown in Diagram 31-18. This drill starts with the coach shooting the ball, and the offensive and defensive players fighting for possession.

When the rebounders, all defensive men, gain possession, they should outlet the ball as shown in Diagram 31-19, and the three players begin the break with a trailer close behind.

Thus, we have a four-on-two situation, and this continues until the two defensive players gain possession and the same process starts again (Diagram 31-20). An important rule to remember is that the middle man and the trailer should always stay on defense.

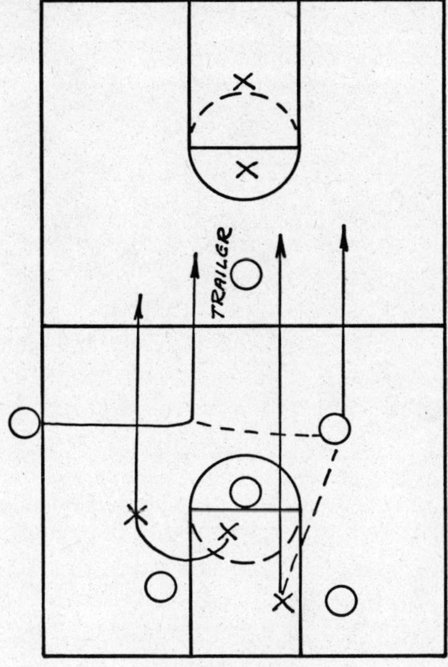

Diagram 31-20

Chapter 32

THE SIDELINE FAST BREAK

by Jeff McCall/John Corona

The best way to attack any defense is to beat it down the floor before the opponent has a chance to set it up. This can be accomplished with the sideline fast break.

The sideline break can be run successfully from a man-for-man alignment, but since each player has a specific responsibility to perform, it is easier to have them nearer their break positions in a zone defense situation.

There are specific strengths and characteristics required at every position. 01 should be an aggressive ball handler and have good vision. He should be a good driver and possess the ability to judge when and when not to attack. He is probably the most important player on the floor. 02 should be a good corner shooter and an adequate passer. 03 must be able to shoot the left-handed lay-up and have good post power moves. 04 should be a good shooter from the short 17-foot area, should have good judgment, and possess at least fair ball-handling skills. 05 must possess good judgment, be a good baseball passer, react quickly to the made basket and be a good rebounder.

The break is run on made shots from the floor and can also be adapted to be run from made free throws. This, combined with the fast break off a missed shot, gives the team a chance to push the ball up the floor on every opportunity other than dead ball situations. Here we will cover the sideline break off a made shot from the floor.

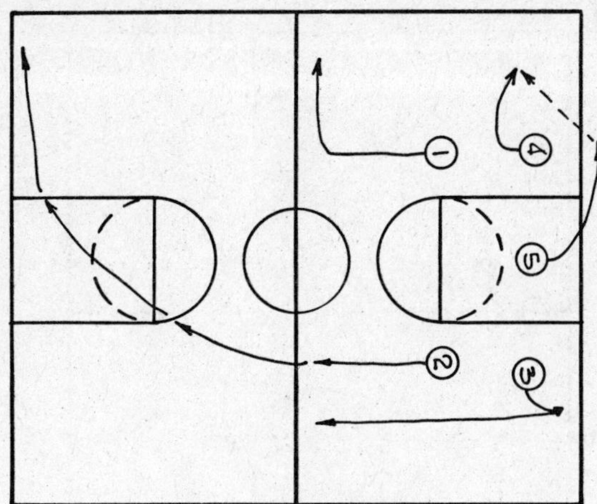

Diagram 32-1

When the opposition scores, each player has the following tasks to carry out (Diagram 32-1): 05 grabs the ball out of the net and throws the bomb to 02 breaking down the floor, hits 01 near half-court, passes to 04 near the sideline about twelve feet off the baseline, or to 03 as a safety valve. In this instance, the pass is to 04. 02 sprints down the floor, looks for the long pass and goes into the strong-side corner. 03 goes to the short weak-side area for the safety valve pass. 04 breaks to the short area to receive the pass from 03. 01 breaks to near half-court, looking for the pass from 05 to 04.

Once the ball goes through the net, all players must get to their spots on the floor as quickly as possible. The faster the ball comes in and the sooner the players are positioned where they are supposed to be, the more effective the break becomes. Once the ball comes in, the following should take place (Diagram 32-2): Upon completion of the inbounds pass, 05 steps in and trails the play. 02 is moving into the corner and if overplayed, can back-cut to the basket. After the ball comes in on the opposite side, 03 fills the left lane and posts up low on the strong side, opposite 02. The move must be timed across the lane so that 03 cuts off the rear of 01. 04 passes the ball to 01 and then comes down the floor to the short

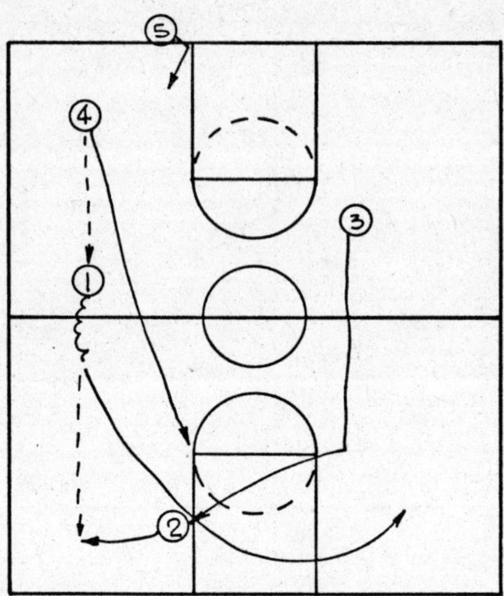

Diagram 32-2

17-foot area around the corner of the key. If the ball comes in straight from 05 to 01, 04 goes to the corner of the key. Upon reception of the ball from 05 or 04, 01 takes one or two dribbles up the sideline and quickly passes the ball to 02 in the corner. 01 then cuts through the key looking for a possible return pass.

With the ball in the corner, 02 has five options (Diagram 32-3); shoot or drive; feed 01 breaking through the key; feed 03 posting up; feed 04 for the jumper from the short 17-foot area; dribble out to run an early offensive pattern or set up the half-court attack.

The sideline break can be run to either side with equal

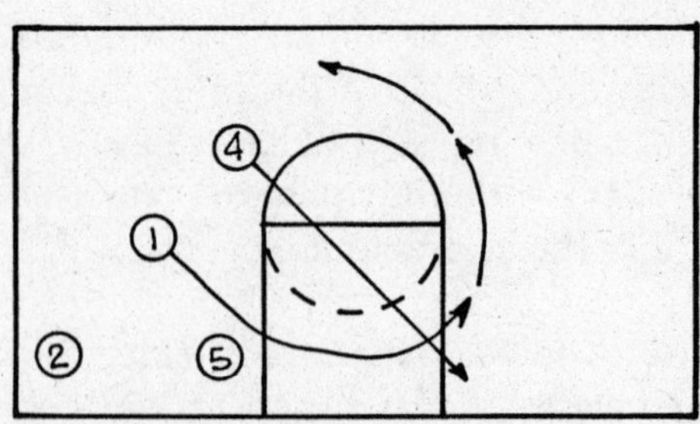

Diagram 32-3

effectiveness. However, if the team is only able to run the offense as diagrammed and is unable to react to situations where the defense will be waiting for them, then the break can easily be slowed down, if not stopped by an alert team. Therefore, it is necessary to have some counters to what the defense attempts to do.

The first area in which the defense may attempt to stop the ball is the short area where 04 is to receive the ball. If this occurs (Diagram 32-4), 05, finding he cannot get the ball to 01, 02, or 04, inbounds the ball to 03 and steps onto the floor for a possible return pass. 01, having gone to the half-court area, hooks back toward 03 for the pass. He then dribbles down the weak side, passes to 02 in the corner and cuts through. 02 breaks down the floor and when he sees that the ball is not inbounded on the strong side, goes to the weak-side corner. Upon reception of the ball, 02 has the same options discussed previously. Seeing the ball come in on the weak side, 04 must release immediately and post up low across from 02. 03 receives the pass from 05 and passes to 01 coming back for the ball. He then fills the lane to the short 17-foot area.

The second point at which the defense will attempt to stop the break is on the pass from 04 to 01. They may attempt a double team

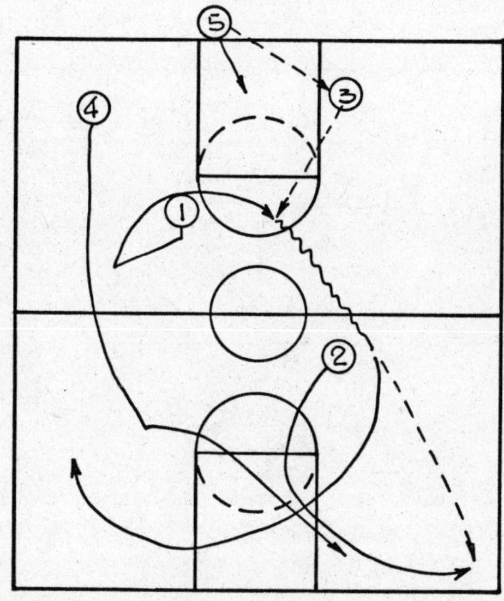

Diagram 32-4

or simply force the dribble. Dribbling is to be avoided if at all possible because the break will fall apart and the team will have been no better off than if they had not run the break at all. If the ball is cut off at the 04 spot (Diagram 32-5), 05 brings the ball in to 04 and steps in. 04, seeing he cannot pass to 01, kicks the ball back to 05. He either passes to 01 bellying back to the ball or to 03 on the weak-side wing. 05 serves as the trailer. As the ball comes in to 04, 03 releases down the floor, keeping good vision to see if the ball goes back to 05. If so, 03 puts his foot down and comes back for the pass, then passes to 01 coming back and fills the lane. 01 goes to half-court and as the ball swings back to 05, puts his foot down and swings back to the ball. He will receive the pass from either 05 or 03. Upon reception of the ball, 01 takes it down the middle. 04 receives the pass from 05, sees that the pass to 01 is cut off, throws back to 05 and fills the lane. 02 goes into the corner on the strong side and back-cuts to the basket.

The third area vulnerable to stopping the sideline break is the area in which 01 receives the ball. The double team is almost a certainty when the opposition tries to stop the ball at this point because the sideline is their ally. If 01 cannot advance the ball, the players react as shown in Diagram 32-6: 05 inbounds the ball to 04

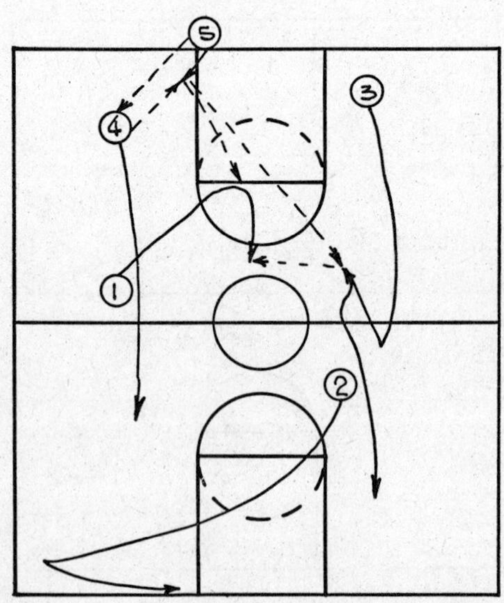

Diagram 32-5

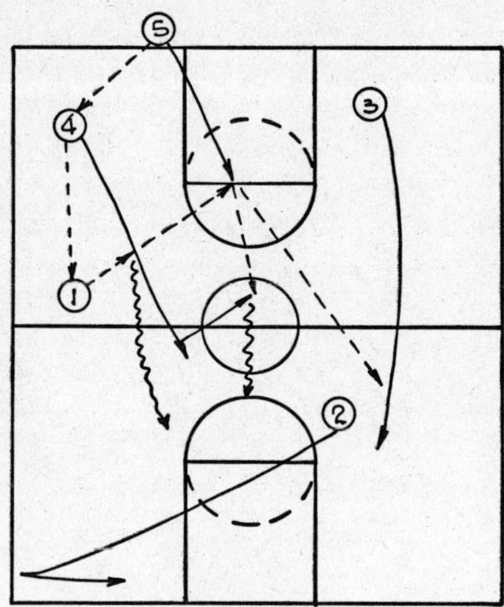

Diagram 32-6

and steps in, becoming the safety. If the ball is kicked back, he passes to 04 posting up at half-court or passes upcourt to 03. When the ball comes into 04, 03 releases and fills the lane. Finding he cannot dribble, 01 remains calm and executes a strong front-pivot out of trouble. He passes to 04 going by or to 05 at the free throw line area. 04 passes the ball to 01. When he sees 01 is stopped, he cuts straight to the basket. If 04 does not get the ball on the cut, he puts his foot down and posts up in the middle of the floor for the pass from 05. 04 then takes the middle if he gets the ball from 01, 05 or 03. 02 goes into the corner and back-cuts to the basket.

The counters rely on reaction from the players on the floor. They must be able to see what is developing as the ball moves up the floor in order to react to what the defense is attempting to do. The counters are designed to handle full- and half-court press situations that might arise. Thus, the sideline break can be used as a press offense as well.

part FIVE

Special Situations

Chapter 33

THE "I" ALIGNMENT FOR CENTER JUMPS

by John Stiver

When your team has a tall center who is reasonably sure of controlling the center jumps, the I alignment can put the opposition at a disadvantage.

The I alignment is designed to: 1) provide an area in which to tip the ball regardless of the opponent's alignments; 2) create a 2-on-1 or 3-on-2 situation as quickly as possible after the tip is made.

The basic alignment for the center jump is shown in Diagram 33-1. The center, 05, is placed in the center jump circle. The best driving wing is placed directly in front of 05 and the other wing, 03,

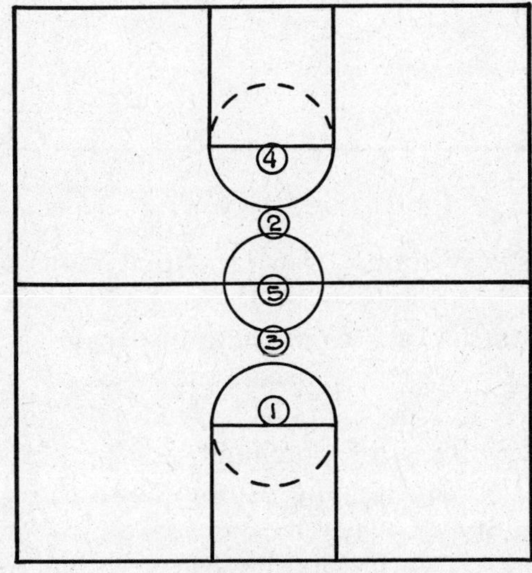

Diagram 33-1

lines up directly behind 05. The strong forward, 04, is placed in the middle of the free throw line facing 05 and the point guard is placed in the middle of the opposition's free throw line.

Where the ball is tipped depends upon how the opposition lines up against the I alignment. If the opposition matches the alignment (Diagram 33-2), then 05 tips the ball high and away from the defender guarding 02. 02 should screen his opponent off, receive the ball and drive to the basket. 04, upon seeing 02 receive the ball, moves opposite from 02 to the side of the free throw lane and breaks to the basket. This creates a 2-on-1 situation that is very difficult to stop. 02 or 04 could score an easy lay-up.

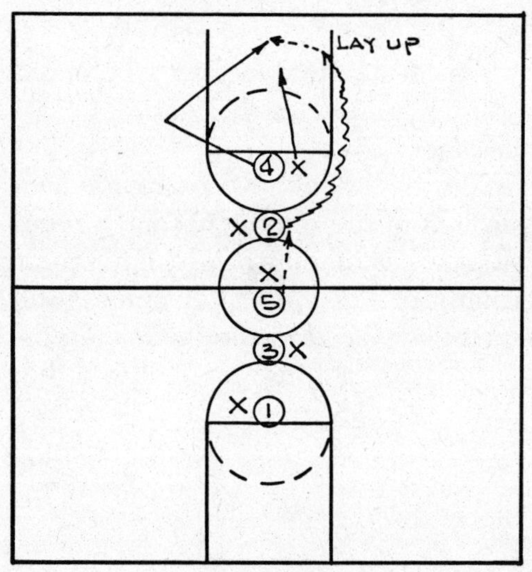

Diagram 33-2

This tip is very simple, yet puts tremendous pressure on the defense. The opposition is forced to change its players' positions or give up two points. Most teams put a player on each side of 02 to take the direct tip away and place a player beside 03, as shown in Diagram 33-3. When this happens, try to tip the ball to 03 breaking to the side away from his opponent (Diagram 33-4). 03 should receive the ball on the run and dribble down the sideline looking for an opportunity to drive to the basket. As in the previous situation, 04 breaks to the side opposite the ball and then to the basket. 02 sprints to the free throw line and looks for a return pass. If executed quickly enough, a 3-on-1 or a 3-on-2 situation results.

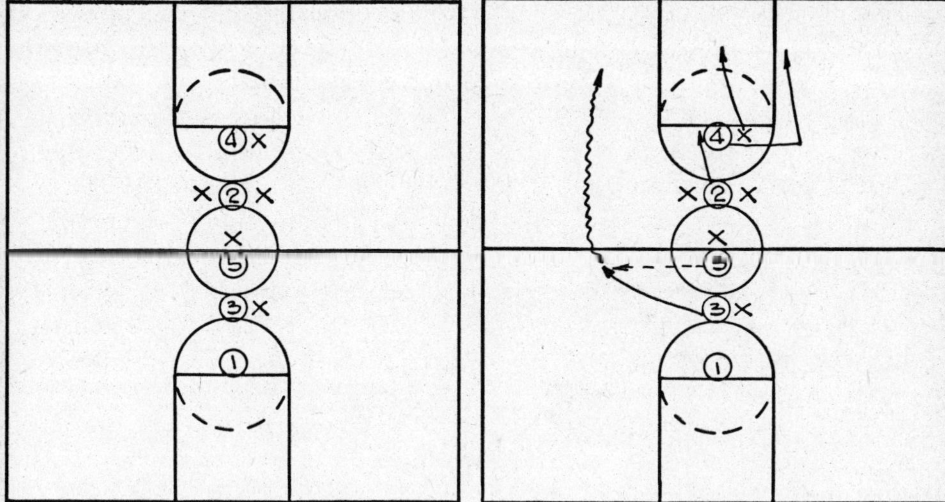

Diagram 33-3

Diagram 33-4

If opposing teams decide to take away our opportunity of creating a fast-break situation, we then become content with gaining possession of the ball. 05 tips the ball back to 01 in any one of three areas as shown in Diagram 33-5.

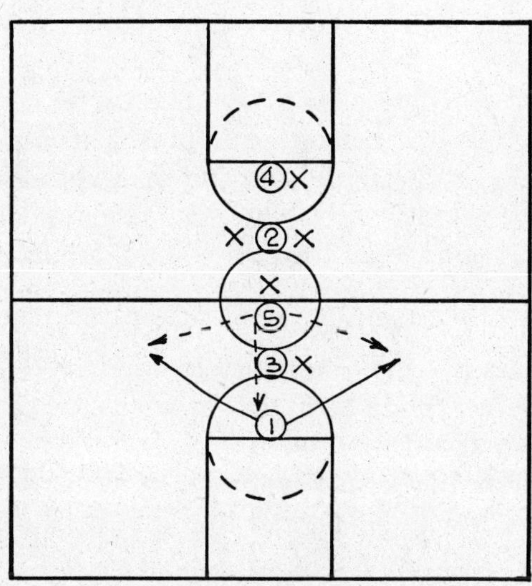

Diagram 33-5

Chapter 34

SCORING WITH OUT-OF-BOUNDS PLAYS

by Charles Batway

In checking back over the films of previous games, a coach will notice that usually between six and ten times per game his team was awarded the ball under its own goal. Why not try to cash in on these possible 12 to 20 points per game? Set up a play that will give the team one of the percentage shots on each play, and also try to have two plays for each game, changing at half-time. After every game, the plays used and the effectiveness of each one are recorded on the game summary. When that team appears again on our schedule, we know which plays were used and the ones that were effective.

No matter what play is used, try to have a player who is a fairly good rebounder take the ball out of bounds. This player should also be a cool-headed, accurate passer. The man out of bounds should make the count silently and when he reaches the four-second count, hit the release man if the cutters have not freed themselves. Most players start to panic when the count is between two and three seconds, and hurry the pass. Also plan to have the player receiving the pass in shoot immediately, because the passer and at least one of the cutters will be in the three-second zone for rebound position, and if a shot is not taken a violation may result.

Some of these plays work well against either a zone or a man-for-man defense, but they all work to the best advantage against a man-for-man. Each play is given a name that will be easily remembered. Try to have the same man on defense on each play and use the same cutters and the same player out of bounds. This procedure cuts down confusion in the players' minds and speeds setting up for the play. In starting a play, either have a verbal starting signal, slap the ball, or raise the ball in the air.

Eight plays are shown in the accompanying diagrams. While there are many more worthy of consideration, let us consider these eight, which will be effective when executed properly.

The box, Diagram 34-1, works well against a man-for-man defense. 02 is the man to try to hit, but 01 or 04 should not be overlooked after the cuts. 03 is the safety man and 05 should step in to rebound after the pass in.

The play shown in Diagram 34-2 works well against a zone defense. 01 cuts first and then 02. After the cuts, 03 goes down the center and if he is not open, finishes up in a good rebound position. 05 steps in bounds after the pass in. 04 stays out for the defense and safety.

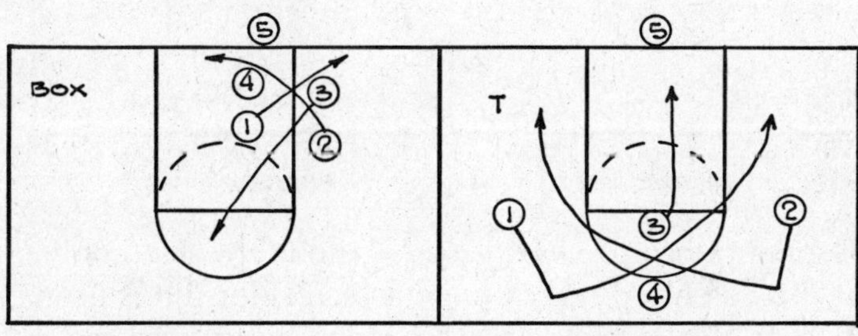

Diagram 34-1 **Diagram 34-2**

In Diagram 34-3, 05 calls the name of 01, 02 or 04. If it is 02, this player breaks for the basket and a drop pass or a lead pass should reach him. If 05 calls 04, then 02 acts as the safety; otherwise 04 is always the safety.

As shown in Diagram 34-4, 01 breaks down the side of the lane

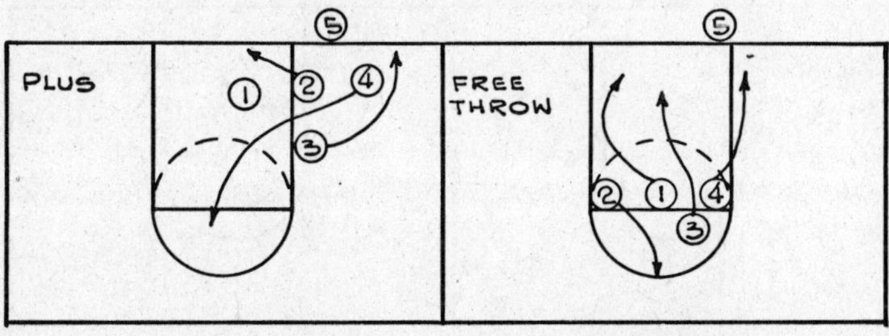

Diagram 34-3 **Diagram 34-4**

and he may open or draw the defense out of the center to clear for 03's cut. 02 is the safety release man.

The play shown in Diagram 34-5 can be used any place on the court and is a good one if the team needs a basket in the closing seconds of a game. The players break in the order of their numbers; 01 goes first, then 02, etc. 05 steps in to rebound after the pass in.

01 can line up on either side of the line (Diagram 34-6). His job is to run his man into the screen formed by 02, 03, and 04. Then 03 breaks to the side opposite the one to which 01 goes. 02 has the defense and safety spot, and 04 and 05 do most of the rebounding.

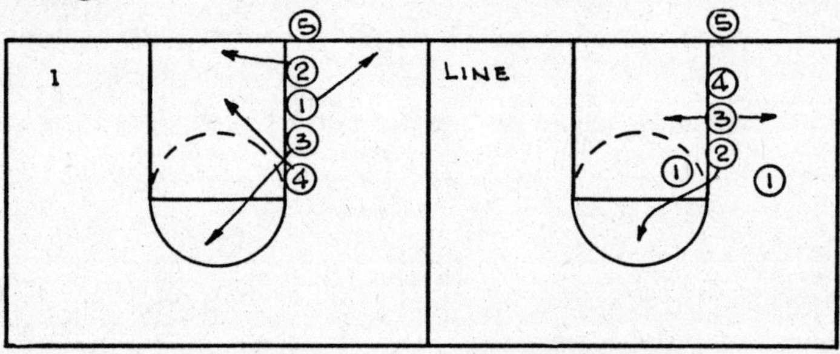

Diagram 34-5 **Diagram 34-6**

The play shown in Diagram 34-7 should be used only on one side, but the defense does not know which side. If it is used on 01's side, 02 takes the defense spot. 05 steps in for rebound position after the pass in.

Diagram 34-8 shows a play that is effective when there are two fast-cutting guards. 01 sets a pick for 03 and rolls for the basket after 04 has broken. Then 02 sets a pick for 04 and acts as the safety release man. 05 passes in and then takes the most advantageous rebound spot.

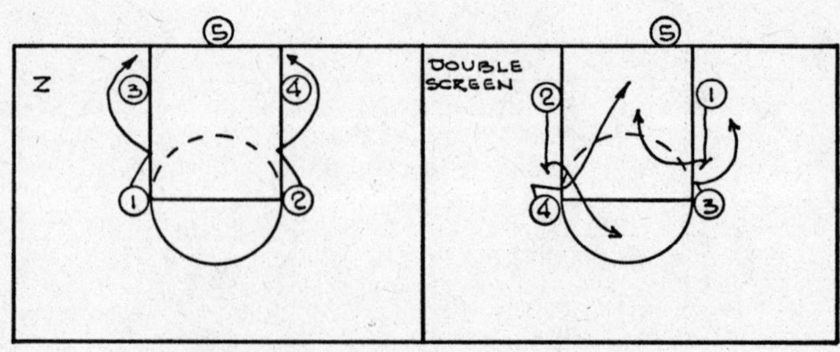

Diagram 34-7 **Diagram 34-8**

Chapter 35

THE SIDE OUT-OF-BOUNDS PLAY

by Al Burkhalter

The basic alignment for the side out-of-bounds play is shown in Diagram 1. 01 and 04 are the forwards, with 01 being the best offensive forward. 02 and 03 are the guards; 02 is the best offensive guard. 05 is the center.

In Diagram 35-1, 01 is at the designated throw-in spot. If this spot is between the free throw line extended and the half-court line, the team will run this play. The guards, 02 and 03, are to be approximately one yard closer to the half-court line than 01; 03 is lined up on the lane line extended and 02 splits the distance between 03 and the sideline. The center positions himself on the middle of the free throw line. 04 lines up in a straight line with 01 and the basket, equidistant to the end line and 01.

The out-of-bounds play always begins when the official hands the ball to the player designated to throw it in. As the team only runs one out-of-bounds play in this situation, there is no predesignated signal such as a ball slap or number call. This type of signal can waste valuable time.

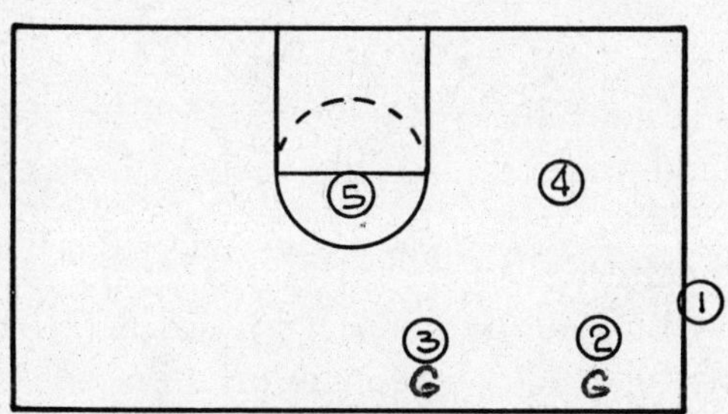

Diagram 35-1

02 and 04 move simultaneously with 01's receiving the ball from the official; 02 moves to set a screen on 03's defensive opponent and 04 breaks toward the basketball (Diagram 35-2). The first option for the inbounds pass is for 01 to pass to 04 and then run the give-and-go, using 04 as a screen (Diagram 35-3). When the center sees 04's handoff to 01, he should clear to the opposite box for a possible pass from 01 or to be in a position to rebound, as shown in Diagram 35-3. If 04's defensive opponent switches to take 01 driving to the basket, 04 should execute the screen and move to receive a return pass from 01. 04 should then drive to the basket (Diagram 35-4). The center would still clear to the box and be in position for a pass, or to rebound.

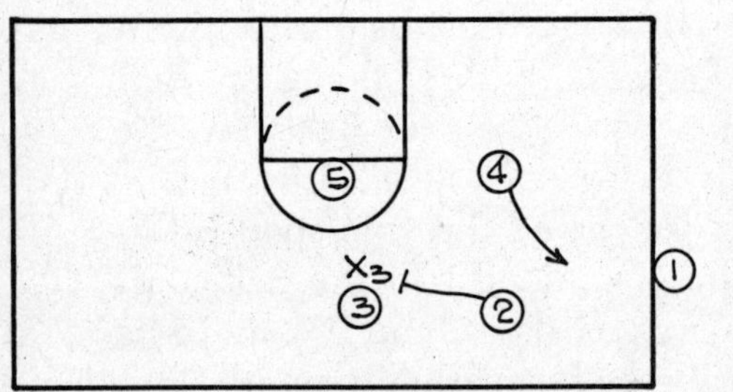

Diagram 35-2

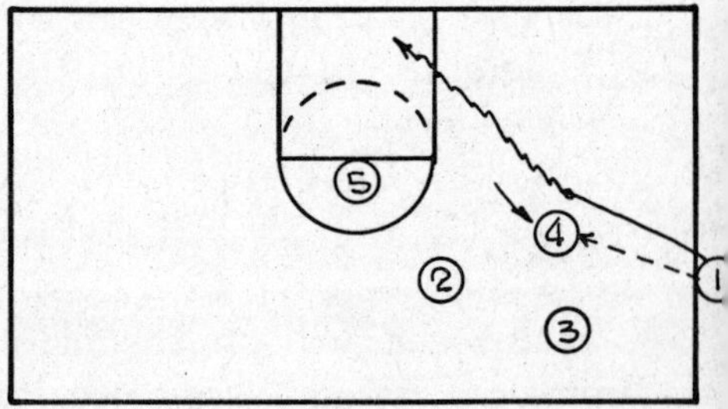

Diagram 35-3

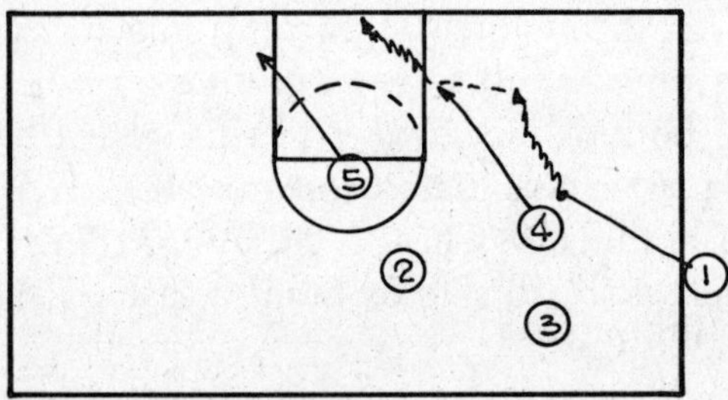

Diagram 35-4

If 04 is unable to make the handoff to 01 and 01 breaks to the basket, he should pivot and face the basket. The center, seeing that no handoff is made, continues out to screen 02's defender. The defense will dictate which defensive player 05 will screen. Some defenses will switch when 02 screens X3; this will allow X2 to take 03 (Diagram 35-5) and 05 would then screen X3. When no switch

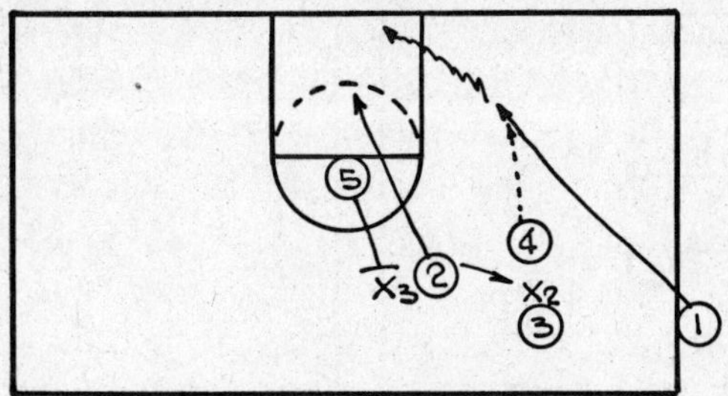

Diagram 35-5

takes place and X3 gets over the screen, 05 will screen X2 (Diagram 35-6).

After pivoting, 04 should look to pass the ball to 01, who is breaking toward the basket. This would be a deeper pass than the handoff, with 01 taking one or two dribbles to score (Diagram 35-5). If 01 is not open for the return deep pass, then 04 should look for 02 breaking down the lane area toward the bottom half of the free throw circle (Diagram 35-6).

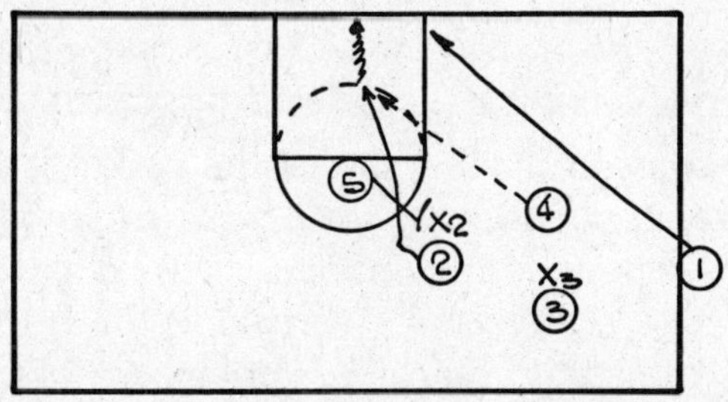

Diagram 35-6

When the inbounds pass is made to 04, if neither 01 nor 02 receives a pass from 04 he clears the lane area to the opposite side (Diagram 35-7). Very often this movement will clear the side of the floor on which 04 is standing. If 04 is to drive in this situation, he must do so before 01 and 02 clear the lane on the opposite side (Diagram 35-8). The center's key to break toward the basket and look for a pass from 04 is after both 01 and 02 have cleared the lane are (Diagram 35-9).

Thus, 04's options after receiving the inbounds pass are as follows: 1) hand off to 01 breaking to the basket; 2) pivot and pass to

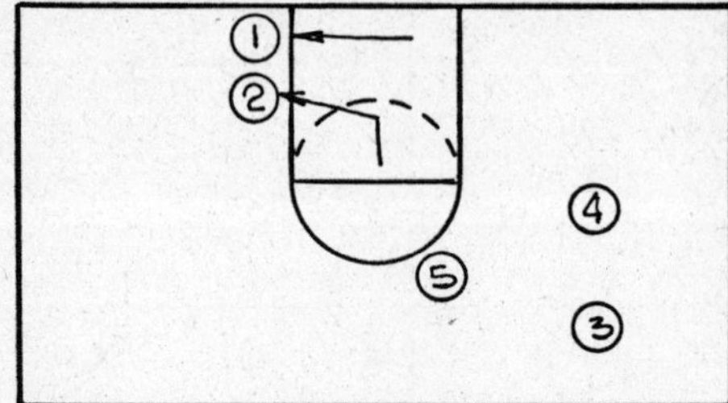

Diagram 35-7

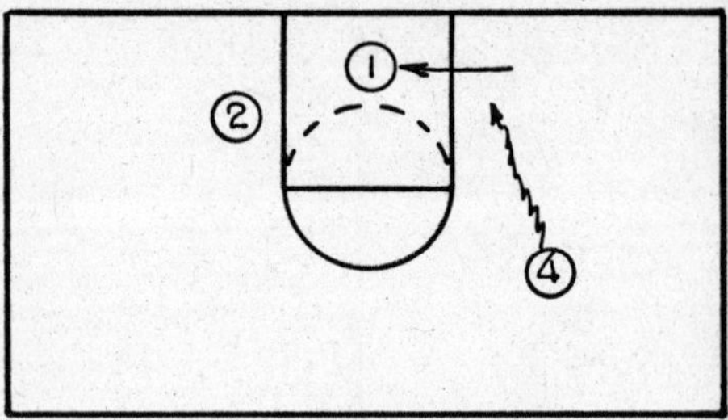

Diagram 35-8

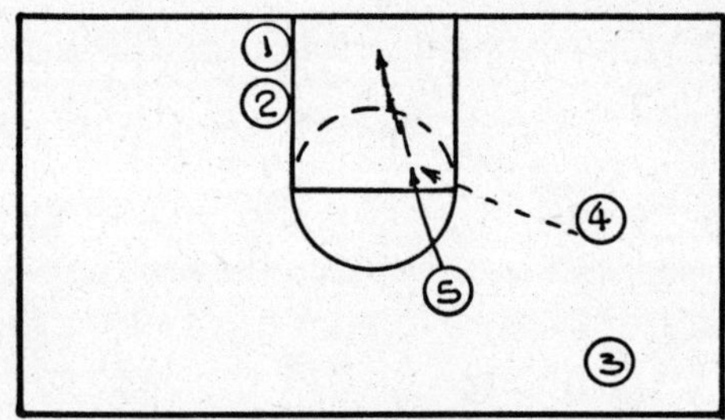

Diagram 35-9

01 deep; 3) pass to 02 near the bottom half of the free throw circle; 4) drive; and 5) pass to the center breaking to the basket. When none of the options results in a shot at the basket, the team adjusts to its half-court set offense.

The second option for the inbounds pass is for 01 to pass to 03, who has used 02's screen and is breaking toward 01. When the inbounds pass is made to him, 03's options are as follows:

1. He may return the ball to 01 who, having used 04's screen, is breaking toward the basket (Diagram 35-10). It is important that

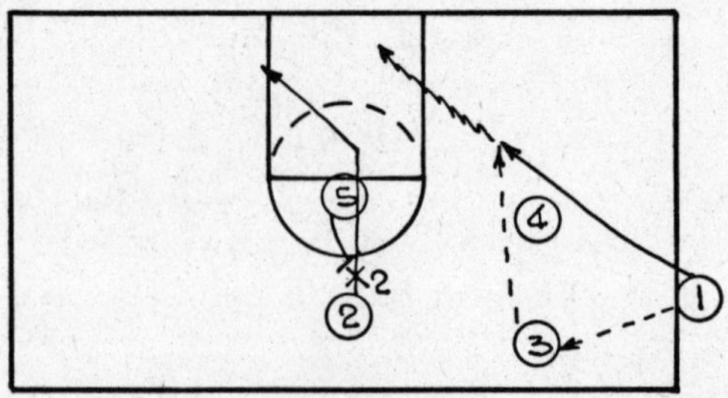

Diagram 35-10

this pass be made before 01 gets to the three-second lane area as this will help minimize the chances of an interception.

2. 03 may pass to 02, who has used 05's screen and is breaking toward the bottom half of the free throw circle (Diagram 35-11). After 02 makes his cut off 05's screen, he immediately looks for the ball. If 04 receives the inbounds pass and does not pass to 02, then 02 clears to the far box, as shown in Diagram 7. If 03 receives the inbounds pass and does not pass to 02, then 02 goes to the box on the ball side (Diagram 35-12). This helps open up the middle so the team can attempt to post 01 inside.

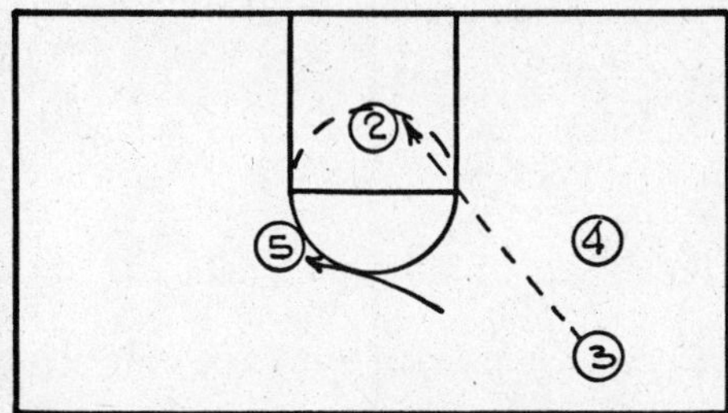

Diagram 35-11

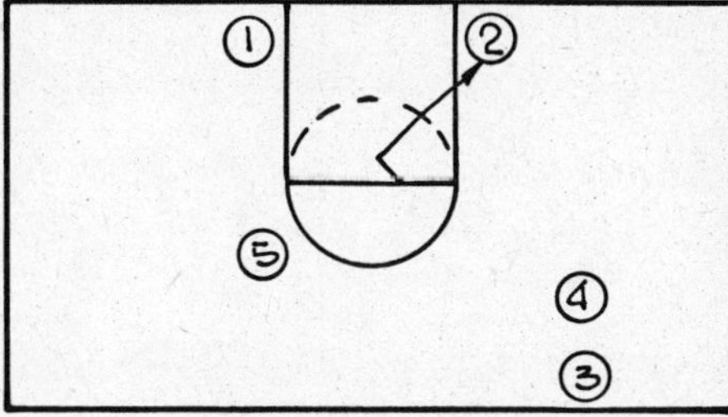

Diagram 35-12

3. When he does not pass to 01 or 02, 03 should look to move the ball to 05 who, after setting a screen on 02's defensive opponent, moves to a spot on the lane line extended and top of the free throw circle (Diagram 35-13). The timing should be such that when 05 receives the ball from 03, 01 is in the lane area ready to receive the ball from 05 (Diagram 35-13). When 01 makes his inbounds pass to 03, 01 should cut his speed upon reaching the lane

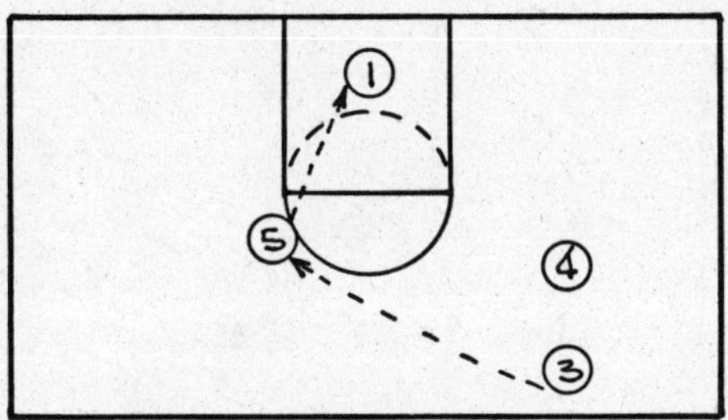

Diagram 35-13

area. This allows him to post inside and thus be ready to receive a pass from 05.

4. When the defense takes away all of 03's options, or if 03 chooses not to use any of them, he will still have the basketball. It is important that he take some time to let these options materialize before putting the ball on the floor. After 03 has had time to check the options of a pass to 01, 02 or 05, then 04 comes to screen 03's defensive opponent (Diagram 35-14). This is 02's key to go to the box away from the ball, ideally creating a clear situation for 03 and 04 to run the screen and roll.

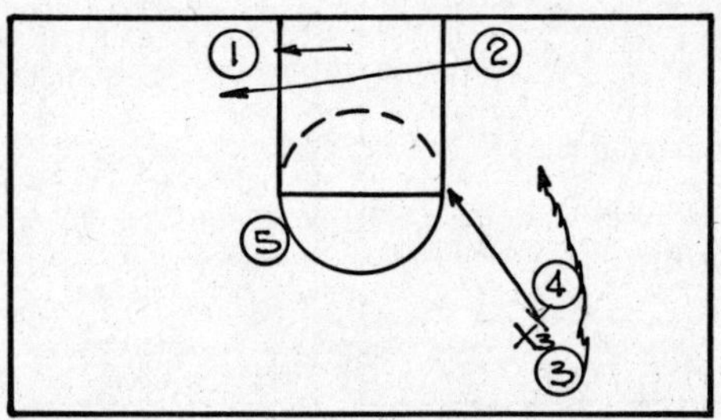

Diagram 35-14

If 03 does not receive the inbounds pass as he breaks toward the ball off 02's screen, he then breaks parallel to the sideline and toward the half-court line. This helps him get open, and also clears the area for 05 breaking toward the ball (Diagram 35-15).

When none of 03's options results in a shot, the team adjusts to its half-court offense. It is the guard's responsibility to control the game offensively; part of this responsibility is to determine when the out-of-bounds play has run its course. Having made this

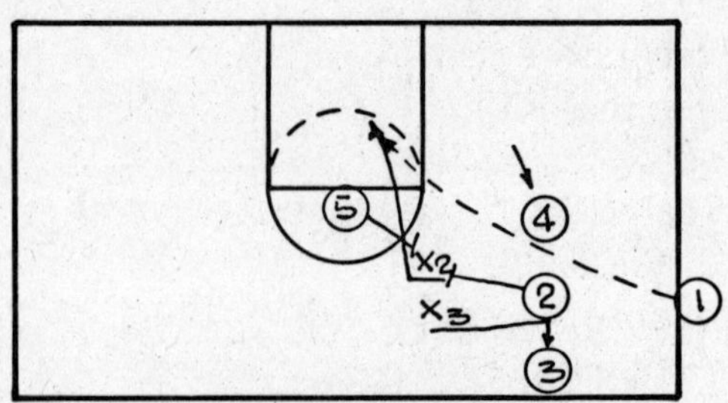

Diagram 35-15

determination, the guards then make the necessary adjustments to their regular half-court offense. This applies to all options of the out-of-bounds play.

The third option for the inbounds pass is to let the play materialize and pass to 02 directly from out of bounds, at or near the bottom half of the free throw circle (Diagram 35-15). This is most often open when the opponents are playing pressure man-for-man defense. It must be emphasized to 01 that this is a difficult pass to execute and should be made only when 02 is wide open, and then only with extreme caution.

The fourth option for the inbounds pass is the pass to 05. 05 has set his screen for 02, seeing that the inbounds pass had not been made; he breaks toward the ball as shown in Diagram 35-16. When 05 receives the pass, 02 clears to the box for rebounding, or to be in a position to receive a pass. 01 uses 04's screeen and breaks to the basket, looking for a return pass from 05; 01 then drives to the basket to score. If 02's defender switches, 01 then passes to 02. When 01 does not receive a return pass from 05, then he clears to the box opposite the ball (Diagram 35-17).

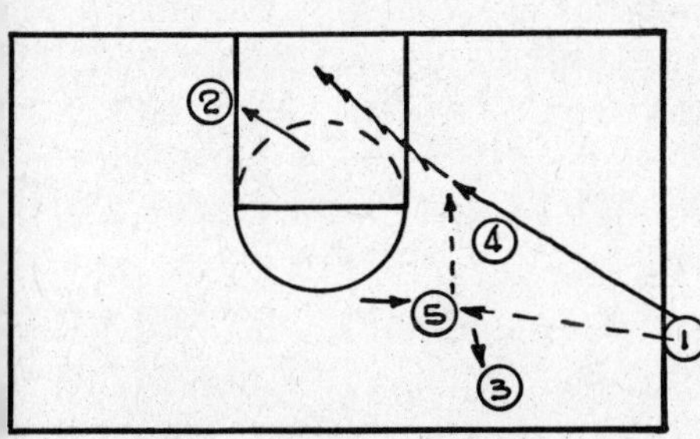

Diagram 35-16

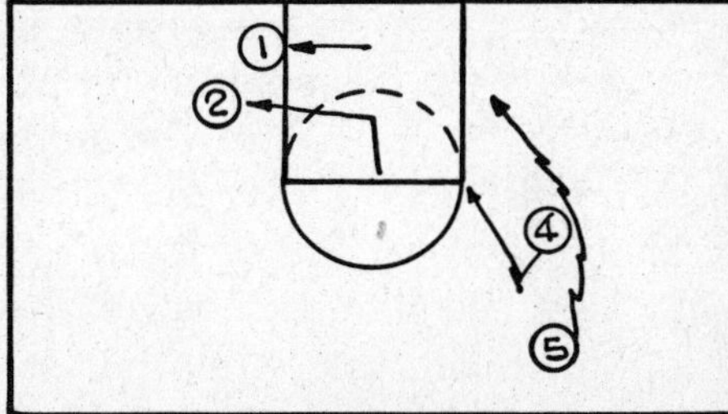

Diagram 35-17

What the team does at this point, when 05 does not pass to 01, depends upon the mobility of the center. If the center can put the ball on the floor, he brings 04 out to screen for 05, and they then execute the screen and roll (Diagram 35-17). If the center is not mobile, 03 takes the ball from 05 on a handoff, and then adjusts to our half-court offense.

When the opponents are playing a zone defense, the players do not go through these movements, but pass the ball in and go directly to their set half-court zone offense.

Chapter 36

THE DELAY GAME

by Dick Vitale

Our offensive delay games are termed: 1) the middle game; and 2) the stacks delay.

In the middle game we define our personnel in this manner: 01 is our point man; 02 is our second guard, while 03 is a forward who can handle the ball effectively; 04 is a forward who can shoot, and 05 is our center. But we also make sure the player filling the 05 position is a fairly good shooter.

In the stacks delay game, it is possible to use two post players; however, the three perimeter players should have the same skills as the 01, 02 and 03 in the middle game. They must be able to penetrate and find open players, and be excellent free throw shooters.

A coach must realize the purpose and strengths of each offensive set, and while our stacks delay and middle game have different objectives, our basic goal is to be prepared to meet all game situations.

Diagram 36-1 shows the basic set for the middle game. Keep the floor balanced in the four corners and have the ball in the center.

In Diagram 36-2, 01 beats his man. As the defensive player guarding 05 gives help, 05 is then open for a pass from 01 and the resultant lay-up.

When 01 starts penetration and the defensive guard gives help, 01 simply passes to 02, who begins his one-on-one maneuver (Diagram 36-3).

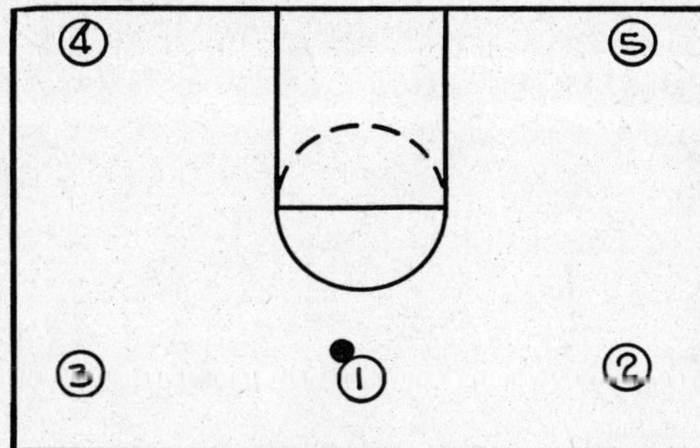

Diagram 36-1

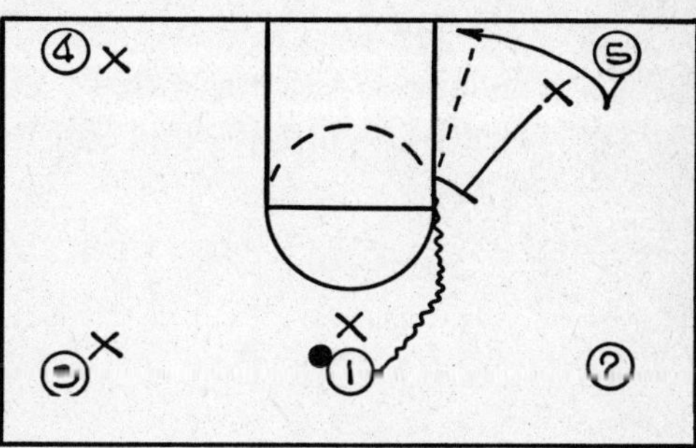

Diagram 36-2

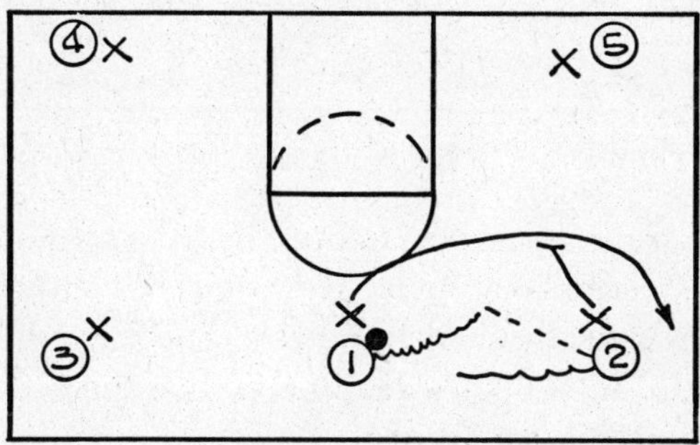

Diagram 36-3

As shown in Diagram 36-4, we flash 04 and have 03 go backdoor, while 01 rotates and 02 becomes the point.

Diagram 36-5 shows the basic set for the stacks delay game. 04 and 05 form a double post.

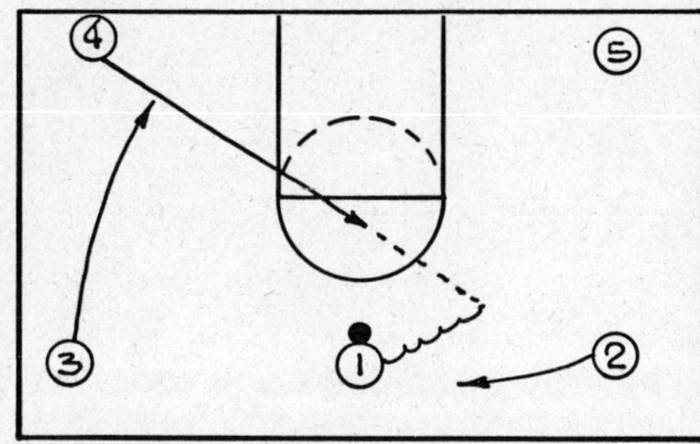

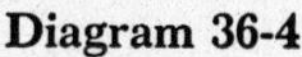
Diagram 36-4

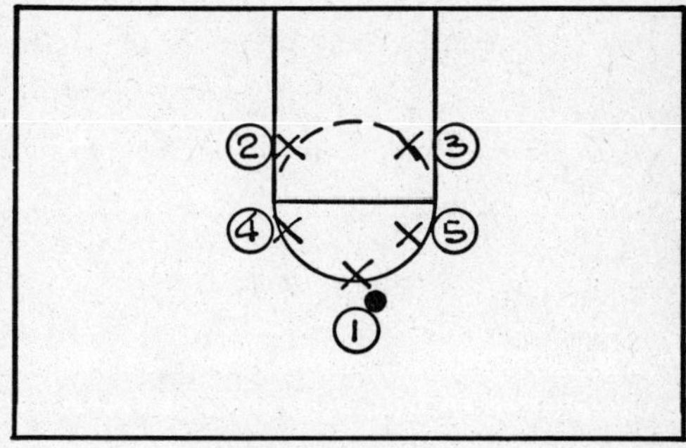

Diagram 36-5

In Diagram 36-6, the ball is entered to the wing, 03, while 01 makes a scoring move to occupy his defensive player. 03 starts dribbling out to replace 01 at the point.

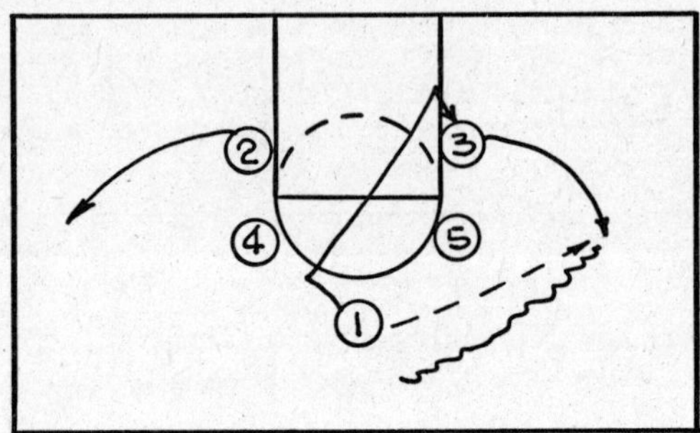

Diagram 36-6

When the defensive player on 01 starts to give help (Diagram 36-7), 05 releases to the goal to take a pass from 01.

In Diagram 36-8, 01 passes to 04. 01 then makes a backdoor cut to take the pass from 04.

The stacks delay set is effective and simple to teach, yet it has been an outstanding addition to our system.

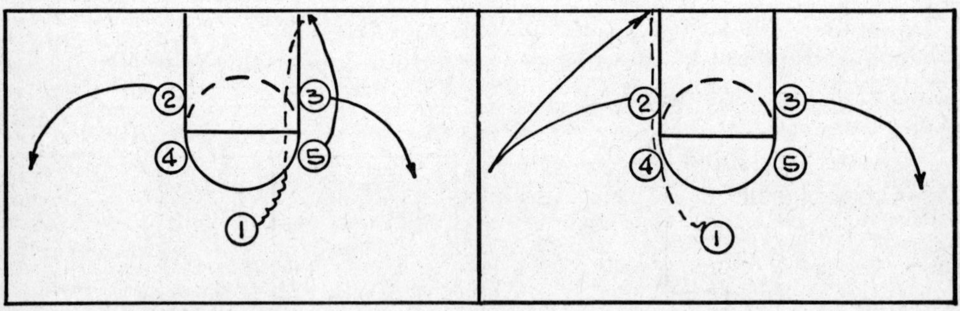

Diagram 36-7

Diagram 36-8

Chapter 37

QUICK SHOT OR LATE GAME OFFENSE

by Roscoe Denney

The quick shot or late game offense has certain criteria which must be met and adhered to in keeping with sound, fundamental basketball: 1) A quick shot, but also a high-percentage shot should be taken at the basket; 2) Offensive floor balance must be maintained; 3) Planned or organized rebounding responsibility is an absolute must; 4) Defensive protection must also be observed; 5) The middle should be kept open to allow ample space for penetration of the defense; 6) The offense should be geared to handle strong defensive overplay; 7) Provisions for single and double clearouts are necessary; 8) No more than three passes should be used; 9) Players should be taught to take full advantage of the threat of the screen; 10) It may be necessary to preempt quick shot plays; 11) This offense should be included in the practice schedule; 12) Personnel placement is just as important as in any other offense.

In keeping with the belief that the middle should be kept open, the 1-2-2 offensive alignment is used as an example (Diagram 37-1).

Positioning within the alignment is even more important than the alignment itself. The wing players should be in a position halfway between the free throw line and the sideline. This allows the middle to be kept open, and also places wing players in a position to receive a pass and shoot the quick, high-percentage shot once penetration of the defense occurs. This is shown in Diagram 37-2 and is referred to as the kickout move.

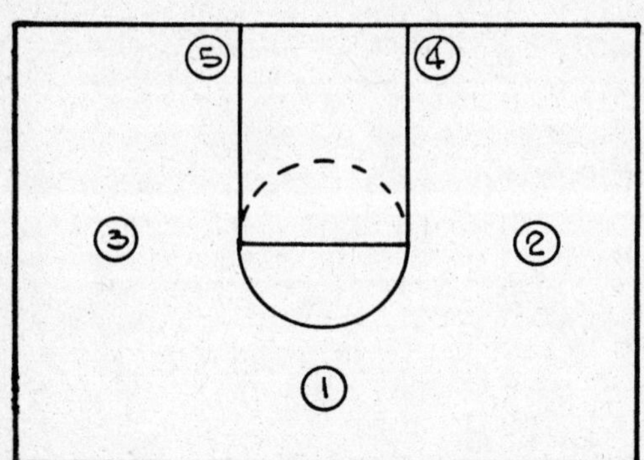

Diagram 37-1

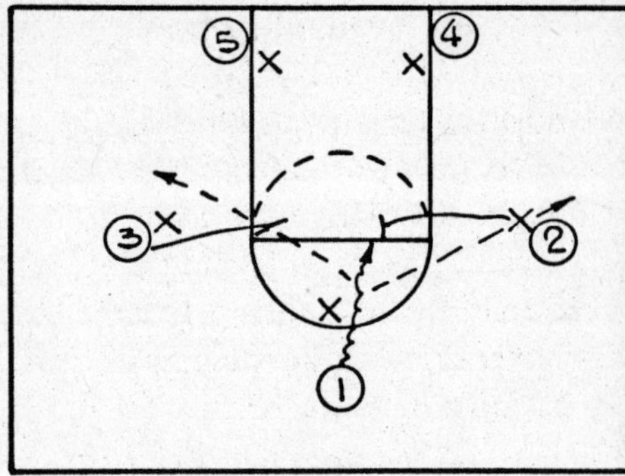

Diagram 37-2

Many coaches, for various reasons, would rather have baseline players either in the corner or at least halfway out on the baseline. We, however, prefer to keep baseline players on the blocks for three reasons. The first is that in the event of further penetration, there is less chance for a charging foul to occur (Diagram 37-3). Baseline players coming to the ball from a position halfway out or farther on the baseline are more apt to charge (Diagram 37-4).

Secondly, one must assume that good defensive players will position themselves in the middle of the lane. Therefore, it is advantageous to have offensive players in that general area. We also feel that this inside positioning will afford us at least a 50 percent chance of rebounding the ball.

The third reason for keeping the baseline players on the blocks is that different personnel are often placed there.

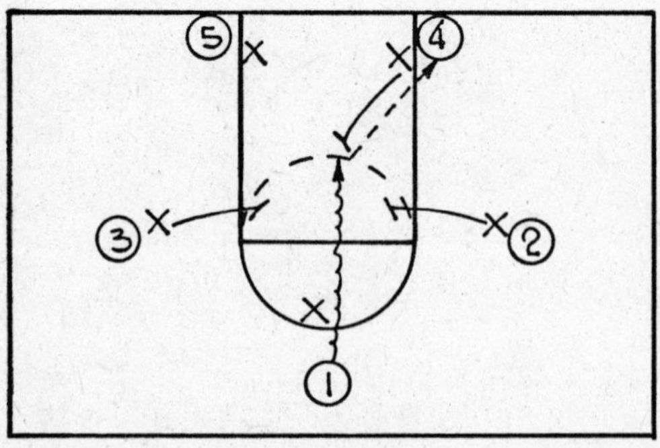

Diagram 37-3

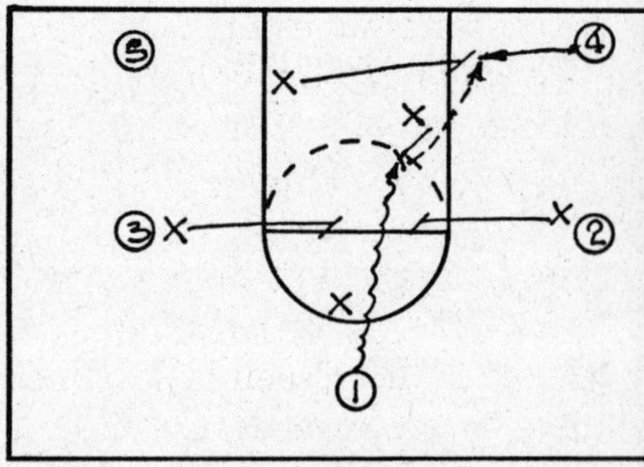

Diagram 37-4

An available option is to place big players (predominately inside players) on the wings, run them down for a pick, post up, and try to get the ball to them. It is also important for the coach to have a player coming over the pick who can score from 12 to 15 feet, especially late in the game and when the team is behind in the score. Again, this may be reason enough for starting big players outside and rotating them inside, as illustrated in Diagram 37-5. Note that inside players are not always placed outside first. Each coach must place his personnel accordingly.

As shown in Diagram 37-5, only one pass is necessary for a subsequent, quick, high-percentage shot. The pass can be made to either side of the floor; inside players assume strong rebounding position, and the point guard takes on the defensive protector responsibility.

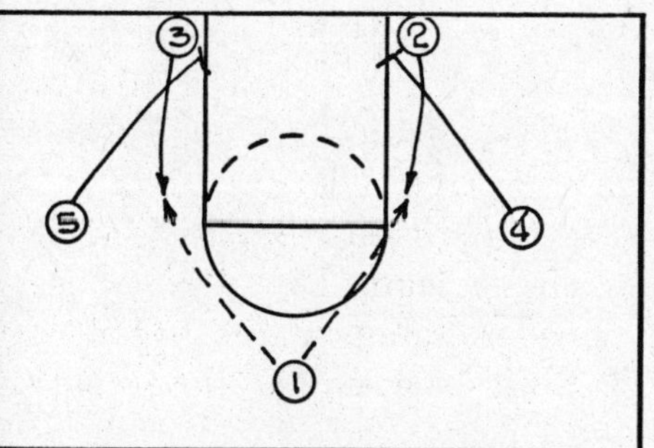

Diagram 37-5

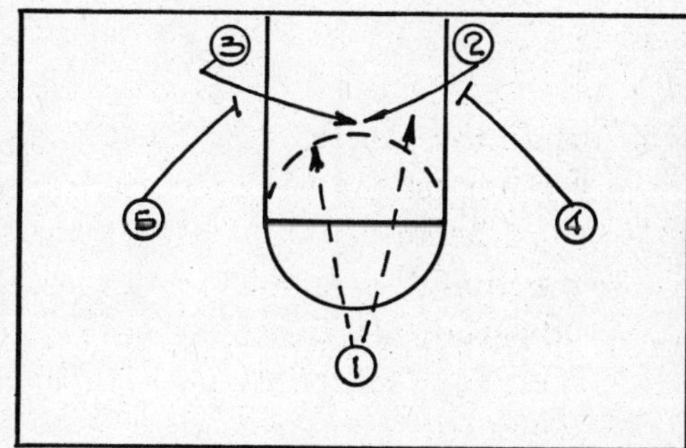

Diagram 37-6

If the value of the double pickdown move is to be fully gained, players must be taught to use and take full advantage of the threat of the screen. If used properly, an uncontested shot will often result. The offensive player must utilize the screen by going over the top, unless defensive adjustments make a different maneuver more practical. When the defense shifts toward the screen to neutralize its effectiveness, the offensive player should use the threat of the screen to free himself (Diagram 37-6).

In other words, the offensive player must read the defense and react accordingly. However, many players do not possess the necessary "savvy" to recognize these situations. For this reason it may prove advantageous for a coach to preempt all of his quick shot plays. By preempting, players merely give the appearance of executing specific plays or patterns, i.e., the double pickdown. Preempting alerts players to the manner in which the defense is guarding and allows them to make a more formidable offensive maneuver.

Another means of preempting the double pickdown is needed to counter automatic switching by the defense. The wing players simply fake the pickdown and flash back to the ball (Diagram 37-7). When teams begin to automatically switch the double pickdown move, do not place the inside players outside first.

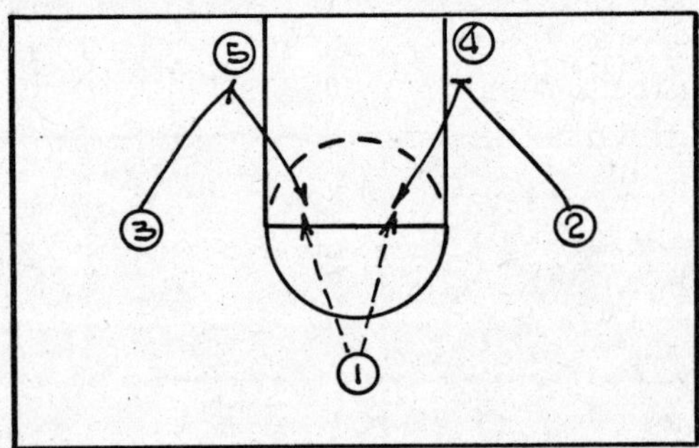

Diagram 37-7

In referring again to offensive rebounding responsibilities and defensive protection duties, players on the blocks, obviously, rebound their respective sides; the shooter follows his shot and rebounds the middle area while the wing player who did not shoot becomes the line rebounder. The wing player and the point guard assume defensive protection responsibilities.

In order to alleviate some defensive overplay in late game situations, we merely go to our double stack low set. After the pass is made to the wing, passing game rules are followed until the ball returns to the point. When the ball reaches the point an automatic double pickdown occurs.

The initial alignment of the double stack low set is shown in Diagram 37-8. The low men on the stack, 02 and 03, break to normal wing positions using 04 and 05 as screens if necessary. The offensive players must again react to the defense and make

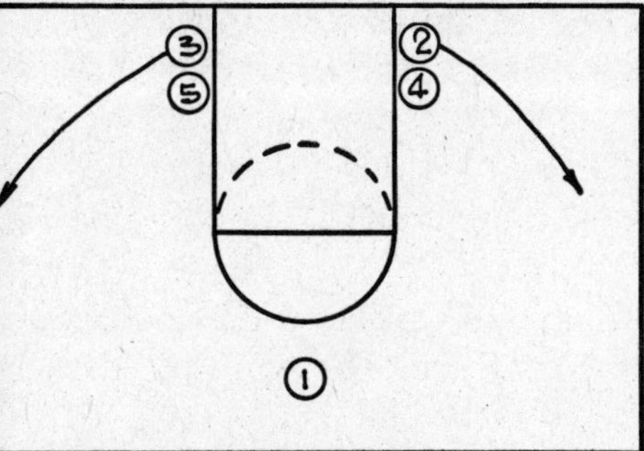

Diagram 37-8

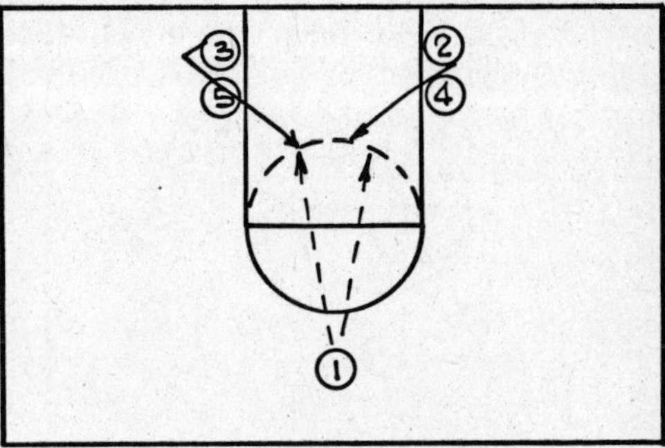

Diagram 37-9

necessary offensive adjustments. In the event that the outside cut is taken away, the inside cut should be available (Diagram 37-9).

Following the pass to wing player 02, the point man, 01, goes opposite and screens for wing player 03. Inside players on the ball side post up in an effort to receive a pass from 02. This is the first option and is shown in Diagram 37-10.

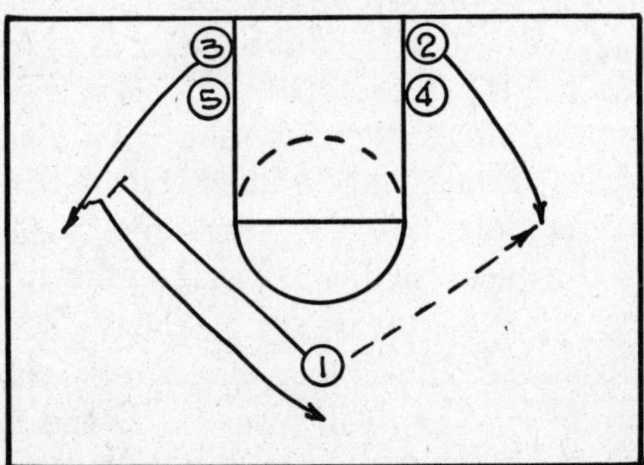

Diagram 37-10

The second option (Diagram 37-11) is for 04 to hold for two seconds and if he does not receive the ball, he rolls opposite and screens for 05. 02 may now make the pass in to 05 if he is open.

If neither of the first two options is available, 02 reverses the ball to the point and a double pickdown takes place. 03 has the option of shooting or passing to either 04 or 05 (Diagram 37-12).

One other criterion that must be given some consideration

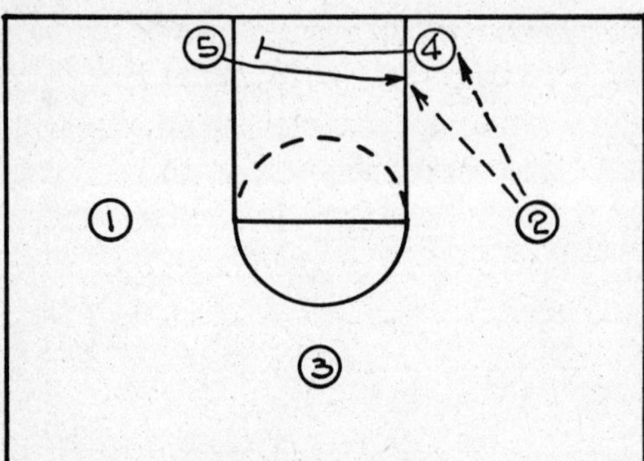

Diagram 37-11

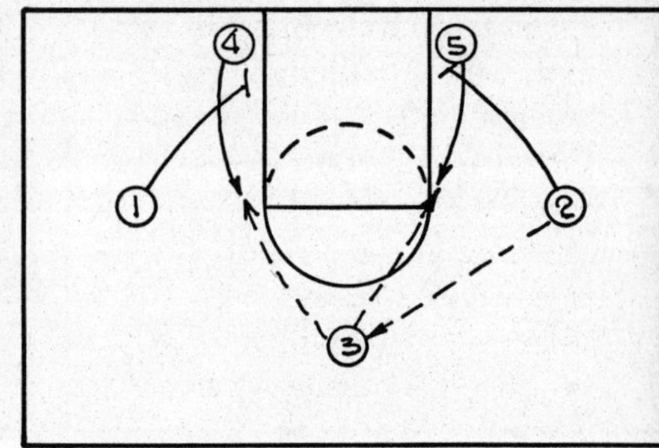

Diagram 37-12

and incorporated into the quick shot offense is the clearout move. Provisions should be made for either a single or double clearout. The clearout can be used as a means of combating pressure or to take advantage of individual abilities by allowing a player to operate in a one-on-one situation. In the 1-2-2 alignment that has been shown here, a double clearout must take place in order to clear a side of the floor. Diagram 37-13 illustrates the clearing process while Diagram 37-14 illustrates subsequent action.

In clearing the left side of the floor, as shown in Diagram 37-13, 01 approaches 03 on the dribble. This is the key for both 03 and 05 to clear the area. Offensive player 03 clears through the middle and rotates to the point, while 05 clears the baseline to the opposite side. If the defensive players assigned to 03 and 05 elect to follow them on the clearout, the left side of the floor will be open

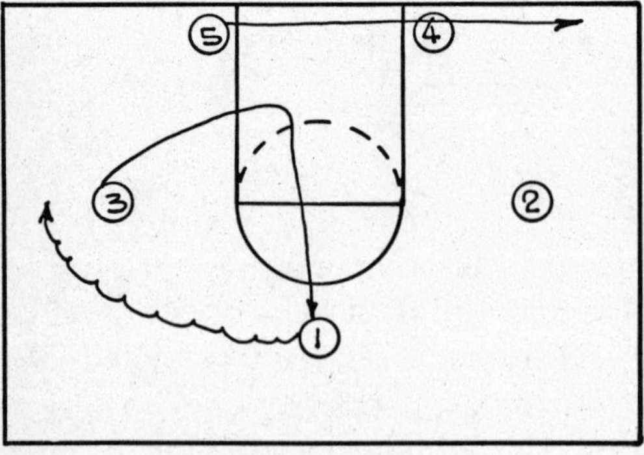

Diagram 37-13

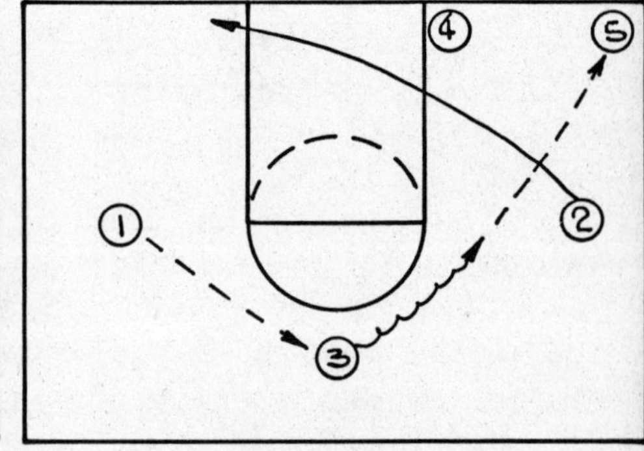

Diagram 37-14

for 01 to operate in a one-on-one move. However, if either one or both of the defensive men choose to stay and help, then ball reversal must be used to counteract this defensive decision. As shown in Diagram 37-14, 01 passes to 03 on the point. As the ball reaches the point, 02 cuts to the ball and basket from his wing position, and if he is open, we naturally pass to him. However, if 02 is covered and no pass is made, we again have offensive floor balance and 02 will rebound that side. 03 takes several dribbles to improve his passing angle, and makes the pass to 05 for the shot. It is worthy to note that 03 is the player most frequently open for the high-percentage shot in the event that ball reversal must be used.

In addition to late game situations, the quick shot offense can be used: 1) as the primary offensive attack; 2) for tempo control, to get a patterned team in a running game; 3) as a last second shot at the end of the quarter, half, etc.; 4) in other special situations such as following a time-out, playing for a specific player, etc.

Chapter 38

BREAKING THE PRESS

by Dennis Fitzpatrick

At a time when pressure defenses are being used more frequently, it becomes increasingly important to have an effective method of breaking the press. With the great variety of presses being used, it is a tremendous advantage to have a press breaker that will work effectively against either a zone or man-for-man press. Not only should a press breaker be simple and adaptable to different situations, but it should provide the opportunity for a quick and demoralizing basket.

In employing the press breaker, adhere to two principles: 1. Spread the defense out as much as possible; 2. Work aggressively for the lay-up. If the other team does not respect the deep players, throw the long pass, which results in a high percentage of lay-ups.

In order for the press breaker to be most effective, it is important that the players be positioned properly. The player who takes the ball out of bounds should be the biggest guard. He must be able to throw long passes accurately. The best ball-handling guard should be working for the inbounds pass. He should set up about as deep as the back of the circle. This will give him enough room to work free far enough from the baseline so as not to be double-teamed by the defender on the baseline. The player who aligns at mid-court should be aggressive in meeting the ball and also be a good ball-handler. A post player who is a good ball-handler would be ideal. His job is to work free between the mid-court and ten-second line, preferably in the center of the court. The two wing spots are filled by the two weakest ball-handlers on the team. Their job is to line up on the five-second line on the offensive side of the court and be prepared to come up and help against the man-for-man press if the ball is taken out on their side of the court.

In breaking the man-for-man press, start from the basic alignment (Diagram 38-1). As soon as the guard touches the ball, the other guard breaks for the ball. The center works to get free in the mid-court region (Diagram 38-2). It is usually desirable to complete the pass to the center, as he has much room to work free and there is not much defensive help. Very often the offensive center overruns the ball, attempting a steal. This becomes a three-on-two fast break.

If the ball goes to the on-court guard, the player who has taken the ball out of bounds streaks for a return pass (Diagram 38-3). If he is ahead of the defender, he will receive a return pass and we will have a four-on-three break.

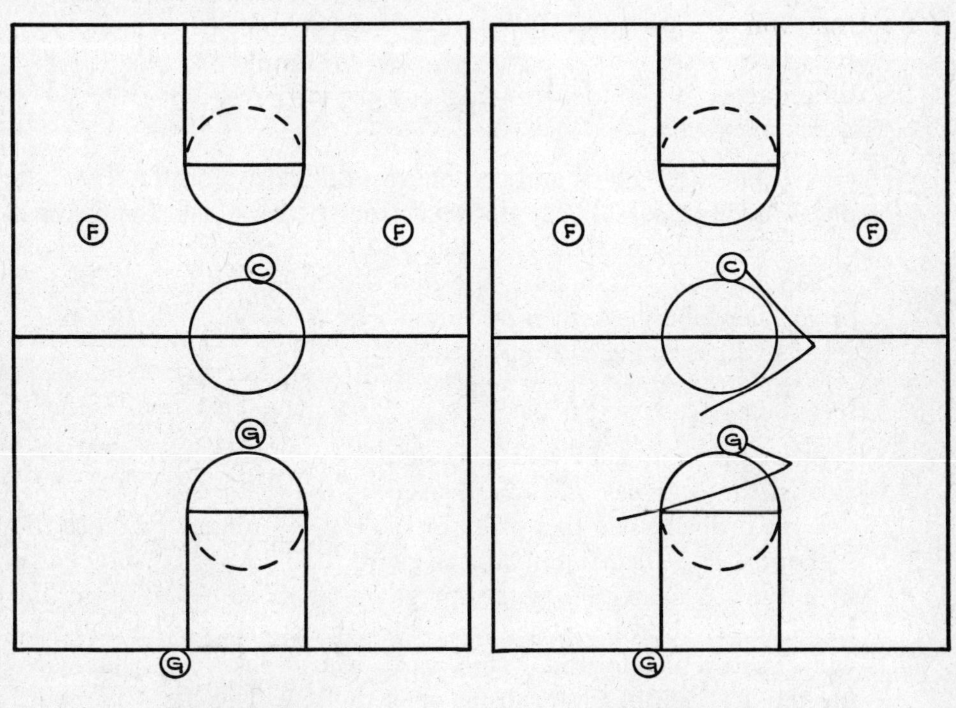

Diagram 38-1 **Diagram 38-2**

Diagram 38-3

If both the guard and center have difficulty working free, the player taking the ball out calls *help*! Upon hearing this, the forward on the ball side breaks for the ball and the center clears backcourt (Diagram 38-4). As before, the guard making the inbounds pass breaks hard for the return pass, and if he is ahead of the defender, receives it, creating a three-on-two.

Against an extremely aggressive man-for-man press or a team that works especially hard on denying the inbounds pass, we use another press breaker that is designed to provide a quick basket against the overplay and thus loosen up the defense.

In order to use this press breaker, the same guard takes the ball out of bounds. We line up the guard, both forwards, and center in a tight I formation with the guard about ten feet from the baseline, as shown in Diagram 38-5. At the slap of the ball, the center sets a pick for the first forward, who streaks for the offensive basket. The center then rolls to meet the ball. The second forward steps out as if to set a pick, but streaks to the opposite sideline instead. The guard then breaks to meet the ball. The first option on

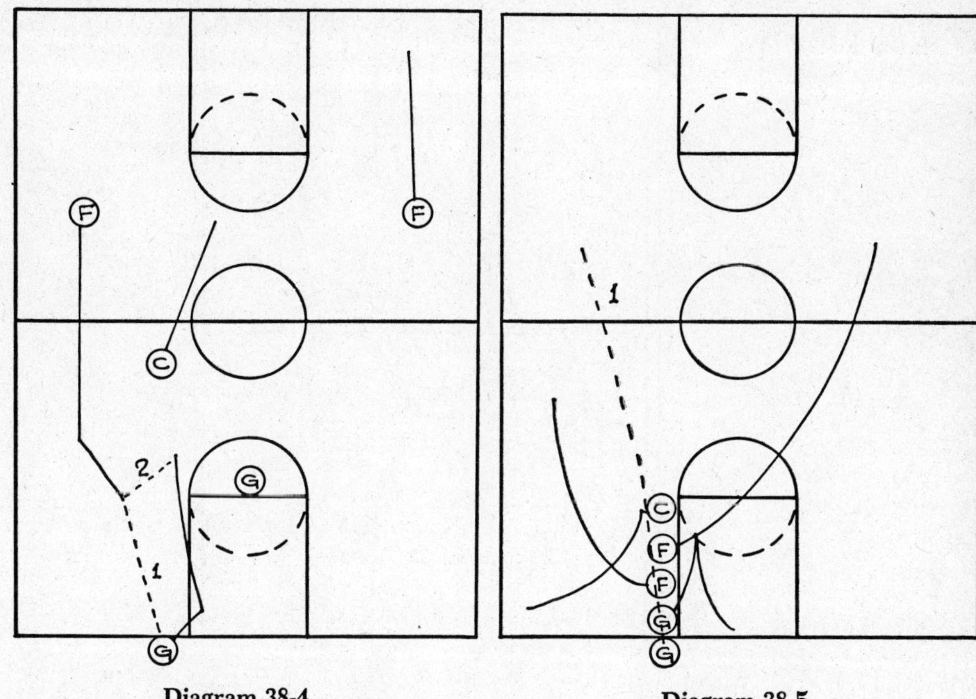

Diagram 38-4

Diagram 38-5

this play is the forward streaking off the center pick. The forward streaking up the opposite side is used in case the defense has only one man back. The guard rolling off the pick from the forward is the third option, and the center is the fourth. After using the standard press breaker, this switch usually catches the defense off-balance and results in a quick basket. It is always successful in loosening up the defense, which makes it easier to bring the ball up the court.

Other special plays can be extremely effective, but only work once. One example of such a play is shown in Diagram 38-6. At the slap of the ball the guard on court steps behind the baseline to take the pass from the out-of-bounds guard. Upon making the pass, the guard cuts behind the pick of the forward and streaks upcourt. The player with the ball will make the long pass, if this man is free. If the forward is not free, the pass can be made to the center, who is working to the baseline, or the cross-court forward who works free in the area vacated by the center. This play has resulted in many baskets, but, as it will be effective only once, save it for critical situations.

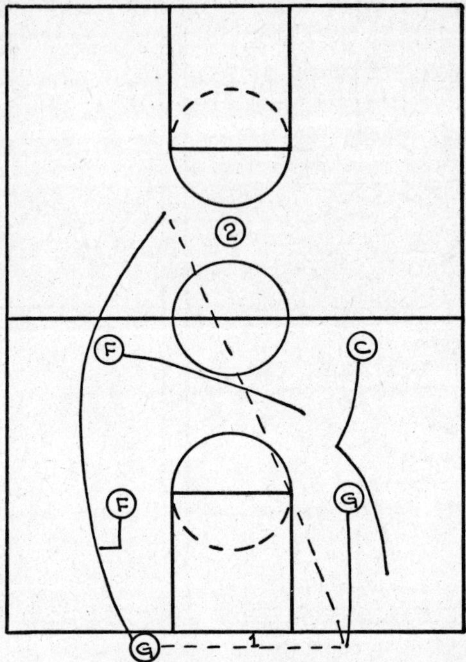

Diagram 38-6

Against the zone press, apply the same principle of spreading the defense as much as possible. Keep the same basic alignment against the 1-2-2, 2-2-1, and 1-3-1 mid-court traps as against the man-for-man pass. Against the 1-2-2 and 2-2-1 traps, if you make the first pass to the center at mid-court, you can get a two-on-one or three-on-two break. Against the 1-3-1 mid-court trap, try for the deep pass to the wings and if completed, you have a two-on-one situation.

Vary the alignment against the 1-2-1-1 press. Move the two forwards up to the mid-court line and slide the center back as deep as the five-second line, as shown in Diagram 38-7. By doing this, the defense must cover two offensive players with one player at the half-court line, and after completing the pass to half-court, you have at least a three-on-two situation. This is merely a matter of stacking your strength at the opposition's weak point.

When the defense prevents the pass to the center, the center slides back and yells *go* which signals the two forwards to come up and work free at each side of the half-court line.

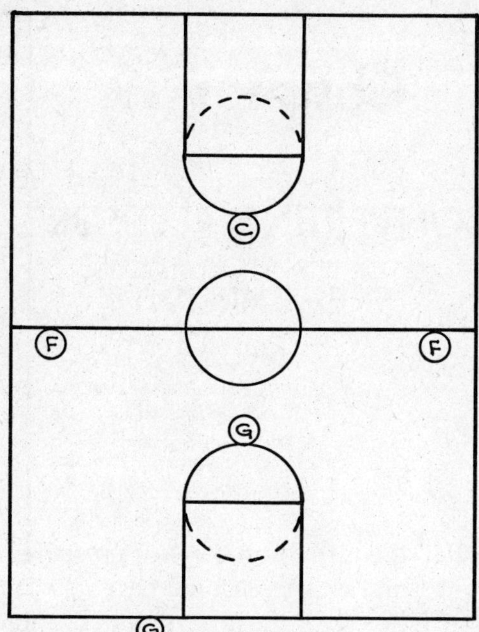

Diagram 38-7

There are a few basic rules to give to the players before installing the press breaker:

1. Make sure you are away from the basket when you take the ball out of bounds.

2. After a basket is scored, make use of the entire baseline when taking the ball out.

3. Don't rush to get the ball after a basket is scored. The five-second count does not start until the ball is touched. This gives the players a chance to set up. (It also gives the defense a chance to set up, but since you have a better chance of scoring against the press, you want them to set up. If, however, you are experiencing difficulty in breaking the press, the ball should be taken out quickly.)

4. Don't set picks in the backcourt. This gives the defense an opportunity to double-team.

5. Always look to pass upcourt. A backwards pass gives the defense an added opportunity to press.

Chapter 39

CONVERTING PRESSURE FREE THROWS

by Doc Scheppler

The basketball team that can convert pressure free throws in an important, tight game can greatly increase its chances of having a successful season. The coach must be able to produce an effective practice situation to bring about positive results. Many factors are present when shooting free throws during a game; crowd noise, self-induced pressure, and physical and mental fatigue. However, in a practice session, the players often work on improving their free throw shooting with these variables missing.

In many of our free throw drills we include, to some extent, the variables that are present in a game situation. Most important are conditioning and shooting in a pressure situation.

There are six drills we use to practice shooting a free throw with game variables involved: 1) free throw sprints; 2) free throw touch lines; 3) team free throw touch lines—consecutive; 4) continuous running and sprinting free throws; 5) variable conditioning free throws, and 6) spotlight free throws.

Free Throw Sprints. The players spread out along the baseline and run a full-court sprint and back. The coach selects a player to shoot a free throw. If he makes it, the players run one sprint; if he misses, they do two sprints. Another player is chosen and if he continues the string of misses, they run four sprints. If he makes it, they run one sprint. The number of sprints continues to double if the string of consecutive misses continues: 1 miss—2 sprints; 2

misses—4 sprints; 3 misses—8 sprints; etc. The drill ends when the team converts the set number of free throws the coach designated at the start of the drill.

Free Throw Touch Lines. This drill is essentially the same as the sprints, except the players run a three-quarter courtliner when they miss and a one-half courtliner if they convert. This drill requires considerably less time than the sprints because of the shortened distance. Note that this drill concentrates exclusively on quick acceleration and changes of direction.

Consecutive Free Throw Touch Lines. This drill involves a team consecutively converting a set number of free throws. A miss constitutes a full courtliner. The drill ends when the set number of consecutive free throws has been made. It is crucial that the coach select the proper number of free throws according to the team's shooting ability and percentage. As a general guideline, players at the junior high level should successfully shoot 2-3 free throws; for high school players the number should be 3-5; and players at the college level should be able to make 5-7 consecutive free throws.

Continuous Free Throws. There are two variations to this drill. Both involve the players running laps around the court until they hear the first whistle (or the word sprint), at which point they sprint until they hear another whistle (or the word stop).

The first variation of the drill involves a set number of free throws to be converted. The coach selects a player to shoot the free throw. Whether he converts or misses, the players still run until the set number has been completed.

The second variation involves all of the players shooting at different baskets. When a player is called to convert his shot and misses, the team runs. If he makes it, another player is selected. The drill should be timed and should last 15 minutes.

This type of free throw drill is especially effective as an early season addition to the practice session, because it provides a foundation for cardiovascular endurance. A total of approximately two to three miles of running and sprinting will be completed if the drill is carried out properly.

Variable Conditioning Free Throws. This drill is identical to the first two drills, except the coach varies the conditioning aspect. We combine the use of hopping, blitz jumps and liners. On the missed shots, players do a full-court hop, 35 blitz jumps (jumping to the fullest height) and three-quarter courtliners. On converted shots, the players do a one-half courtliner, 20 blitz jumps and a one-half court hop. After completing the designated conditioner, the coach selects a player to shoot the free throw. Whether he makes the shot or not, proceed to the next conditioner. This type of free throw drill is the least tiring, but it specially utilizes the muscles involved in playing basketball.

Spotlight. This drill is used during the regular free throw practice time. The coach randomly selects the players to convert their free throws. A miss constitutes a touch line sprint. The free throw practice time ends when everyone has shot a spotlight free throw.

Successful game free throw shooting is not by any means guaranteed by utilizing these drills. Obviously, the players should be fundamentally sound in their shooting styles. These drills are designed to prepare the players to shoot free throws in a game situation when fatigue and pressure are additional factors.